The Power of the Pen

From the Unconscious to the Conscious

An anthology produced by

The American Handwriting Analysis Foundation

Edited by Sheila Lowe, MS, CG, CFDE

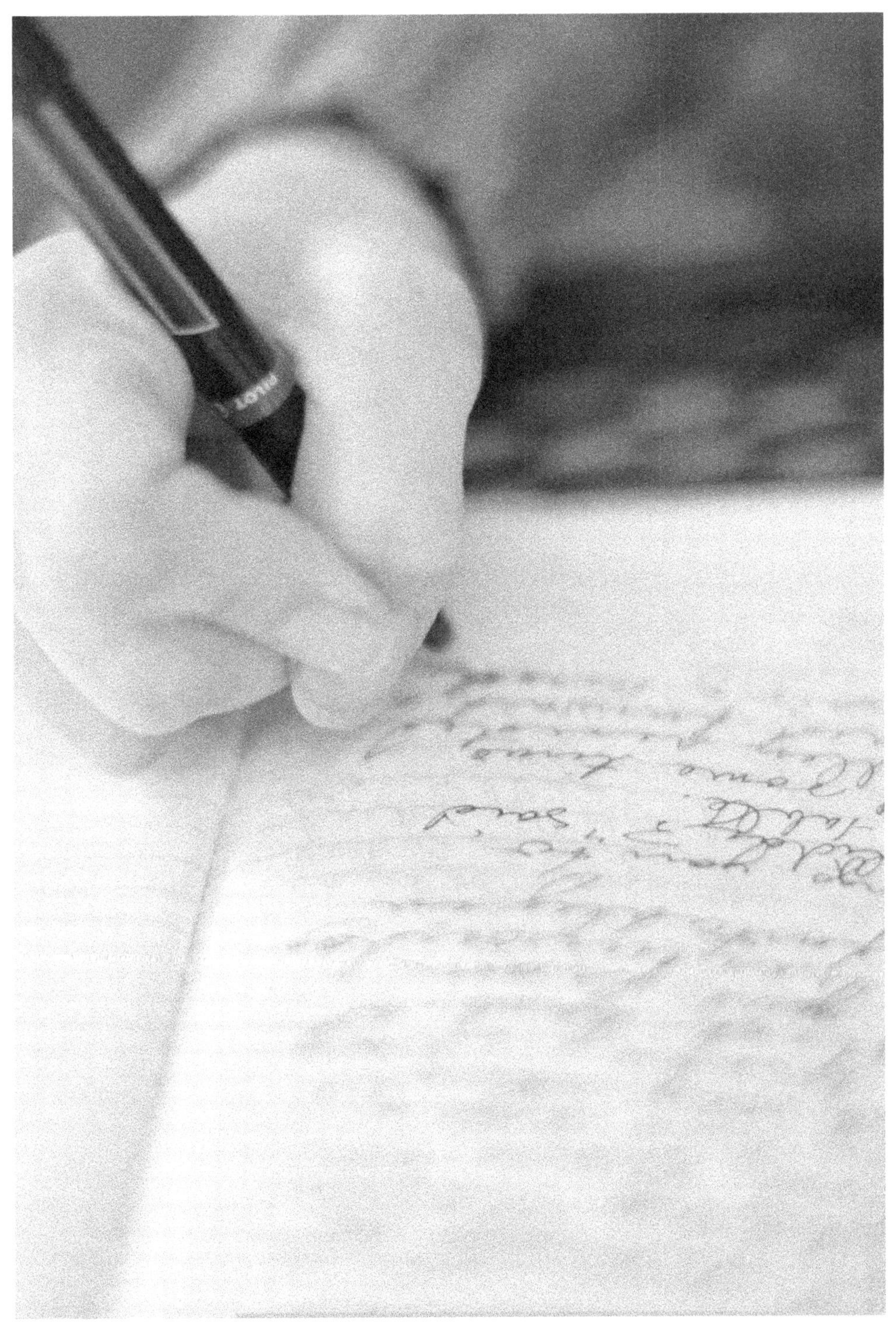

DEDICATION

This book is dedicated to Camillo Baldi, Abbé Jean Hippolyte Michon, Jules Crépieux-Jamin and other early researchers and teachers who introduced us to graphology. And to Ludwig Klages, Max Pulver, William Preyer, Robert Saudek, Ania Teillard and their successors on whose shoulders we stand. They widened and made this important area of study more accessible to practitioners. And of course, to Felix Klein and Roger Rubin for being our very best modern-day teachers.

ACKNOWLEDGMENTS

It is with profound and grateful thanks that I wish to acknowledge the authors for their educational and entertaining entries to this anthology: Roger Rubin, Marc Seifer, Linda Larson, Edda Manley, Ruth Holmes, Sarah Holmes Tucker, Adam Brand, John Beck, Jane Yank, Lena Rivkin, Victor Clark, Lauren Mooney Bear, Kathleen Dickinson, Teresa Abram, Barbara Donato, Marion Rollings, Annette Poizner, Jane O'Brien, Cynthia Crosson, Ashira Gobrin, Macjob Oladipupo, Tricia Clapp. I added my own contribution as an analysis of Michael Ondaatje's handwriting.

Special thanks to Teresa Abram, who did all the initial legwork and so much of the followup; to Marion Rollings for taking on the tedious work of formatting the bibliographies; and to Lauren Mooney Bear who, as current president of AHAF, served not only as an adviser, but whose professional artistic eye helped create the cover design.

Thanks also to Dr. Mark Noble, skeptical but open-minded in generously agreeing to write the Foreword.

And finally, thanks to the readers, some of whom will become the future of handwriting psychology.

TABLE OF CONTENTS

PREFACE

"The message behind the words is the voice of the heart."

Rumi

When the original idea for a handwriting analysis anthology started percolating in my mind, it felt like an important project that could make a difference in the way the world perceives the field. However, that was 2012 and I was the newly elected president of the American Handwriting Analysis Foundation. There were numerous important initiatives for my board to address, not the least of which was the then-recent release of the Common Core Curriculum. The CCC set academic standards for US public schools, and removed the requirement to provide handwriting training. So, at that time, our greatest area of focus was to see cursive training returned to the curriculum.

Over the next ten years AHAF achieved some major successes, but it was not until after I left the presidency in June, 2022 that the idea of an anthology was resurrected and now, is finally coming to fruition.

Respected handwriting professionals from around the world were invited to participate and their essays cover a wide range of topics and writing styles. I trust you will enjoy reading the personal stories and learning more about depth handwriting psychology from some of the top graphologists of our time.

The American Handwriting Analysis Foundation (AHAF) is a non-profit educational organization established more than 50 years ago in 1967. Founded by Charlie Cole, who vowed never to serve in office, but who tirelessly supported the organization in many ways, AHAF has grown to international status with members in nearly twenty countries.

The all-volunteer AHAF board – its leadership team – provides innumerable free resources to its members, ranging from an online library/archive, online study group and chapter, *The Vanguard* quarterly publication, and the Campaign for Cursive committee, whose dedicated volunteers have worked tirelessly to help bring handwriting training back to the public school system and who run the annual Cursive is Cool contest.

The 2022 AHAF leadership team is comprised of President Lauren Mooney Bear, Vice-President Ashira Gobrin, Treasurer Aaron Goodman, Secretary Blaine Bergeson, Research Chair Jane Yank, Communications Chair Teresa Abram, Librarian/Archivist Tricia Clapp, Ethics Chair, Donna Whipple, Immediate Past-President/*Vanguard* Editor Sheila Lowe.

Compiling and editing this book has been a true labor of love, and it is my great desire for the efforts of every contributor to be recognized as such, too. Seeing this ten-year-old dream come to publication is more gratifying than I can adequately express. As your editor, I wish you good reading.

Sheila Lowe, MS, CG, CFDE
Immediate Past President

FOREWORD

Writing by hand: A simple gift with complex benefits

"The true alchemists do not change lead into gold – they change the world into words"

William H. Gass

Every author who contributed to this book knows one of the human species greatest secrets – which is that the effects of writing on the writer are so powerful they seem like magic. Yes, writing is critical in communicating with others, in creating a historical record, in enabling books and plays and love letters and instruction manuals and legal contracts (and also in enabling endless amounts of spam and angry invective in all corners of the internet). It is impossible to imagine the development of even a rudimentary civilization without the invention of some form of writing. But – and this is the key point– even without all those social benefits, the benefits of writing on the writer are enough reason to embrace this activity.

Writing can engage our thinking and improve our learning like little else can do. Many people have noted that writing helps organize their thinking. For example:

- The French theologian John Calvin cited St. Augustine of Hippo when he wrote "I count myself one of the number of those who write as they learn and learn as they write."
- Arthur Krystal, essayist and screenwriter, wrote "when the work is going well, I'm expressing opinions that I've never uttered in

conversation and that otherwise might never occur to me. Nor am I the first to have this thought, which, naturally, occurred to me while composing. According to Edgar Allan Poe, writing in Graham's Magazine, "Some Frenchman—possibly Montaigne—says: 'People talk about thinking, but for my part I never think except when I sit down to write.'"

- Joan Didion, essayist and pioneer of New Journalism, noted "I write entirely to find out what I'm thinking, what I'm looking at, what I see and what it means."

Along with enhancing our thinking, writing enhances our learning, and particularly so when it's combined with the slow analytical thinking required for solving novel problems. Slow analytical thinking differs from the reflexive reactions that are the currency of most of our thoughts. Those reflexive reactions, often referred to as fast thinking, seem to represent 95-98% of what most people call thinking. But fast thinking expresses the interpretations and predictions we already believe to be true. Such interpretations and predictions express a model of the universe that we already have. They are the writing that (sadly) so often typifies much of what appears on social media sites and other situations where someone is expressing an opinion based on their pre-existing emotional responses rather than on careful analysis of a problem.

It's slow thinking that's critical for learning something we did not already know and solving problems for which our current answers are not sufficient. We don't have to use writing to do this kind of thinking, but using writing as a component of slow thinking helps us solve problems, gain new insights and learn new information more effectively.

One reason writing has such a powerful impact on learning is that our human brains are specialized for dealing with visual information. Our attention to visual information is so great that some scientists suggest that more nerve cells of the human brain are involved in processing visual information than smell, taste, touch and hearing combined. Whether or not these numbers are precisely correct, vision is central to the human ability to obtain information from the world.

When you write, your attention is further enhanced in part because your visual system is focused on a small area in space, and that physically focused attention increases the release of neurotransmitters that enhance the learning process. When these changes are combined with the added attention of the slow thinking process, a brain state is created where the natural processes of learning are harnessed more effectively.

The enhanced learning associated with writing and slow analytical thinking also is associated with enhanced retention, a consequence of more effective learning. At higher levels of function, the writing activates multiple brain centers that organize and store knowledge for efficient retention.

Writing also changes the way in which we can use active memory processes. Once you've written something down, you don't have to spend effort trying to keep it in your active memory. Our conscious minds are only able to work with a fairly small number of items of information at one time.[1] If you've written something down, you can move on to the next thought without having to keep what you've already written in your active memory. You can modify what you've already written and also keep a record on the evolution of your thinking. In all these ways, writing is like adding a powerful extra memory storage device to your brain.

Writing lets you modify each thought with ease, and to build further on that modification. Writing also lets you quickly go to any thought that you want to revisit precisely as you wrote it, without spending time and energy trying to remember what you thought. From changing words and phrases, to changing your conclusions and using the first versions as a path to a better understanding of whatever topic you're focused on, writing makes a constant revisiting of your thoughts something that's easy to do. Because writing is almost always associated with editing and rewriting, you are effectively entered into a discussion with yourself, and that discussion further reinforces learning.

But is it just the act of writing that's critical, or is writing by hand special? One way to investigate whether the thought processes of writing are sufficient on their own to provide the benefits presented so far, or whether the mental processes and physical actions of writing by hand are also important, is to compare the effects of writing by hand with writing on a computer. In doing this, we can investigate how each approach affects the brain and whether one or the other provides a more effective learning process.

1 Current estimates on the top number of thoughts you can keep in active awareness at one time are seven or so. Writing things down enables you to increase this number as much as you'd like.

Multiple studies on this problem indicate that writing by hand provides many more benefits than writing on the computer, even though both are useful. For example, the brain responds differently to writing by hand and on the computer, and writing by hand seems to activate more brain regions. Writing by hand creates greater activity in sensorimotor parts of the brain. Multiple senses are activated by pressing the pen on paper, seeing the letters as they are written and even hearing the sounds made when writing. These sensory experiences activate circuits that connect different parts of the brain, which further enhances learning.

People writing by hand more effectively use their reticular activating system, a part of the brain that automatically emphasizes whatever the writer is focusing on at that moment. Writing on paper also is associated with more brain activity in areas associated with language, imaginary visualization, and in the hippocampus, an area of the brain critically important for memory and navigation. The increased activation of the hippocampus suggests that writing by hand contains richer spatial details that can be recalled and navigated in the imagination than does writing on a computer.

The memory functions involved in forming letters and words by hand also are tied to the movements required to make each letter. The intricate hand movements involved in shaping letters requires utilization of fine motor skills and senses. In contrast, writing with a keyboard uses the same movement for each letter. Hitting different letters on a keyboard thus does not activate the brain in the same way as writing by hand.

People who write by hand also are more likely to remember important information than those typing on a computer, and show a better understanding of the concepts that they are learning. Using pen and paper, which activates more brain regions, seems to provide the brain more 'hooks' on which to hang your memories. In contrast, pressing buttons on a keyboard activates fewer areas of the brain, and we forget what we've typed faster. This might be what helps the memory of what we've written by hand hang around in our brains a bit longer.

Writing by hand and writing on a computer are both also multimodal experiences, and multimodal learning is one of the most effective learning strategies. The use of multiple sensations and parts of the brain help to enhance learning.

It appears, however, that writing by hand brings more brain processes to bear on a task than writing with a computer. For both types of writing, memory and analytical thinking are used to summarize information and choose the right words. Yet there are important differences. Memory, including muscle memory, is used to hold the pen and form the letters and words and to shape the words and letters correctly when you are writing by hand. The sequence of finger movements required to form letters activates multiple brain regions associated with processing and remembering information. Complex analytical, motor and visual functions are at work here in multiple ways, and research suggests that the uniquely complex spatial and tactile information associated with writing by hand on physical paper may be critical in leading to improved memory.

In brief, writing by hand is a very special activity with multiple benefits. It is one of the great enhanced technologies of the mind.

The power of writing by hand brings us to the topic of this book, which is that we all write in different architectures, not just in the geometry of our thoughts but also in the physical shapes of our writing. Some people write in beautiful shapes and others can barely read their own writing (which also may be unintelligible to others). The shapes of sentences on the page, and the shapes of editing also differ from individual to individual. Such differences are not present when people write using computers. The structures of thought still may be different, but the physical structure of letters and words and even the page itself lacks the individual characteristics of writing by hand.

The different physical architectures associated with writing by hand bring us to the subject of graphology, the topic of this book. Are the different shapes of writing by hand meaningful? Does the physical structure of our writing change its benefits? And why do we write differently? Is it just training or is there more going on?

In all honesty, I haven't yet made up my own mind on the question of how much is revealed by the physical shapes of our writing. Whether the shapes of your letters and words reveal deep insights into your personality is an ongoing and fascinating discussion, even though the fact that writing is one of the most powerful tools in the toolbox of learning is without doubt.

Because the authors contributing to this book got the benefits of writing their views on the topic of graphology, however, and you, dear reader, have the benefits of their thoughts in front of you, you get to make up your own mind about the interpretation of the many physical shapes of handwriting. That need to think about different possible interpretations and make up your own mind is what life is all about. All we each can ask is whether particular ideas help us interpret the world and offer more accurate predictions about the future. Don't believe or disbelieve ideas about graphology – or anything else - because of who wrote them or because of prior beliefs embedded in your fast thinking and reflexive reactions. Believe these ideas – or not – because of whether or not they enable you to interpret information in such a way as to better understand whatever it is that's the focus of your attention. Pay attention particularly to whether you are able to use your interpretations to make more accurate predictions about future events. Ask whether the shape of someone's handwriting adds to your understanding of that person in a way that you can test, and what the results are of conducting that experiment.

The experiment of writing by hand is guaranteed to work. The question of whether the physical architecture of our handwriting provides insights useful in understanding such matters as our emotions and proclivities remains a topic of active discussion. The authors of this book have provided you with their carefully thought-out views on this intriguing topic, which has long been of interest in different cultures around the world.

Mark Noble, PhD.

BIOGRAPHICAL NOTES

Dr. Mark Noble is Professor of Genetics and Neuroscience at the University of Rochester Medical Center. He's best known for his work as one of the pioneering figures of stem cell biology. His current laboratory is engaged in development of improved treatments for traumatic injury to the nervous system, more effective and safer treatments for various types of cancer, and discovery of new molecular pathways involved in development of the nervous system.

Following disturbing discoveries in his laboratory on the toxicity of some widely used antidepressants, Dr. Noble reached out to Dr. David Burns in 2017 to understand new high-speed medication-free approaches to the treatment of depression and anxiety that represent the newest stages in the evolution of Cognitive and Behavioral Therapy (CBT). This new treatment approach is called TEAM CBT (an abbreviation for Testing, Empathy, Addressing Resistance and Methods). After observing the remarkable changes that occur in high-speed therapeutic sessions, he began interacting with Dr. Burns and his colleagues to understand how TEAM CBT can produce such rapid change, even in people for whom other therapeutic approaches failed to provide benefit for years, or even decades. This work has led to new hypotheses on the neuroscience of effective psychotherapy, as well as to experiments on molecular aspects of chronic stress that feed back into Dr. Noble's research on cellular and molecular approaches to understanding normal development and treating disease. Additional thoughts on the analysis of TEAM CBT from the perspective of brain function can be found in podcasts that are part of the free weekly series provided by Dr. Burns as part of providing training in this therapeutic approach. At Dr. Burns' invitation, Dr. Noble also contributed a chapter on the neuroscience of TEAM CBT for Feeling Great, which is the guide to TEAM CBT written by Dr. Burns. [1]

Dr. Noble proposes that one of the critical contributions to the effectiveness of TEAM CBT is its extensive use of writing. This topic is discussed in two guides to TEAM CBT that are available for free download on the web. His thoughts on the importance of writing in TEAM CBT led to the invitation to provide this introductory essay on the magic of writing by hand.[2]

1 Podcasts on TEAM therapy from the perspective of how the brain works are at https://feelinggood.com/2018/08/06/100-the-new-micro-neurosurgery-a-remarkable-interview-with-dr-mark-noble/ and https://feelinggood.com/2019/11/18/167-feeling-great-professor-mark-noble-on-team-cbt-and-the-brain/ andhttps://feelinggood.com/2022/01/03/275-a-spectacular-advance-featuring-professor-mark-noble/ . The chapter in *Feeling Great* is Chapter 30.

2 https://feelinggood.com/wp-content/uploads/2021/12/AAAB-Brain-Users-Guide-to-TEAM-Therapy.pdf and https://feelinggood.com/wp-content/uploads/2021/12/AAA-Exploring-the-Daily-Mood-Log.pdf

Some advice from AHAF's Librarian/Archivist

Tricia Clapp, CG

If you are reading these words, you have an interest in handwriting analysis (graphology). As a librarian/archivist and bookseller, my best advice is this: don't wait to explore that interest, start today. Go to your local bookstore or public library and look for books about graphology, then read every one you find. Thrift stores, as well as new and used book stores, are excellent resources.

You will also want to start collecting handwriting samples for practice. Ask friends and relatives for their handwriting, and here are a few other suggestions:

- ☐ Browse biographies, history, memoirs and any other book that might contain handwriting samples
- ☐ Find inspirational books by multiple authors. Many contain the handwriting of each person
- ☐ In Google Images search on 'handwriting.' If you have a particular topic in mind, add that. E.g., 'handwriting+artists.'
- ☐ Art books are often a treasure trove of handwriting

Once you have decided to begin a formal study of handwriting analysis, where can you go to find a good teacher or course? AHAF does not offer its own course, but www.ahafhandwriting.org, lists some that we recommend.

Note: some organizations are highly proprietary about their study materials. We urge that whatever courses or method of graphology you choose to study, you make sure there is no caveat that forbids reading any materials but theirs.

As you start out, I recommend that you learn from every source you can find and reference as many books and articles you can on each topic. For example, as you start learning and the course work covers margins, read every book that deals with margins (there is an article on margins in this anthology!).

And as you learn, looking into books that are not specific to graphology, but where the handwritings famous people, sportspeople, celebrities, politicians, etc., are included, ask yourself whether what you are learning is consistent with what you know about that person. If it is not, ask yourself why not–what is different? See if you can get new insights about the person beyond what the book tells you.

Joining the American Handwriting Analysis Foundation will give you unlimited access to lists of books to study, as well as monographs (detailed papers focused on a particular subject) that you may borrow. You'll have a treasure trove of study groups and chapters to join and build your education. We look forward to your active membership.

BIOGRAPHICAL NOTES

Tricia Clapp began her study of handwriting in the 1980s with Wanda Peters. She was a founding member of the AHAF Tucson chapter and has been active on the local and the AHAF national board ever since. She has presented at numerous conferences and events, and has made a study of the Enneagram typology and how it relates to handwriting. As co-owner of Mostly Books in Tucson, Arizona since 1988, Tricia is well equipped to guide those who need help building their handwriting analysis reading list.

booksmostly@gmail.com

The Uses and Abuses of Insecurity: a Graphological Perspective

Roger Rubin, BA

Before beginning a discussion of some of the effects and results of insecurity, it would be helpful to first establish a baseline idea of what creates security.

A. First and foremost, there must be a symbiotic or dual union established during the child's first fifteen months. The child needs a face with accepting eyes to reflect and mirror his 'self' back to him. Whatever is in the nurturing person's eyes becomes the core and foundation of the child's identity.

B. Getting his narcissistic needs met. Physical and emotional needs are not thwarted or frustrated but, instead, are satisfied and gratified.

C. Warm contact from an emotionally available person to establish a sense of trust. If we can feel the touch and warmth of a caring person, we can believe the world is friendly and warm and we can depend on what is out there to get our needs met.

D. The need for physical space and autonomy or the opportunity to differentiate ourselves from our parents. Starting at around 15-18 months, children begin the process of separation and individuation. Only after a successful bonding between mother and child can we make a successful separation. This is the first of a lifetime of 'going off on our own.'

E. An environment that is dependable and predictable. Children need reliable parents to count on as they begin to test their personal limits and create their own identity. They need to discover and trust in safe and stable boundaries.

F. Experiencing pleasure, fun, and stimulation that are age-appropriate at every stage of development.

G. The need to experience appropriate pain and suffering in order to learn in a healthy way from experience.

H. The feeling that one's dependency needs will be met in a reasonably predictable manner. In other words, a mother and father with a firm identity who can be relied on to be there for the child.

Getting these security needs met allows us to establish self-value, self-esteem, and an underlying sense of worthiness. It is the basis for achieving any degree of self-actualization, and it is the basis for self-love and self-acceptance. Further, it is the foundation for happiness and the love of others.

John Bradshaw has been quoted and paraphrased extensively for this paper, as has Alice Miller, Gershen Kaufman, and others who believe that the core of what we experience as insecurity comes from the feeling of shame which, when carried to an extreme, becomes "toxic" and dehumanizing. Kaufman writes:

Shame is the affect which is the source of many complex and disturbing inner states: depression, alienation, self-doubt, isolating loneliness, paranoid and schizoid phenomena, compulsive disorders, splitting of the self, perfectionism, a deep sense of inferiority, inadequacy or failure, the so-called borderline conditions, and disorders of narcissism. (*Shame: The Power of Caring*)

Shame, healthy and unhealthy

A few comments about healthy shame and unhealthy shame might be useful here. Healthy shame lets us know that we are limited. We are not omnipotent and grandiose in our being or in our power. Limitation is our essential nature and it is OK to entertain some level of self-doubt.

According to Erik Erikson, a sense of shame is part of the second stage of psychosocial development. The first stage is when the child needs to develop a sense of basic trust. This is done through our primary caretakers. They need to be predictable, mirroring, comforting and trustworthy.

It is in the second stage, from about fifteen months to three years, that the child begins to develop autonomy and starts testing the limits of the world around him and begins to discover his own limits. It is in this process that healthy doubt and shame are developed. This creates the feeling of core boundaries and limits which never allows us to believe that we know it all. Also, at this time, shyness occurs, which as a healthy feeling of shame is a reluctance to expose oneself.

The basis for blushing is established here, too. Blushing results from being caught off guard unexpectedly, and a degree of healthy shame.

Unhealthy or toxic shame, which Bradshaw calls "the shame that binds you," is experienced as the all-pervasive sense that one is flawed and defective as a human being. "Toxic shame is no longer an emotion that signals our limits, it is a state of being, a core identity. Toxic shame gives one a sense of worthlessness, a sense of failing, a falling short as a human being. Toxic shame is a rupture of the self with the self," experienced as inner torment, a sickness of the soul.

Merle Fossom and Marilyn Mason in their book, *Facing Shame: Families in Recovery,* describe it this way:

> *Shame is an inner sense of being completely diminished or insufficient as a person. It is the self-judging of the self. A moment of shame may be humiliation so painful or an indignity so profound, that one feels one has been robbed of his or her dignity, or exposed as basically inadequate, bad, or worthy of rejection. A pervasive sense of shame is the ongoing premise that one is fundamentally bad, inadequate, defective, unworthy, or not fully valid as a human being.*

Shame and guilt

At this point, it would be useful to contrast shame with guilt so the difference between the two is better understood.

Healthy guilt is the emotional core of our conscience. It is emotion which results from behaving in a manner contrary to our beliefs and values. According to Erikson, the Third stage of psychosocial development is the polar balance between initiative and guilt. Guilt presupposes internalized rules and develops later than shame. Developmentally it is more mature than shame. Fossum and Mason write:

While guilt is a painful feeling of regret and responsibility for one's actions, shame is a painful feeling about oneself as a person. The possibility for repair seems foreclosed to the shameful person because shame is a matter of identity, not of behavioral infraction.

Any human emotion can become internalized. When internalized, an emotion stops functioning in the manner of an emotion and becomes a characterological style, the core of the person's character, his identity. In the case of shame, internalization is the result of identification with unreliable and shame-based models and the trauma of abandonment which binds feelings, needs, and drives with shame. Parents abandon children in the following ways:

- □ By physically leaving them
- □ By not being there to affirm their children's expression of emotion
- □ By not providing for their children's developmental dependency needs
- □ By physically, sexually, emotionally abusing them
- □ By using children to take care of their own unmet dependency needs
- □ By using children to take care of their marriage
- □ By hiding and denying their shame secrets to the outside world, the children must protect these covert issues in order to maintain the family balance
- □ By not giving them their time, attention, and direction
- □ By acting shameless

The job of parents is to model. Modeling includes how to be a man or woman; how to relate intimately to another person; how to acknowledge and express emotions; how to have physical, emotional, and intellectual boundaries; how to cope with life's problems; how to be self-disciplined; how to love oneself and others.

Dysfunctional parents can't do these functions well or at all. They don't know how. They were themselves children of dysfunctional families and were deeply wounded or deprived. It has been observed that 96% of all American families are dysfunctional to a greater or lesser degree. Although unprovable and startling, it is likely true. The level of dysfunctional behavior around us is extraordinarily high and pervasive.

Shame as alienation

Dysfunctional parents produce dysfunctional children. Children cannot know who they are without good reflective mirrors. When mirroring is defective, they experience abandonment. This is also caused by neglect of developmental dependency needs or abuse of any kind. One of the most common results is a sense of alienation.

Alienation means that one experiences parts of one's self as being separate, apart and disconnected from the self. As an example, if you were never allowed to express anger in your family, your anger becomes an alienated part of yourself. You experience toxic shame when you feel angry. This part of you must be disowned or severed. The condition of inner alienation and isolation is accompanied by a low-grade chronic depression. This has to do with the sadness of losing one's authentic self. This also applies to the expression of sexual feelings, sorrow, being afraid and of feeling joy.

Shame as the false self

Exposure of the self to the self lies at the heart of neurotic shame, so escape from the self is necessary. This is accomplished by creating a false self, which is always more or less than human. It could be a perfectionist or a slob, a family hero or family scapegoat. Layers of defense and pretense are so intense that one loses awareness of who one really is.

Whether the role chosen is that of a super achieving perfectionist or an addict in an alley, the core motivation is the neurotic shame that drives them to assume family roles and life roles that reflect a deep sense of self rupture. To name but a few of the many roles children play in dysfunctional families: hero, little parent, surrogate spouse, victim, caretaker, saint, athlete, peacemaker, scapegoat, the perfect one, the problem, the rebel, lost child, achiever. These roles allow one to survive and feel a sense of control and protection.

Shame as co-dependency

As Bradshaw uses the concept, co-dependency is a loss of one's inner reality and an addiction to outer reality. As part of the abandonment process a child gives up his own reality in order to take care of the parent (s)or the needs of the family system. The child survives by the defense of not-being-there. It is easiest to see co-dependence in the activity addictions such as alcohol or drug addiction. Co-dependents try to make themselves indispensable by taking care of others, by enabling them to continue the addiction. They are willing to do whatever it takes to be loved or worthwhile.

Shame as the core of compulsive/addictive behaviors

Our society seems to be in serious trouble. Twenty-five percent of the US population is either alcoholic or addicted to other drugs. This is a conservative figure which does not include nicotine or caffeine. There may be as many as 60 million sex abuse victims. Some claim that as many as one in eight women are battered. Eating disorders are rampant. Workaholism is a widespread condition.

Bradshaw defines compulsive/addictive behavior as "a pathological relationship to any mood-altering experience that has life damaging consequences." And, "any process used to avoid or take away intolerable reality."

Because it takes away intolerable pain the behavior becomes the user's highest priority. It takes time and energy from other parts of life; thus, its life damaging consequences.

The intolerable pain the behavior takes away is the shame-based feeling of utter aloneness, grief, and sense of being flawed all the way to one's core. Shame begets shame. The more one seeks solace, the more one becomes ashamed of the very seeking of it. Alcohol, sleeping pills, and tranquilizers are depressants; they numb feelings. Stimulants such as cocaine, hallucinogens, nicotine, and caffeine create an artificial strength, freedom, and control.

Food addictions are divided into four categories: obesity, anorexia nervosa, bulimia, and the fat/thin disorder. It is estimated that at least 34 million people are obese, 61% of them women. Obese people are shame-bound in either their angry or sad feelings. They feel empty and lonely and eat to be filled or full in order to numb their painful underlying emotions.

Anorexics take control of the family with their starving and weight loss behaviors. Rigidly controlled, they deny all feelings, especially sexuality, are super-achieving, and live behind a wall of pretense. They renounce their emotions by refusing to eat.

In bulimia, the binge cycle intensifies the underlying shame, which then triggers the purge cycle, which adds self-disgust and self-contempt. Vomiting is a way to cleanse themselves of the *shameful* amount of food just devoured. In the fat/thin disorder, by constantly thinking about eating or not eating, one is distracted from real feelings.

Bradshaw mentions feeling addictions whereby an undesirable feeling is replaced by what was a family-authorized feeling. The most common addiction to an emotion is a form of intensified anger called rage. Rage is the only emotion that cannot be controlled by shame. When we are raging, we feel unified within, no longer split, no longer inadequate and defective. We are mood-altered.

Other feeling addictions are addiction to sadness, fear, excitement, religious righteousness; even to guilt, which keeps one working endlessly on oneself, analyzing every event and transaction ad infinitum.

Activity addictions are buying, hoarding, sex, reading, gambling, exercising, watching sports, watching TV, and caring for pets. The addiction to work allows the workaholic to avoid painful feelings of loneliness, inadequacy, and depression.

Defenses against shame

There are many defenses against deep shame such as the primary ego defense of denial which is the attempt to deny the pain. Fantasy bonding, which is clinging to the illusion that there is somebody there who loves one, which is a way of clinging to the abuser. Repression is used to numb out feelings.

Dissociation is the defense that splits one from the tormenting reality by substituting another for it at the same time. This is seen in cases of severe sexual or physical abuse, may manifest in dissociative identity disorder. Others include projection, somatic conversions, and reaction formations.

A more complex defense against toxic shame is to act shameless. This is a strategy which becomes a characterological style.

Perfectionism is also one of these. Perfectionism is learned when one is valued only for doing and performing and when this is the basis for parental love. Kaufman writes:

> *"When perfectionism is paramount, the comparison of self with others inevitably ends in the self feeling the lesser for the consequence. Comparing and judging lead to a destructive kind of competitiveness which aims at outdoing others and being one up on them, rather than being the best one can be."*

Striving for power and control is another defense. Power is a form of control and those who must control everything feel vulnerable to being shamed, being exposed so it can be seen that they are flawed and defective. They need to be higher on the pecking order to feel adequate and superior. Only by having power over others can one reverse the role of early childhood. It is a reenactment of their original victimization. Control means attempting to limit other people's thoughts, feelings, and actions. It destroys intimacy and equality. In its most neurotic form, it is an out-and-out addiction. Individuals spend all their energies planning and scheming for position in order to climb the ladder of success.

Criticism and blame are perhaps the most common ways that shame is transferred inter-personally. If one feels put down and humiliated, the feeling can be reduced by blaming and criticizing someone else. When your mother says, *"You never think of anyone but yourself,"* you are likely to feel deeply shamed and may grow up to treat those around you in the same way.

Caretaking and helping are activities that distract one from feelings of inadequacy. This occurs when the goal of the caretaker is the caretaking and not the good of the person being cared for and leads to enabling or rescuing, and is characteristic of co-dependency. Parents often enable or rescue their children, doing for them what they could not do for themselves. The children wind up feeling inadequate or defective.

People pleasing and being nice is often a way to avoid real emotional intimacy and contact. By avoiding intimacy, the people-pleaser makes sure that no one sees him as he really is, suffering from feelings of shame and inadequacy. This behavior is characteristic of Pollyanna types, religiously righteous people, and those who behave in a compulsively positive manner.

Bradshaw says that to heal our toxic shame we must come out of hiding. As long as our shame is hidden, there is nothing we can do about it. In order to change it, we must embrace it. "The only way out is through."

The last half of *Healing the Shame that Binds You* is devoted to ideas and methods for externalizing the internalized shame that most of us carry around. Bradshaw believes very much in using groups, especially those that use the twelve-step program originated in Alcoholics Anonymous, as well as in intensive personal work.

ILLUSTRATIONS

#1 - Female. 50. Right hand. Successful artist, wife, and mother. Fairly well-adjusted, warm, nurturing, and creative personality. Conventional, yet expressively original. Positive, healthy symbiotic union. As a result, is well-integrated and balanced. Strong rhythm, right slant, pastose stroke, original letter forms, simplification.

ILL. #1

Dear Mr. Rubin –

Having thought about what these two paragraphs would (should) say for the past few days, naturally I've waited until the last possible moment before catching a plane to Washington to write. This of course means that I'm in a frantic rush and not being especially careful.

#2 (next page)- Female. 75. Right hand. Very successful psychiatrist with strong interest in aesthetics. Mature, developed personality. Balance between intellectual and emotional areas. Brought up by a cold mother (angular PPI) but a loving

I know that this is wrong. but I feel that I am slipping badly and that I better stop now to try too much before I will be forced to do it.
I wish I had my old self-confidence
So please tell me

nanny and a loving father (garland forms). Good early security pattern. Movement, form, and space rhythms are strong. Strong simplification with legibility, balanced zones, well organized.

#3 - Male. 65. Right hand. Retired psychiatrist. Art and antique collector. Superior analytic intelligence (highly simplified with angular forms). Emotionally detached, controlled, irritable (mixed slant, variable size). Narcissistic needs thwarted and frustrated (PPI emphasis on mother. Extreme angularity and strong rightward lower zone strokes suggest hostility, independence and defiance towards father and other authority figures

ILL. #3

8/27/84

Dear Ms. von Zweck—

I regret that Jessie gave you my name without consulting me. If she had told me her intentions, I would have flagged her down.

I have lived here some 11 years, and at first liked it. For the past 3 or 4 years I have soured on the place completely, and, when I can get my affairs & possessions organized, I plan to move to Virginia. As a matter of fact, I will be busy doing just that, and may actually be on my way when you arrive here in September.

#4 - Male. 46. Right hand. High-powered investment banker. Narcissistically deprived. Over-controlled as child. Toilet trained at age twelve months. Parents were intellectual, cool, and avoided touching him (wide word space). Competitive, aggressive, and intelligently exploitative (angularity, i-dots in the form of sharp dashes or accent marks). High level of tension and poor release pattern (strong emphasis on angular rather than rounded/angular forms, PPI. Very tall upper zone .

#4

Dear Roger,

I am writing to ask you to analyze my handwriting from the sample I am writing now and from a previous 1977/78 sample I dug out at random; and, finally, I include a recent letter from my father to my wife which will provide the requested sample of his handwriting.

I could not come up with a sample of my mother's script, nor could I find any from college days of my own.

While I am interested in any comments

#5 - Female. 32. Right hand. Jewelry designer and crafts artist (extreme simplification in original forms; 'lyrical d'). Moderately successful but working below capacity. High intelligence and awareness levels (wide open spatial arrangement, simplification; emotionally underdeveloped.) Little warmth and touching from mother, resulting in feelings of rejection and deep self-doubt. Unresolved identity issues interferes with being fully productive. Feels flawed and isolated (unfinished lower zone forms)

ILL. # 5

[illegible] more expensive, and finely finished woven
patterns from Europe, and offer many
novelty cloths and printed ribbons to our
customers.

Our largest customer base is
florists, followed by craft accounts.
The gift trade, which most consumers
commonly associate our product with
is our least profitable market.

Hope this little piece on

.#6 - Male. 60's. Right hand. Father of Fig. #5. He is emotionally unavailable to himself and others (variable PPIs, twisted lower zone). Main motivation and activity is directed towards creating success in the business world (strong rightward-directed rhythm, tall capitals, extremely long t-bars).

ILL. # 6

Alice —
I hope you find this useful
in your quest for identity
Love
Dad

#7 - Female. 50's. Mother of Fig. #5. Became a psychotherapist in later life. Emotionally cool, detached (extremely wide word spaces, undeveloped lower zone). High intelligence but withholding (simplification, no parental figures on PPI).

ILL. # #7

Dear Alice,
I hope that you not only find the right answers, but discover the right questions —
Love
Mom

#8 - Female. Mid 40's. Right hand. Successful primal therapist. Narrowness, wide word spacing and high upper zone/long lower zone indicate repression, inhibition, and fearfulness, poor sexual identity. Strong tension and weak release causes anger and frustration. Mother was critical, rigid, and impossible to please, a guilt dispenser. This writer has an overdeveloped superego (rigidity, too-tall upper zone, extreme word spacing) and a weak ego; is guilt-ridden, and tends to blame others for her problems (extreme upper zone).

ILL. #8

Kimberley, B.C. is situated about 200 miles north of Spokane, Washington
It is near Trail, B.C, Fernie, B.C, Nelson, B.C, Kelowna, B.C
I attended twelve years of school there and then went to the
University of British Columbia which is in Vancouver, B.C, 700 miles away
Married my highschool boy friend at age 21, had Pamela at age
24, Scott 17 months later, lost one baby at age 29 and that
is why I adopted Darryl. My husband and I divorced after

#9 - Male. 46. Right hand. Was a ranking police officer, now a lawyer and a writer. Both parents were alcoholic, resulting in severe early abandonment problems for him. He is currently dealing effectively with his own substance abuse issues (difficulty controlling the writing instrument). His somewhat chaotic inner life leads to instability in emotional relationships (the overall writing looks chaotic, released rhythm. Strong intelligence and intuition seen in the simplification, open upper zone, fast speed). Strong variability in slant and size plus extremely long t-bars indicate a struggle for control).

I want to see you because
I believe this to be a moment of
transition in my life, of roads to
be taken and not taken. Maybe
there are answers in the
There are answers in one's handwriting, no doubt, but to read them is
the problem. Therefore, I come to you
now for guidance, a reading, an
insight, or maybe no more than a
hint. In any case, help. I enclose an
Army document with
my father's signature.

#10 - Male. 27. Right hand. substance abuser. Part time stockbroker and part-time graduate student in psychology. Intelligent but underachieving (simplification with slack rhythm makes the writing too soft). Mother overprotects him and father rejects him. Early disturbance led to identity confusion especially in sexual areas ('feminine' appearance, too few angles). Low levels of concentration and impulse control. His cleverness and manipulativeness (slack rhythm) are a partial cover for a damaged ego.

ILL. #10

DON'T GO THROUGH THE PAIN
AND NOT LEARN THE LESSON

Don't go through the pain
and not learn the lesson
because each time you don't learn
the lesson, the pain is more severe

#11 Female. 36. Right hand. Eating disorder. Serious weight problem based on unfulfilled oral needs in infancy. Works as advertising salesperson with

ILL. #11

Thank you for scheduling me
in Tuesday. I hope you enjoy
your trip to San Francisco.
Truly looking forward to
meeting you!

modest success. Strongly underachieving (forms too elaborate). Emotional immaturity severely restricts her social skills and satisfaction (childish writing).

#12 - Male. 42. Right hand. Successful documentary film maker. Poor parenting resulted in severe emotional alienation and distancing (extreme spacing–rivers, stick PPI). Very intelligent and creative but emotionally underdeveloped (simplification, originality, cut off lower zone).

Here is what I have of our handwriting. Here is my own too, for Ron's mother!
I have a couple of very nice lady friends who are looking for someone nice - perhaps we might have dinner sometime when I get back from St. Thomas (I am off to a film festival wed - Sunday

#13 - Male. 49. Left hand. Highly successful business executive. Emotionally deprived and poor1y nurtured as a child (odd, illegible forms, leftward trend.) Feelings are detached and out of touch (left slant, wide word spaces). He is a driven workaholic, absorbing high levels of tension and stress.

ILL. #13

You had asked how the fact that DLJ can delay placing the business with us can cause us problems because we would be paying out to brokers under the min. provisions of their contracts. This is handled in the agreement by restricting to 100,000 contracts the amount they can delay so we are

BIOGRAPHICAL NOTES

Roger Rubin is a past president of the National Society for Graphology. He began his studies in graphology in 1971 with Felix Klein. As a court-qualified handwriting expert and handwriting analyst he has worked with a wide variety of clients for more than forty years. Roger is the author of several monographs dealing with various aspects of handwriting psychology and has been a frequent speaker at national and international conferences. In addition to being featured in a wide variety of newspaper and magazine articles, he has appeared on many radio and television programs, including Sixty Minutes.

rogwrite@aol.com

BIBLIOGRAPHY

Bradshaw, John. *Bradshaw On: The Family*. Deerfield Beach, FL. Health Communications.

Bradshaw, John. *Healing the Shame that Binds You.* Deerfield Beach, FL. Health Communication.

Erikson, Erik. *Childhood and Society*. New York: W.W. Norton.

Fossum, M. and Mason, M. *Facing Shame.* New York: W.W. Norton.

Kaufman, Gershen. *Shame: The Power of Caring.* Cambridge, MASS. Schenkman Books.

Miller, Alice. *The Drama of the Gifted Child.* New York: Basic Books.

Satir, Virginia. *Conjoint Family Therapy*. Palo Alto, CA: Science and Behavior.

A Copybook Surprise

Edda Manley

In the 1800's having the ability to read and write by hand was considered a cherished skill and an indication that a person had received an education.

People who were fortunate enough to be taught the fundamentals of handwriting knew that continued practice in writing was necessary to improve and develop the script they desired to have. To facilitate such practice, people would purchase the very basic supplies of straight pen, ink and a lined book called a Copybook. Many hours would be spent writing one's signature repeatedly until it was easy to write the signature the way you wanted it to appear.

Just like today when handwriting analysts ask a person to write something for a sample of handwriting, it can be difficult for the writer to think about what to write. It is also interesting to see what people wrote in copybooks to practice their handwriting.

Below are a few samples of handwriting from a copybook written in the late 1800's which show the things that were chosen to write and they style of writing from that time.

Capital/upper case letters of the alphabet

Writing upper case letters gave the writer practice at creating the embellishments of an earlier era that indicated a more refined person. You can see between the first and second line of the alphabet letters that different formations were being experimented with.

Listing the names of various metals gives more practice with both upper case and lower-case letters. These names and the proper spelling of them would have been taught in school. The last line of writing would be a more free-flowing thought which gives a good example of the writers' regular handwriting.

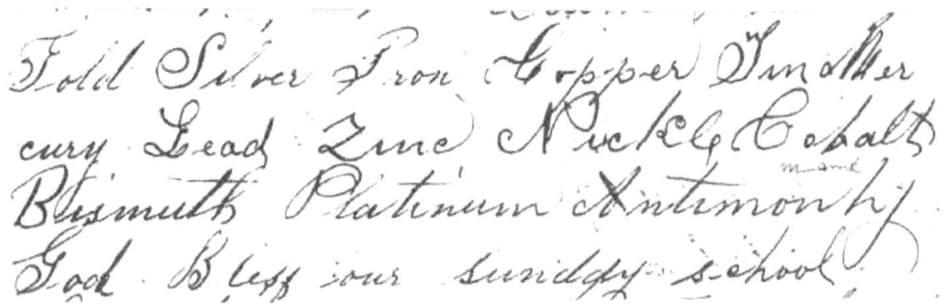

Gold Silver Iron Copper Tin Mer
cury Lead Zinc Nickel Cobalt
Bismuth Platinum Antimony
God Bless our Sunday school

Writing random words that require upper case and lower-case letters gives more practice in writing long words that contain various letters. Notice the improvement in the writers' ability to control the inkflow of the pen by the time the third line is written. This is indicated by the absence of dark spots, such as seen in the first and second line.

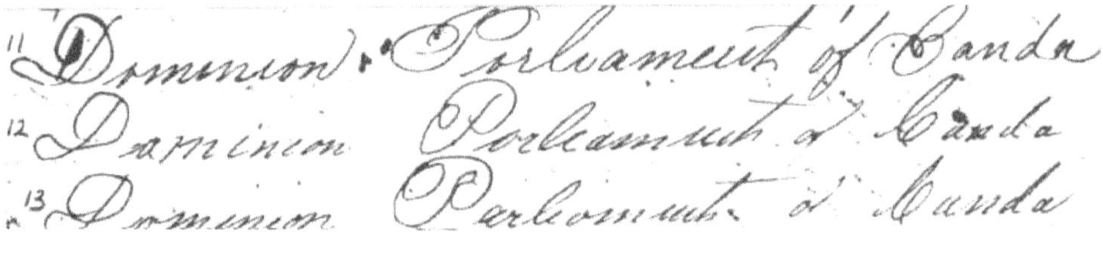

11 Dominion Parliament of Canda
12 Dominion Parliament of Canda
13 Dominion Parliament of Canda

Sayings concerning religiosity were frequently written to reinforce positive thoughts.

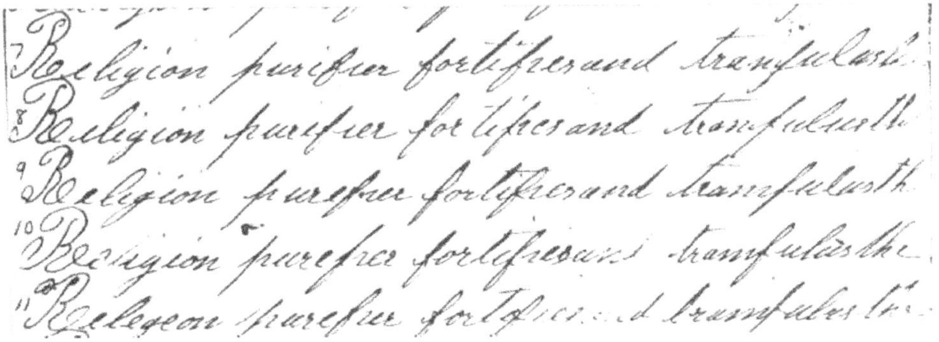

Poetry and short sayings, we would call them affirmations, were very popular during these times, as they are today. This one below reads:

That love and happiness in union glows
This in that heart where goodness flows.

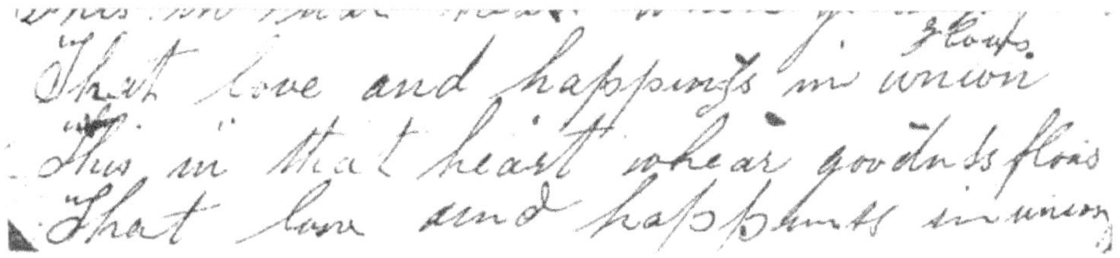

The Copybook

My graphology partner, Suzanne McPetrie, and I were contacted by a member of well-known family in Ontario, Canada. A copybook that was used for practicing penmanship had been found in the attic of a house belonging to a relative. Their request was for us to analyze the contents of the book and give whatever information we could about the people who had written in this copybook, which is dated 1874.

We were allowed to make a photocopy of the original copybook, and to access to the original copybook should we need it. In all, it contained 28 pages of handwriting.

It was obvious that several people had written in this copybook at different times. This was a common practice because writing supplies were fairly expensive and not readily available in all households. Some entries showed one writer practicing his formal signature, a male name, so there is no doubt about gender. Other pages had delicately written entries that led us to speculate that it possibly may have been a female writing.

Another writing was mournful prose we called the *Ode to Rosanna*. We felt that Rosanna was possibly a housekeeper who had left the service of the household, and the writer of this entry deeply missed her. There was a darkness on the photocopy of this page, and we were unsure of how that was created.

We requested to view the original to see if we could learn more from a closer look at the page. When Suzanne saw the original, she quickly determined that it was likely that wine had spilled onto that part of the page.

Her remark when she saw it was, "He was in his cups," a saying from that era when a person was drunk. This also explained the deterioration of the handwriting as the writer wrote more on the page.

Several of the entries on various pages had repeated signatures that only had the first or first and second initials before the last name. Practicing one's signature was important because your signature on documents would reflect to others the status of the person signing.

The signatures were written quite large with curled flourishes on the capitals, reflecting this writer's desire to be seen as important. Bold, embellished signatures were mostly produced by people who considered themselves to be pillars of the community.

A page-by-page summary of similarities in the handwriting was made, each page ending with our opinion on who wrote that specific page. In total we were certain that four people had written in this copybook at various times.

Further research provided copybook scripts from the time period in which the writers may have been taught. We could not be sure that they were in fact taught these scripts, but at least we had examples of the general style of handwriting that was used at this time.

The puzzle pieces were now beginning to start to fit together. We were able to put all the writings of the same writers together, even though the person's writing appeared on many different pages. This then gave us the most handwriting available for each writer. Now we could begin analyzing the handwriting and putting together a personality profile for each writer.

A brief analysis was done on personality characteristics we could determine for each writer. We presented our analysis of the handwriting and the personality profiles we were able to construct for each writer and were able to answer any questions the client might have had.

As we have often been counseled, a graphologist does not have a legal right to use the diagnostic terminology used by the psychology profession to describe certain specific conditions of mental health. We can, however, describe what we see in the writing.

One of the handwritings had such strong and frequent indicators of a specific behavior that we believed not mentioning it would leave out an important aspect of this writer's personality. Specifically, we saw that the writer had "moments of extreme elation followed by moments of severe despondency." There is a clinical term for such behavior when diagnosed by a qualified person in the field of psychiatry. Without actually stating this term, we were able to state that the writer of this sample would display such behavior.

The analysis was well received, and we left knowing that we had done the best work we were able to do for this client. Payment for our work was received, and we hoped our information would be of use to them. This is where our role as a handwriting analyst usually ends.

Several months later, I received a package in the mail. When I opened it, I was delighted to see it was a copy of the genealogical study that had been constructed on the entire family–a beautiful hard-cover book with family photos and an abundance of information. Inside the front cover the book was signed by the family member who had contracted me to do the analysis of the copybook.

To my complete surprise, chapter ten was titled *The Copybook*. When I read this chapter, I learned that this copybook, and our analysis of the handwriting, had led to the discovery of a family secret that had been kept from many family members for more than 100 years. So here, as they say…is the rest of the story.

The rest of the story

The information we had shared about this specific behavior led the family to research further. During the mid to late 1800's many people had, what we would today term as severe mental health issues. In those days, it meant that a person suffering such an affliction would be placed in what was then called, an asylum for the insane. There were several such facilities here in Ontario at that time.

The family researched records from this time period at the asylum closest to where this family had lived, and were shocked to find in the official records that both a father and son from their family tree during that period had been admitted to such a facility. The father had been admitted during 1874 and released a few months later. The son, unfortunately, was recorded as having his condition deteriorate and finally dying in an asylum.

Living relatives had no knowledge of what happened to this family member. Mental illness was considered a disgrace and not something that was openly spoken about. The family had kept this person's life a secret. There was a record that he had been buried, but there was no tombstone on his grave site the book revealed.

Further research also determined who the sole female writer in this copybook was. She was not a relative, but rather, a family friend who visited the home of this family at various times.

Through the years this has been a very private story for me. This was my first experience with a genealogy request. I knew when I first held the copybook in my hands that it was something to be revered and treasured. From the very beginning I was honored to have the opportunity to analyze this handwriting from a time period when people valued the ability to write by candlelight whenever they had a few minutes to spare.

Signatures were repeated on several pages to develop the style and "look" they were pleased with. Some of the writing was of high quality both in form and correct spelling and grammar. Other writing showed errors that might have been from lesser education, or thinking skills that were not well-developed. All this information assists us in doing a handwriting analysis. How wonderful, I thought, that someone had the foresight to save this copybook, a true family treasure!

More than anything else, this handwriting analysis assignment taught me that we never know when the work we do might truly change peoples' lives. I had no idea that information we shared could have such an impact on the family history.

Those who have lost relatives and never know what happened to them, have a void in their lives that stays with them forever. I, too, have a cousin who lost his life in a maritime accident at a port near Montreal Quebec, and his body was never found.

For me, it was a risk to make the decision to "go where angels fear to tread." I am not qualified in psychology. Through the years, though, at conferences and other learning opportunities with colleagues, we acquire some knowledge about mental conditions. In this case, the indicators we saw in the handwriting were so strong that I was confident that what I was observing was accurate. Leaving out such significant information was simply not in the best interests of the family.

Privacy issues

The family name in this story has not been revealed, as I do not have the permission from the family. I would not request such permission because it is a deeply private matter. I believe it is important for me to preserve the entire family's privacy, and am glad this story can be told without revealing the family name..

Confidentiality is another aspect of the graphology profession that needs to be respected and maintained. We can share experiences that may be learning opportunities for others, and still keep details that preserve the privacy of those involved from being revealed. As has often been said of our profession, it involves both science and art.

In sharing this story, my hope is that others in the general public may see how interesting and rewarding our work as handwriting analysts can be. One never knows when the opportunity to make a significant difference in other people's lives might occur. In 2003, when I was first contacted to do this handwriting analysis, I never thought that almost twenty years later it might possibly encourage others to pursue working in this most amazing profession.

BIOGRAPHICAL NOTES

Studying all aspects of handwriting and handwriting analysis has been a passion for Edda for over thirty years. Currently, she serves AAHA (American Association of Handwriting Analysts) as Regional Chair II - Canada. She is also a member of AHAF (American Handwriting Analysis Foundation). Edda has given numerous presentations to organizations who were interested in learning more about handwriting analysis. In March 1997, Edda and her mentor, the late Suzanne McPetrie, gave a one-day workshop, *The Basics of Handwriting Analysis.* From this group, many went on to further study of handwriting analysis and complete their certification exams with AAHA.

eddamanley@cogeco.ca

Handwriting: essential for learning, memory, and self-esteem; research reveals why

Jane Redfield Yank, Ph.D.

Definitions. For purposes of this essay, the term handwriting refers to visible traces produced by hand that consist of graphemes or orthographic forms representing letters, diacritics, and words. Pictographs and writing produced by foot, mouth, thought, other effectors, and assistive devices are not included in the definition used in this essay due to limited research on those applications.

The information presented in these comments apply to both cursive ("joined-up") handwriting and manuscript printing (disconnected writing based on "ball-and-stick" writing forms).

Shapes, sizes, spacing, and alignment of letters, words, and punctuation on a writing surface (paper, digitizing pads, tabletop devices, and similar items), speed, and pressure are important factors in evaluating the quality of the written form.

Is handwriting more accurately described as brainwriting?

Although popular articles describe handwriting as brainwriting, writing by hand involves much more than a one-directional process beginning in the brain and ending with the written trace. Handwriting involves multiple brain centers associated with language, memory, emotion, cognition, sensory inputs from vision, hearing, proprioception, and haptics, spatial and temporal patterning, and motor functions interacting with environmental constraints to produce recognizable symbols that have been established by a culture to convey meaning and knowledge.

Milestones in handwriting research

In the first half of the 20th century, the topic of handwriting generated little interest from experimental psychologists and neuroscientists. Still, a handful of studies investigating central processes in handwriting were published by pioneering researchers. June Downey, professor of psychology at the University of Wyoming (USA), published experimental findings on the effects of changing visual and tactile conditions on handwriting (1908).

In the decades between the two world wars, Robert Saudek, a lecturer at various European universities, conducted experiments on handwriting measurements of under different conditions of speed, pressure, and letter formation (Saudek, as cited by Marano et al., 2020). At Harvard University, Gordon Allport and Philip Vernon attempted to catalog personality traits from handwriting and movement in their research published as *Studies on Expressive Movements* (1933).

Researchers from Columbia University, Thea Stein-Lewinson from the New York Psychiatric Institute at Columbia and Joseph Zubin, biometrics lab director and professor of psychology, published a comprehensive set of objective scales for measuring temporal features of handwriting, described as rhythm (1942). Despite exceptions such as these, most handwriting research performed before 1980 focused on methods for teaching penmanship, holding a pen, and encouraging proper arm position and posture.

In the late 1970s, handwriting became recognized as a readily accessible skill for studying fundamental sensorimotor and cognitive mechanisms such as motor programs and the role of feedback/feed-forward loops in motor control (Keele, 1968; Schmidt & Wrisberg, 1973). These theories motivated teams of experimental psychologists at the Nijmegen Institute for Cognition and Information (NICI) at Radboud University (formerly known as

Katholieke Universiteit Nijmegen) and their international colleagues to develop a research program to develop and explore unifying perceptual-motor theories on handwriting skills.

At the same time, the theory of dynamical systems and considerations of the effect of the environment and the body on thinking and behavior gave rise to theories of embedded cognition. Cognitive scientists discovered that "writing is a cognitive technology par excellence" (Mangen et al., 2015, p. 228), offering many avenues for exploring the interdependent nature of cognitive and motor processes in skilled movement.

The increased use of keyboarding in education spurred research to understand the effects of digital technology on communications and cognition. Separately, computer scientists envisioned new applications of computing that would rely on handwriting and gesture, and began efforts to develop handwriting and hand motion recognition algorithms to enhance computer operations.

As a result, research on the perceptual, motor, and cognitive aspects of handwriting has rapidly grown over the last several decades — indeed, more than 1000 peer-reviewed articles have already been published and listed in the EBSCO discovery service database in the first ten months of 2022 alone.

Contributions from brain sciences to psychophysical processes in handwriting

Expanded interest in handwriting yielded rich opportunities to test and observe brain activations corresponding to sensory, spatio-temporal, perceptual, and motor control processes necessary for handwriting. At the same time, researchers acknowledged that handwriting is not simply a problem for understanding central movement processes but involves thought, intent, planning, and information retrieval and transmission (Alves et al., 2016). Investigating the manner by which writing by hand integrates sensori-motor and cognitive functions has revealed the intricate coordination of processes required for producing meaningful, skilled handwriting.

Early studies on brain activity during handwriting began with the premise that both sensorimotor and cognitive functions, including language, were mapped to specific areas of brain anatomy. The frontal motor cortex, the superior parietal lobule, and inferior temporal gyrus (fusiform gyrus) and mid fusiform gyrus with specialization in Exner's area within the posterior middle frontal gyrus appear to link the motor and cognitive aspects of written language such as spelling, punctuation, and capitalization (Hazem et al., 2021). Sensorimotor components of handwriting such as vision, proprioception, hearing, and haptic sense for controlling grip and sensing friction have been associated with the intraparietal lobule/superior parietal lobule and the cerebellum (See Yang et al., 2020).

As this research progressed, scientists discovered more complexity in the development and integration of the sensorimotor and language aspects of handwriting than the traditional mapping scheme for neuronal activity would suggest. Separate brain structures for language and motor functions and one-directional transmission of impulses from brain structure to corresponding effector fails to provide an adequate explanation of how handwriting is produced.

Instead, recent research conducted with functional magnetic resonance imaging (fMRI) technology has revealed that the motor, sensory, cognitive, language, and emotional functions required for handwriting are not fully localized in specific brain areas (Planton et al., 2017). As a result of these findings, several neuroscientists are promoting a new model that proposes that movement and cognitive operations depend on patterns of activity within an interconnected network of brain structures (Pessoa, 2022; Thiebaut de Schotten & Forkel, 2022).

They contend that such network activity connects and expands neural connections that extend into the shoulders, arms, hands and fingers to produce skilled, intentional movement. According to Vinci-Booher, Cheng, and James (2019), such patterns or activity within interrelated sensorimotor subsystems "…support both the motor and cognitive components of handwriting (that is, "the full behavior" [of writing]) in different ways" (p. 138) while enabling the writer to adjust to environmental constraints and fulfill task demands.

Studies by handwriting researchers have also discovered that intentional practiced movement in handwriting has a reciprocal influence on the development of neural structures. Pagliarina et al. (2017) observed that "the intimate link between culture and biological organization can be interestingly noticed in recent evidence showing how handwriting profoundly changes …our brain" (p. 7). In other words, handwriting has been shown to strengthen brain development and function in different cultures, despite diversity in language, writing systems, and socioeconomic conditions (Hervais-Adelman et al., 2022, Vinci-Booher & James, 2021.)

To demonstrate this relationship, fMRI studies have shown that handwriting has significant advantages over keyboarding for increasing blood flow and neuronal activity to the brain areas associated with memory, learning, comprehension, letter recognition, and reading in both Latin and Chinese alphabets (Cao et al., 2013; Ihara, et al., 2021; James, 2017; James & Berninger, 2019; James & Engelhardt, 2012; Umejima, et al., 2021).

Repeated studies have found that handwriting activates more cognitive processes than does keying in both children and adults for cognitive tasks as diverse and multifaceted as synthesizing and recalling information, engaging in abstract and nuanced thinking, comprehension, symbol recognition (Christensen, 2009; Longcamp et al., 2008; Mangen et al., 2015; Mueller & Oppenheimer, 2014; Wiley & Rapp, 2021; Zemlock, Vinci-Booher, & James, 2018), developing a sense of identity, and increasing empathy (Doug, 2019; Johanessen et al., 2021; Mangen & Kuiker).

Should digital technology eliminate the use of handwriting?

Despite the advantages described above and others that are beyond the scope of this essay, the use of handwriting is in sharp decline in school and everyday life. Parents and educators alike understand the importance of ensuring that students write effectively with all the tools available to them, including digital devices, keyboards, and emerging brain-to-text technologies (Makin, Moses, and Chang, 2020; Willett et al., 2021). But the cognitive costs of replacing handwriting with digital technologies could be high. Greenfield (2009) observed that "[no] one medium can do everything. Every medium has its costs and weaknesses; every medium develops some cognitive skills at the expense of others. Although the visual capabilities of TV, video games, and the Internet may develop impressive visual intelligence, [these gains are offset by] the cost…to deep processing: mindful knowledge acquisition, inductive analysis, critical thinking, imagination, and reflection" (p. 71) - skills that are enhanced through handwriting.

As these examples show, mounting research evidence supports the benefits of handwriting over tapping devices for performing cognitive tasks, fostering understanding, and facilitating learning. With this information, we should be reluctant to discard the skill of handwriting, which contributes significantly to individual and species development, even as we embrace new writing systems.

Longcamp, Tanskanen, and Hari (2006) have described the trace left when writing by hand as an "imprint of action" that evokes implicit rules of movement that key tapping does not, providing an explanation for the difficulty in reading written documents reported by those who no longer write by hand. They cautioned that the differences in brain function when writing by hand and tapping on digital devices may have profound implications for literacy, language, comprehension, communication, and productivity that we should acknowledge when debating the need of handwriting in the future (Askvik et al., 2020).

As Pagliarini et al. (2017) noted, "the act of writing is so easily taken for granted that we forget what an astonishing accomplishment and elaborate process it is" (p. 7).

References

Allport, G. W. & Vernon, P.E. (1933). *Studies in expressive movement.* Macmillan.

Alves, R. A., Limpo, T., Fidalgo, R., Carvalhais, L., Pereira, L. Á., & Castro, S. L. (2016). The impact of promoting transcription on early text production: Effects on bursts and pauses, levels of written language, and writing performance. *Journal of Educational Psychology*, 108(5), 665–679. https://doi.org/10.1037/edu0000089

Askvik, E. O., van der Weel, F. R. R., van der Meer, A. L. H. (2020, July 28). The importance of cursive handwriting over typewriting for learning in the classroom: A high-density EEG study of 12-year-old children and young adults. *Frontiers in Psychology*, 11, 1810. DOI: https://10.3389/fpsyg.2020.01810

Cao, F., Vu, M., Chan, D. H. L., Lawrence, J. H., Harris, L., N., Guan, Q., Yi, X., & Perfetti, C. A. (2013). Writing affects the brain network of reading in Chinese: A functional magnetic resonance imaging study. *Human Brain Mapping*: 34(7), 1670–1684.

Christensen, C. (2009). The critical role handwriting plays in the ability to produce high-quality text in writing. In R. Beard, D. Myhill, J. Riley, & M. Nystrand (Eds.), *The SAGE book of writing development.* pp. 284-299. Sage.

Doug, R. (2019). Handwriting: Developing pupils' identity and cognitive skills. *International Journal of Education and Literacy Studies*, 7(2), 177-188. Retrieved from https://eric.ed.gov /contentdelivery/servlet/ERICServlet?accno=EJ1219559

Downey, J. E. (1908). Control processes in modified handwriting: An experimental study. *The Psychological Review*, 9(1). 1-148.

Greenfield, P. M. (2009). Technology and informal education: What is taught, what is learned. *Science*, 323(5910), 69-71. DOI: https://10.1126/science.1167190

Hazem, S.R., Awan, M., Lavrador, J. P., Patel, S., Wren, H. M., Lucena, O., Semedo, C., Irzan, H., Melbourne, A., Ourselin, S., Shapey, J., Kailaya-Vasan, A., Gullan, R., Ashkan, K., Bhangoo, R., & Vergani, F. (2021). Middle frontal gyrus and area 55b: Perioperative mapping and language outcomes. *Frontiers in Neurology*, 12. DOI=10.3389/fneur.2021.646075

Hervais-Adelman, A., Kumar, U., Mishra, R. K., Tripathi, V. N., Guleria, A., Singh, J. P., Huettig, F. (2022, October 17). How does literacy affect speech processing? Not by enhancing cortical responses to speech, but by promoting connectivity of acoustic-phonetic and graphomotor cortices. *Journal of Neuroscience*, JN-RM-1125-21; DOI: 10.1523/JNEUROSCI.1125-21.2022.

Ihara, A. S., Nakajima, K., Kake, A., Ishimaru, K., Osugi1, K., & Naruse, Y. (2021). Advantage of handwriting over typing on learning words: evidence from an n400 event-related potential index. *Frontiers in Neuroscience*, 679191. DOI: https://doi.org/10.3389/fnhum.2021.679191

James, K.H. (2017). The importance of handwriting experience on the development of the literate brain. *Current Directions in Psychological Science*, 26. 502-508. DOI: https://10.1177/0963721417709821

James, K. H. & Berninger, V.W. (2019). Brain research shows why handwriting should be taught in the computer age. *LDA Bulletin*, 51(1), 25-30.

James, K. H., & Engelhardt, L. (2012). The effects of handwriting experience on functional brain development in pre-literate children. *Trends in Neuroscience and Education*,1, 32–42. 10.1016/j.tine.2012.08.001.

Johannessen, C. M., Longcamp, M., Stuart, S. A. J., Thibault, P. J., & Babere, C. (2021). The look of writing in reading: Graphetic empathy in making and perceiving graphic traces. *Language Sciences*, 84. https://doi.org/10.1016/j.langsci.2021.10136

Keele, S. W. (1968). Movement control in skilled motor performance. *Psychological Bulletin*, 70(6, Pt.1), 387–403.

Longcamp, M., Boucard, C., Gilhodes, J.-C., Anton, J.-L., Roth, M., Nazarian, B., & Velay, J.-L. (2008). Learning through hand- or typewriting influences visual recognition of new graphic shapes: Behavioral and functional imaging evidence. *Journal of Cognitive Neuroscience*, 20(5), 802–815. https://doi.org/10.1162/jocn.2008.20504

Longcamp, M., Tanskanen, T., & Hari, R. (2006). The imprint of action: Motor cortex involvement in visual perception of handwritten letters. *NeuroImage*, 33(2), 681-688. http://dx.doi.org/10.1016/j.neuroimage.2006.06.042

Makin, J. G.., Moses, D. A., & Chang, E.F. (2020). Machine translation of cortical activity to text with an encoder–decoder framework. *Nature Neuroscience*, 23, 575–582.

Mangen, A., Anda, L.G., Oxborough, G.H., & Brønnick, K. (2015). Handwriting versus keyboard writing: Effect on word recall. *Journal of Writing Research*, 7(2), 227-247.

Mangen, A. & Kuiken, D. (2014). Lost in an iPad: Narrative engagement on paper and tablet. *Scientific Study of Literature* 4(2). DOI:10.1075/ssol.4.2.02man

Marano, G., Traversi, G., Gaetani, E., Sani, G., Mazza, S., & Mazza, M. (2020). Graphology: An interface between biology, psychology and neuroscience. *Psychological Disorders and Research*, 3(3): 1-13. doi: 10.31487/j.PDR.2020.03.05

Mueller, P. A. & Oppenheimer, D. M. (2014). The pen is mightier than the keyboard: Advantages of longhand over laptop note taking. *Psychological Science*, 25(6). 1159 1168. DOI: https://10.1177/0956797614524581.

Pagliarini, E., Scocchia, L., Vernice, M., Zoppello, M., Balottin, U., Bouamama, S., Guasti, M. T., Stucchi. (2017). Children's first handwriting productions show a rhythmic structure. Scientific Reports, 7(5516). 1-10. DOI:10.1038/s41598-017-05105-6

Peck, M., Askov, E. N., & Fairchild, S. H. (1980). Another decade of research in hand writing: Progress and prospect in the 1970s. *Journal of Educational Research*, 73(5), 283–298.

Pessoa, L. (2022). *The entangled brain: How perception, cognition, and emotion are woven together.* MIT Press.

Planton, S., Longcamp, M., Péran, P., Demonet, J. F., & Jucla, M. (2017). How specialized are writing-specific brain regions? An fMRI study of writing, drawing and oral spell ing. *Cortex*, 88, 66-80.

Schmidt, R. A., & Wrisberg, C. A. (1973). Further tests of the Adams' closed-loop theory: Response-produced feedback and the error-detection mechanism. *Journal of Motor Behavior*, 3, 155-164.

Stein Lewinson, T. & Zubin, J. (1942). *Handwriting analysis : a series of scales for evaluating the dynamic aspects of handwriting.* Crown's Press.

Thiebaut de Schotten, M. & Forkel, S. J. (2022). The emergent properties of the connected brain. *Science*, 378(6619), 505-510. DOI: 10.1126/science.abq2591

Umejima, K., Ibaraki, T., Yamazaki, T., & Sakai, K. (2021, March 19). Paper notebooks vs. mobile devices: Brain activation differences during memory retrieval. *Frontiers in Behavioral Neuroscience.* DOI: https://doi.org/10.3389/fnbeh.2021.634158

Vinci-Booher, S. & James, K. H. (2021, November 19). Protracted neural development of dorsal motor systems during handwriting and the relation to early literacy skills. *Frontiers in Psychology*, 12:750559. doi: 10.3389/fpsyg.2021.750559. PMID: 34867637; PMCID: PMC8639586.

Vinci-Booher, S., Cheng, H., & James, K. H. (2019). An analysis of the brain systems involved with producing letters by hand. *Journal of Cognitive Neuroscience*, 31(1), 138–154. https://doi.org/10.1162/jocn_a_01340

Willett, F. R., Avansino, D. T., Hochberg, L. R., Henderson, J. M. & Shenoy, K. V. (2021, May 12). High-performance brain-to-text communication via handwriting. *Nature.* DOI: https://10.1038/s41586-021-03506-2

Yang, Y., Tam, F., Graham, S. J., Sun, G., Li, J., Gu, C., Tao, R., Wang, N., Bi, H., & Zuo, Z. (2020). Men and women differ in the neural basis of handwriting. *Human Brain Mapping*, 41(10), 2642–2655. https://doi.org/10.1002/hbm.24968

Zemlock, D., Vinci-Booher, S., & James, K. H. (2018). Visual-motor symbol production facilitates letter recognition in young children. *Reading and Writing*, 31, 1255-1271. DOI: https://10.1007/s11145-018-9831-z

BIOGRAPHICAL NOTES

Jane Redfield Yank is a psychotherapist and researcher with a Master's Degree in Social Work (University of Wisconsin-Madison) and Human Development (St. Mary's University of Minnesota) and has worked as a licensed psychologist and clinical social worker. She studied handwriting analysis with Felix Klein and obtained a PhD from the University of Minnesota in kinesiology with a concentration in statistics, studying the effects of cognitive stress on handwriting. She has taught movement sciences, social work methods, and research, assisted researchers in health sciences, business, and education, and has published in several journals. Dr. Yank is the current chair of the Research Committee for the American Handwriting Analysis Foundation and a member of the International Graphonomics Society.

jane.yank@gmail.com

Past, Present, Future: living on the edge of your margins

Barbara R. Donato, MS, GGA, CG

Handwriting provides an outward symbol of the inner personality at the time of the writing. Writing by hand is a neuromuscular activity that handwriting analysts refer to as 'brain writing,' and the way we write paints a picture of how we think, feel, and act.

Think of a blank piece of paper as your environment and the writing you create on the paper as symbolic of how you behave in that environment. For example, when you enter a room where you don't know anyone, do you breeze in confidently and proclaim, HERE I AM!? Or, do you quietly walk in, move over to a corner of the room, and wait for people to come up to you? Specific indicators in your handwriting provide clues as to how you will respond in this situation.

Most young people in the U.S. learn to write by following the copybook writing style taught in school. As you mature, your life experiences affect the personality and handwriting changes accordingly. The closer you write to the copybook style you learned in school, the more comfortable you are conforming to society's rules. When the handwriting moves away from the copybook style, it demonstrates originality.

Analyzing your handwriting to determine your personality type and potential for behavior is like putting together pieces of a puzzle. To develop an initial impression, we first look at the holistic aspects of the writing, which include space, form, and movement. Space includes the spacing of words, letters, lines, and margins, and tells us how much breathing room you give to yourself and to others. The form of your writing shows us if and how you want to connect with other people. And the movement of your writing indicates if you are on an even emotional keel or if something is out of balance.

To identify additional aspects of your character, we also look at other factors in your handwriting, such as size, slant, pressure, loops, zonal balance, mental processes, individual letters, and your signature. Each of these traits influences the surrounding traits, the same way that individual people contribute to their team's overall performance. Also, each trait can have a light side and a shadow side, depending on how it is used. We carefully prepare a personality profile based on your handwriting by assembling all of the pieces and evaluating how they work together.

Creating Boundaries

Margins signify boundaries and are one of the first things we notice in the layout of your writing. We examine the left, right, top, and bottom margins on all pages of your writing to understand how you orient yourself to the past, present, and future, as well as to other people. In *Handwriting: A Key to Personality,* Klara Roman notes that margins represent your outlook on time and space in relation to your inner world and the external environment. (Roman, page 303) In this sense, your margins express how you perceive and feel about your station in life.

Handwriting analysts agree that the left part of the page represents the past and the self, the middle part represents the present, and the right represents the future and other people. Using this parameter, you can determine your orientation to space, time, yourself, and others by looking at your margins to see where you start and end each line of writing.

In the U.S., students are taught that the standard width of all four margins on an 8 $^{1}/^{2}$ x 11 piece of paper is about one-inch. How close you start each line of writing on the left margin is a conscious act and tells us how comfortable you are with yourself and your past.

The right-hand margin is made more unconsciously than the left margin, and gives clues about how you organize your time and how comfortable you are with other people and the future. The top and bottom margins tell how you relate to the recipient of your letter in particular and to society in general. The more your writing falls inside a "frame" of one-inch margins on all four sides of the paper, the more you respect your own and others' space.

Left-Hand Margin

Unless you are writing a headline or chapter heading, your left-hand margin is the starting point of your page of writing. Where you place your writing instrument on the first line sets the tone for the left-hand margin and all of the lines to follow. Since the left represents the past, where your margin falls–either before, on, or after the standard one-inch margin line–provides insight about your desire to stay on the familiar terrain of your past, or to venture forward into the unknown. Here are some explanations of left-hand margin variations.

- **Ground Zero:** If you start your left-hand margin on the one-inch mark, you are comfortable with your past and generally harbor no desire to stay there; you are ready to embark on new experiences.
- **Wide:** If you begin your left-hand margin after the one-inch mark, you are confident about the future and long to move away from the past. The farther away this margin is from the one-inch mark, the more you want to flee the past and move forward.
- **Narrow:** If your left-hand margin starts before the one-inch mark, you are fearful of moving forward and prefer to stick with what you've already experienced.
- **Widening:** If you start each successive line underneath the first line increasingly toward the right, you may be spontaneous and/or impulsive. You are eager to move forward and accomplish your goals.
- **Decreasing:** If you start each line after the first line closer to the left side of the paper, you fear the future and long for the security of the familiar. It's hard for you to let go of your past.
- **Rigid:** If you start each line after the first line precisely beneath the first line of writing, you care deeply about appearances. You don't allow yourself or others to deviate from what's expected at home or at work.
- **Irregular:** If your left-hand margin is variable and waivers before and after the initial line, you march to the beat of your own drum and may be seen as unpredictable and unreliable.

- **No left margin:** If your left-hand margin abuts the left edge of the paper, the past has a profound influence on you. Moving away from what you know into unknown territory can terrify you, leaving you afraid to embark on new experiences.

Illustrations of left-hand margins

Left-Hand Margins

Ground Zero Left-Hand Margin

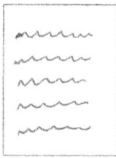

Decreasing Left-Hand Margin

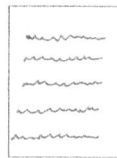

Wide Left-Hand Margin

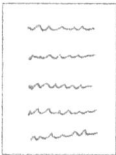

Rigid Left-Hand Margin

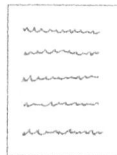

Narrow Left-Hand Margin

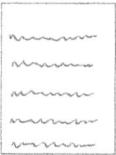

Irregular Left-Hand Margin

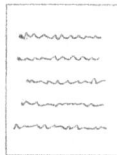

Widening Left-Hand Margin

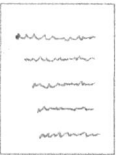

No Left-Hand Margin

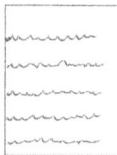

Right-Hand Margin

Where you stop writing on each line at the right side of your paper shows how you feel about your future, whether you're fully embracing it or tentatively tiptoeing toward it. The right margin tells how careful you are when interacting with other people. According to *The Complete Idiot's Guide to Handwriting Analysis,* the right-hand margin shows how you manage time, energy, and money. (Lowe, page 92) Here are some explanations of right-hand margins:

- **Rigid:** It is unusual to end each line directly beneath where the first line ends, but if you do this, you are organized, have tremendous self-control, and may have an aesthetic appreciation of space. Strictly adhering to the rules is a joy for you.
- **Wide:** If your right-hand margin ends before the final inch of your paper, you are reserved and hesitant about the future. The more the margin ends before the one-inch mark, the more you want to avoid the unknown.
- **Narrow:** If your right-hand margin ends after the one-inch mark, you are bold and confident about moving forward. Marc Seifer, in his book, *The Definitive Book of Handwriting Analysis*, notes that a narrow right-hand margin also indicates you are buoyant and self-assured. (Seifer, page 112)
- **Widening:** If you end each line below the first line increasingly before the right edge of the paper, you may start out confidently, but fear and hesitation may prevent you from achieving all you set out to do.
- **Decreasing:** If you end each line below the first line closer to the right edge of the paper, you are self-directed and eager to move forward to accomplish your goals. You welcome the opportunity to explore new things.
- **Irregular:** It is not unusual to see some variability in the right-hand margin. However, if your right-hand margin is widely variable and moves erratically before and after the end of the initial line, it indicates you don't like following the rules. It can also signal that you're feeling emotionally unbalanced.
- **No right margin:** If your right margin crashes into the right side of the paper, you are moving full steam ahead! Your enthusiasm may make it difficult for you to plan and organize your time efficiently.

Illustrations of right-hand margins

Rigid Right-Hand Margin

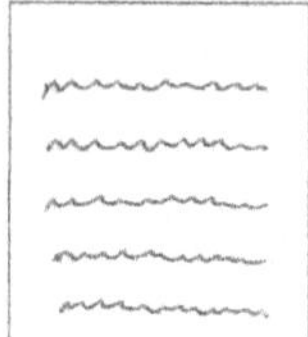

Decreasing Right-Hand Margin

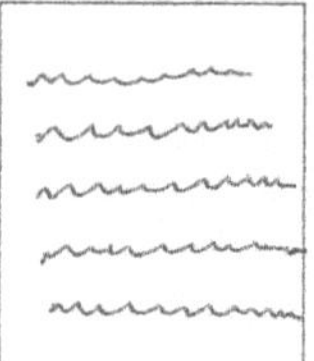

Wide Right-Hand Margin

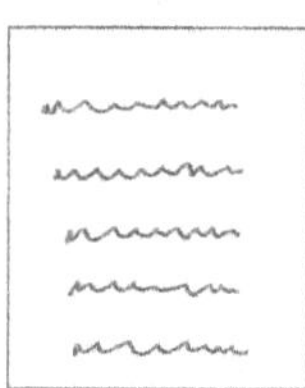

Irregular Right-Hand Margin

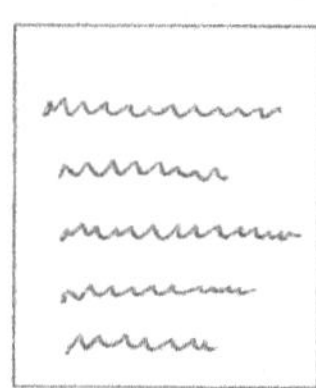

Narrow Right-Hand Margin

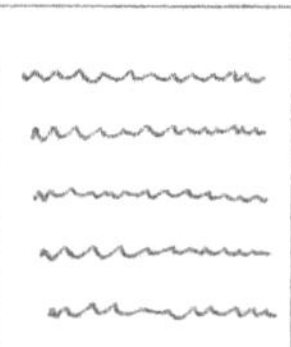

No Right-Hand Margin

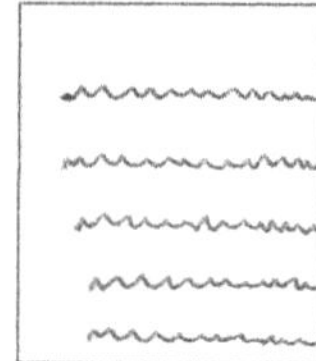

Widening Right-Hand Margin

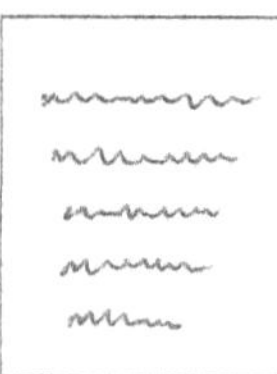

Top Margin

The top margin shows us how much esteem you give to the person to whom you are writing.

- **Large Upper Margin:** Although students are taught to make one-inch margins all around the page, when writing letters, we learn that leaving a little more space at the top of the page shows respect for the letter recipient. If you make the upper margin more than three inches below the top of the page, you are acting in a formal manner and showing great esteem for the person receiving your letter.
- **Narrow Upper Margin:** If you start your letter at the top of the page with little breathing room, you are showing disrespect for the person to whom you are writing.

Bottom Margin

The bottom margin shows us how you plan and how you interact with others.

- **Large Lower Margin:** If you have plenty of words to fill a page, yet leave an overly large margin at the bottom of the page, you avoid contact with those outside of your inner circle and are not interested in fitting in with society at large.
- **Narrow Lower Margin:** If you make a very narrow margin at the bottom of the page, you stretch social boundaries and like to surround yourself with lots of other people. You may also be feeling down.

Balanced Margins

Having balanced margins on all four sides of the page indicates that you honor your own personal space as well as other people's boundaries. You also pay attention to appearances, and care about how you, your home, and your work environment appear to others. You have an artistic sense and aim to have everything in its proper place.

Wide Margins All Around

If you have lots of white space and wide margins all around, you may be withdrawn and living in a fortress. In her book, *Instant People Reading*, Anne Conway notes that if you write with wide margins, you are stuck in neutral and can move neither forward nor backward. This type of inertia may cause you to wait for life to occur on its own, rather than extend yourself to make it happen under your own direction. (Conway, page 152)

Narrow Margins All Around

If you leave minimal breathing room on all four sides, you act in a forward, uninhibited, and thoughtless manner. You may be seen as grasping or overly frugal.

No Margins

If you write with no left or right margins, according to *The Psychology of Handwriting*, you may be preoccupied with money. You may be focusing on your funds because you fear the future, even if you are comfortable financially. (Olyanova, page 68)

In addition, if you write with no margins on all four sides and fill up the whole page with writing, it indicates that you will invade others people's boundaries by talking too much, getting too physically close, or being too involved in their personal affairs.

In the 1990 reprint of his classic book, *Personality in Handwriting*, Alfred O. Mendel states that if you don't use any margins at all, you have a desire to fully immerse yourself with the world, leaving no distance between yourself and others. Mendel adds that people may view your behavior either positively or negatively and, depending on their own personalities, may regard you as either sympathetic or meddling, considerate or tactless, generous or miserly, or genuinely interested or simply nosy. (Mendel, page 59)

Miscellaneous margins

Balanced Margins

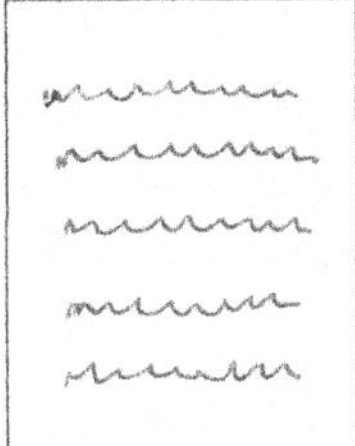

Narrow Margins All Around

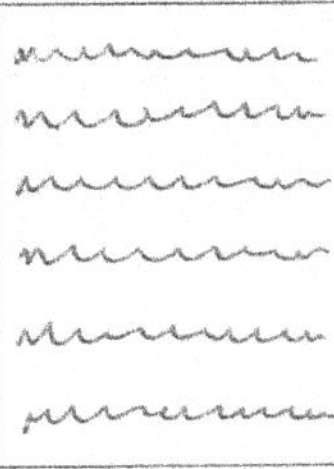

Wide Margins All Around

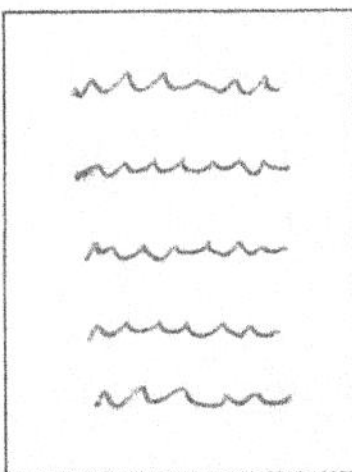

No Margins

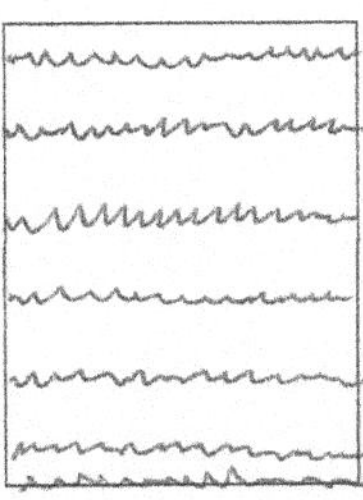

Summary

No handwriting can be fully analyzed by considering only the margins. That said, the layout of your handwriting gives important clues about the inner workings of your personality. Your margins show us how you relate to your past, to yourself, to the future, and to other people. They give us insight into how likely you are to initiate a new project and follow through on its completion. They tell us about your spontaneity, organizational skills, if you can stay on course, and how generous or frugal you are. They also let us know how intimately you are linked to your previous experiences, and how comfortable you are with charting unknown territories. Finally, your margins tell us if and how you want to interact with other people, the type of respect you give to others, and whether you will honor their personal space or immerse yourself in it.

With this information, look at your own handwriting and decide how you are living on the edge of your margins. Use this simple and effective tool to understand if you are focusing your energy on the past, present, or future, and decide if that's where you really want to be.

BIBLIOGRAPHY

Amend, Karen and Ruiz, Mary S., *Handwriting Analysis -The Complete Basic Book*, Newcastle Publishing Company, Inc., CA, 1980

Conway, Anne, *Instant People Reading Through Handwriting*, Newcastle Publishing Co., Inc., CA, 1991

Lowe, Sheila R., *The Complete Idiot's Guide to Handwriting Analysis*, Alpha books, NY, 1999

Mendel, Alfred, O., *Personality in Handwriting*, Newcastle Publishing Co., Inc., CA, 1990 (reprint of 1940 classic)

Olyanova, Nadya, *The Psychology of Handwriting-Secrets of Handwriting Analysis*, Wilshire Book Company, CA, 1960

Poizner, Annette, *Clinical Graphology – An Interpretive Manual for Mental Health Practitioners,* Charles C Thomas Publisher, Ltd., IL, 2012

Roman, Klara, *Handwriting a Key to Personality,* Pantheon Books, NY, 1952

Seifer, Marc, *The Definitive Book of Handwriting Analysis*, New Page Books, NJ, 2009

Teillard, Ania, *The Soul and Handwriting*, Scriptor Books, 1993

BIOGRAPHICAL NOTES

Barbara R. Donato, MS, CGA, CG, CZT, holds a Master of Science degree in public relations from Boston University, and a Bachelor of Arts degree in sociology from Merrimack College. The International Graphoanalysis Society certified her as a handwriting analyst in 1998, and the American Handwriting Analysis Foundation in 2014. In 2013, she became a certified Zentangle® teacher. As an officer of the New England Society for Handwriting Analysis (NESHA), Ms. Donato participates in events featuring renowned graphologists. She uses her graphology skills to help clients identify their strengths and challenges, and to enlighten and entertain diverse audiences.

barbara.donato@comcast.net

Handwriting as a window to human potential

There is always more than what we see at first

Ashira Gobrin, CG

"Adaptation is crucial for survival. Adaptation is a symptom from the natural design of evolution. If an individual is unable to adapt, then that individual will perish through natural selection." -Lloyd R Shisler

As humans, we build shelters to protect us from natural elements and all kinds of potential threats. We have for thousands of years created physical defense mechanisms to help us adapt, or to survive. For the same reasons, we also create emotional and psychological defense mechanisms. Freud described an emotional defense mechanism as a psychological strategy that is unconsciously used to protect the ego from being overwhelmed by anxiety. Adaptation is a crucial part of our development into well-adjusted and creative beings, but when the adaptation is a distortion or self-imposed defense, it can be an inhibitor rather than an internalized and integrated aspect of our character and personality. In other words, we can use adaptation as a weapon, or as a tool.

As we grow from child to adult, we strive to be healthy, secure and conscious of our worth. The foundation of this expressive adult requires a strong sense of belonging. This is a space in which to expand ourselves, to explore our abilities and to reach our full potential. The security of the family, our mother and father figures, form the skeleton of our character development off which this creativity can develop. A secure person is comfortable expressing herself through her innate and acquired talents, skills and capabilities.

In contrast, when a child feels rejected and unloved, the secure foundation of family is fractured, and a contraction of self occurs through withdrawal and regression. A child can experience loss through neglect, rejection or death. A single parent or adoptive parent cannot always heal the acute experience of abandonment and often the child must attempt a series of adjustments to seek connection that doesn't seem to satisfy. If she is constantly criticized without the equivalent sense of security, love, or worse, she is rejected repeatedly, she becomes frustrated and insecurity is the result. This child will develop superficial relationships and will find comfort in the boundaries of the past rather than trust the unknown adventure of the future.

Analysis of a writing

Let us explore the journey of development of one individual through exploration of her handwriting. The writer of this sample, which appears on the following page, is female, right-handed, aged 43 at the time of this writing, using medium pressure.

Figure 1

The overall impression of this writing (on the next page) is one of caution and careful reserve. The writer is a compulsive character, as we can easily see in what appears on initial review to be mechanized regularity. This is a classic example of unspontaneous, overly disciplined writing. What appears to be rigid regularity, points to an element of will. She is functional as determined by her clear space picture, although her margins pull to the left side of the page and avoid the right. Her tendency towards the past holds her back and she operates with an abundance of caution. Change will have to come slowly and in an organized way.

The writer has a rounded form, with simple, clearly defined uncontaminated letters. Her precise form demonstrates a clarity of thought and communication, she communicates directly, is conscientious, loyal and wants to learn and make herself understood. A dominant middle zone highlights her methodical, and practical capability, lacking in enthusiasm. She likes to do things in her own rhythm, a change to which reduces efficiency and tends towards losing her temper.

Dear Ashira,

Thank you for agreeing to do this for me I am curious to learn more about myself through this exercise I will tell you a little bit about my day so far I awoke to a chilly morning with a beautiful orange sky just beginning to apear I set about to my morning journal routine before a quick workout My workout is always a bit of an obstacle course with the cat and dog trying to help out I grabbed a quick glass of water and lugged into work After a fast and furious morning, I enjoyed some lunch while catching up on some textbook reading for school After another few hours of work, I took a quick break to write this letter and do some artwork

Thanks for your work!

JB

May 11 1978, right handed

With further examination of the writing, we notice a persona carefully guarding and protecting the sensitive personality underneath. The upright slant keeps the emotional door closed, but with insufficient emotional release, there is frustration beneath the veneer of careful control.

The wide spacing between words and especially on either side of her PPI (Figure 2) keep a carefully calibrated distance from other people. Although she is sensitive, her carefully disconnected writing, the wide spacing between words, letters and lines, and the vertical slant tell us that she holds her feelings in check. She is indeed influenced by emotional experiences, but does not express her feelings easily. She instead controls her emotions and maintains poise and an impartial outlook. She does not easily trust and she is protective of who she lets into those carefully crafted boundaries.

Figure 2

orange sky just beginning to apear set
about to my morning journal routine before
a ~~quick workout. My~~ workout is always a
bit of an obstacle course with the cat and
dog trying to help out grabbed a quick
glass of water and ~~Jogged into~~ work. After
a fast and furious morning enjoyed some
lunch while catching up on some textbook

Some parts of the handwriting are better developed than others. Every now and then the attempt to connect shows through (Figure 3). The writer has learned a great deal about adapting to her circumstances through overcoming her inhibitions and her tendency towards the past. She has a desire to connect to people but finds it difficult. She can integrate her ideas but doesn't do it constantly, and so we understand that the intelligence accessible to her has not yet been fully developed. Her inhibitions are preventing her from developing her true abilities due to her past orientation.

Figure 3

beautiful letter

before furious

A closer look at the picture of space reveals some irregularity in baselines that are wavier than they first appear (Figure 4). The irregularity is tempered by control as she makes multiple minor adjustments to try keep her baseline spacing regular. Her compulsive structure is working to manage against depression, illustrated by the upward baseline movement—an attempt to be cheerful and optimistic. But gravity is strong and pulls her down, so with a single word at times sitting on different baselines, she lives in two different realities at the same time: the reality of where she is, and the reality of where she wants to be.

Figure 4

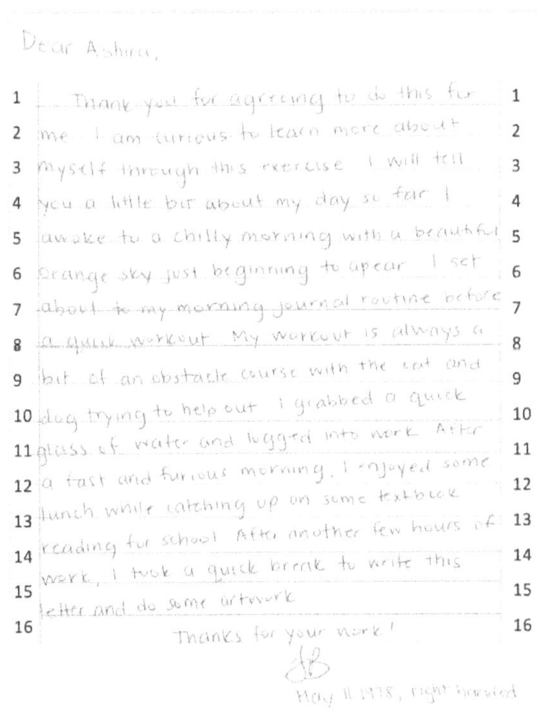

Dear Ashira,

Thank you for agreeing to do this for me. I am curious to learn more about myself through this exercise. I will tell you a little bit about my day so far. I awoke to a chilly morning with a beautiful orange sky just beginning to apear. I set ~~about to my morning~~ journal routine before a quick workout. My workout is always a bit of an obstacle course with the cat and dog trying to help out. I grabbed a quick glass of water and logged into work. After a fast and furious morning, I enjoyed some lunch while catching up on some textbook reading for school. After another few hours of work, I took a quick break to write this letter and do some artwork.

Thanks for your work!

JB

May 11 1978, right handed

The variability in her middle zone exposes the variability of her own self-concept (Figure 5). She is sometimes more confident in herself and at other times embroiled with self-doubt.

She has a propensity to underachieve, highlighted through her low t-bars, likely due to underestimating herself and a fear of not being good enough, which holds her back from truly showing what she is capable of.

Figure 5

quick workout textbook

The frozen movement in her writing is revealing that she has not let go of her past, which is in turn, holding her back from her future. What is she holding back, and why?

Anxiety, insecurity, ambivalence

Graphologist and psychologists understand ambivalence, unresolved emotions and experiences impair a person's inner freedom. When inner freedom is threatened, anxiety results. Pulver stated, "anxiety, in the broadest sense, is always existential in nature, and refers to the loss of inner freedom, of safety, of security; anxiety also refers to a situation that is associated with such experiences, namely, problems of loving support."

The study of early recollections gives clues to understanding the writers' perceptions about herself in her present relationship to her environment. By selectively focusing on issues of the present, or unresolved ones from the past, the feelings associated with these recollections both conscious and subconscious always serve a purpose and have impacts in the 'here and now' of who the person has become.

Defense mechanisms

Accepting that this writer is a product of what happened to her as a child, we can conclude that she has experienced something significant in her past that has taught her to adapt in order to survive. In the case of this writing, we see some obvious defense mechanisms including:

- Caution: dependency and reluctance to leave the security of the mother and the past, revealed in a narrow left-hand margin, wide word spacing, slow and precise movement.
- Suppression: deliberately preventing dangerous or painful thoughts from entering the consciousness, revealed in occasionally retraced downstrokes by upstrokes above the baseline.
- Emotional isolation: operating as if emotions did not exist, to feel

with the mind instead of the heart revealed by wide word spacing, especially around the PPI.
- Independence: The desire to separate from her mother on an emotional level, and of becoming more reliant on herself, revealed in the stick form PPI, upright slant, wide word spacing.

The defenses in this writing stem from early development stages where the writer experienced a profound lack of her mother's love. Maternal deprivation occurs through many situations, all resulting in experiences where the child cannot physically or emotionally experience love, and therefore cannot mature emotionally. To be deprived of her mother's love causes fear, insecurity, mistrust. The earlier it occurs in childhood, the greater the impact of the trauma. Physical deprivations such as a lack of normal physical comforts—food shelter and clothing—also cause emotional disorders.

The child who has insecure relationships with her mother and, at later developmental stages, with her father, feels rejected and unworthy of her parents' approval. Since she cannot win their approval, she loses self-esteem. She underestimates her own worth. Insecurity and fear of repeated failure is counteracted by keeping her goals at a low level, thus avoiding failure in the eyes of others.

The human desire for growth and development

Despite this experience, this young woman can feel her deficiency and is desperately searching to find a better version of herself. The intuitive air stroke connections between some of her letters and the o, a, g's that are at times open to the top in her writing show that she is open to ideas and possibilities. Rena Nezos writes about these open oval formations as receptivity, the need to talk, to express oneself. In a favorable writing she says this can demonstrate altruism even to the point of self-denial. In a homogeneous writing, it also indicates melancholia and a sense of loneliness.

There is ambivalence here in her orientation towards others as she makes sufficient contact with others to fulfill her needs, but at the same time, she keeps a careful distance between herself and most others due to the lack of clarity about herself and her inability to eliminate her judging of herself and others. She is searching as demonstrated by the mid zone letters digging into the lower zone, and she is frustrated by her lack of success as seen in the angles and ticks that occur rather frequently despite the roundness of her handwriting. (Figure 6)

Figure 6

Ticks and angles

while orange morning

Digging into LZ

some

In fact, when this writer presented her handwriting for her analysis, her request was "Is there any information on how I can best change? Or how I can learn most effectively?" Her eagerness and perseverance are certainly commendable; however, if she were able to free her inner self, she would accomplish much more than she does in relation to the energy she expends. Without greater release, she will have to start pushing her boundaries carefully and with a lot of support. In this regard, the writer's situation is somewhat tragic. What a difficult struggle life is for this person.

Character Structure

To gain a deeper understanding of the underlying personality, it would be helpful to understand the difference between an emotional response and a formed character structure. In a paper you can find in this anthology, The Uses and Abuses of Insecurity by Roger Rubin, he states: "Any human emotion can be internalized. When internalized, an emotion stops functioning in the manner of an emotion and becomes a characterological style, the core of the person's character, his or her identity. In the case of shame, internalization is the result of identification with unreliable shame-based models and the trauma of abandonment which binds feelings and needs and drives with shame."

Renate Griffiths, in her paper *Early Childhood Disturbances*, discusses character structures as a grouping of traits, behaviors, responses, unconscious attitudes and an amalgam of defense mechanisms. Each structure serves to defend the person or help a person adjust and survive to a given set of realities that she must deal with. No one is one pure type but often we have one or two dominant types. The ability to identify the underlying character structure, gives insight into the individuals basic conflicts and the period in which they were created. In this writing we find two character structures that work both harmoniously to compliment each other and cause tension in their conflicts.

Depressive Character Structure:

Depressive structure occurs during oral stage and is found among other traits in significantly rounded writing. As we have learned, anxiety arises from the fear of a mother abandoning the child. The mother is not available when needed, and the helplessness and dependency of the child rings deep. If only the child is good enough, the mother won't leave. If the mother leaves, it must be because the child wasn't good enough. Depressive characters often can be helpful, altruistic and are empathetic and nurturing. (Figure 7)

Figure 7

Grounded in a fear of abandonment, the child develops a desire for nearness and reassurance while at the same time, the distrust from previous episodes of abandonment makes them incapable of genuine partnership through the ability to be vulnerable and codependent. The depressive character feels at the mercy of others. Guilt feelings run deep and create a fear of self-development. The conflict of wanting relationships that remain out of reach means they experience fear of loss, but they can't maintain relationships. In order to earn a place in the good books of those they desire to be close to, they can be empathetic, helpful, devoted, loyal, and frequently give more than they get.

Compulsive Character Structure:

Compulsive structure occurs during a more conscious stage when the child learns the difference between her will and the will of others. The compulsive person mistrusts warmth and tenderness. Emotions are connected to dependency feelings that suggest helplessness and stimulate a fear of ridicule and rejection. She must appease her conscience and control impulses and cannot be allowed to experience joy because of unconscious guilt. The price that is paid is loneliness and social isolation as she avoids connections with feeling or emotion. Through concentration, willpower, and determination, the compulsive character can find achievement.

An existential fear of losing control creates a low tolerance for change. The compulsive character creates safeguards, uses strong principles, and an abundance of caution. Their drive to achieve means they can be diligent with a sense of duty, perseverance, commitment, and loyalty that ensures they will get a job done no matter what.

With the combination of these character structures, we can better understand this writer's use of persona to protect herself from the impacts of her past emotional experiences as she adopts the "good girl" persona. A fracture occurs in the developmental foundations when the parent lacks attunement to the child's needs. In place of true nurturing in the form of the ability to predict and preemptively fulfill the needs of the child, the parent instead demands that the child live up to strict or unrealistic expectations. The child grows up with the feeling of deep fear that it will not be fed or loved or attended to unless it conforms to the wishes of the parent at the expense of its own desires. An existential anxiety develops based on fear of deprivation and denial of care. "If I don't conform, I will be abandoned, pushed out into the cold and I may not survive." The child decides to be "good" by living up to the expectations of the parents, and by behaving as if she were happy. She lives in a dual reality.

Persona as a defense

Persona can be a used as a defense—a mask to protect the trauma of the self, or as a disguise, or to hide the darker parts or a self. Which it is depends on the gestalt. For these individuals, the persona is a false self defense, a suit of armor, like a mask hiding the person underneath, or the hard shell of a crab protecting the soft body underneath. The persona protects the injured and traumatized true self, from further injury.

Using careful and considerate form with very little deviation from a school form in the writing, we find little originality, and no rebellion. Her writing is less spontaneous, pretty in a contrived way, conforming to school type models, using a high degree of regularity and uniformity of forms, and diminished creativity.

Learned emotional control, holding back present gratification for future rewards, suppression of anger, compliance through following the rules, achieving goals to prove her value to the parents, doing things well to the point of being a perfectionist, fear of criticism, guilt of doing something wrong are the hallmarks of the "Good Girl," and all of these traits are found in this writing.

Of course, the tragedy of the good girl is that she is never good enough. There is always something not quite right with her performance. She feels that she is not good or perfect enough to win the love she seeks. She will become critical of others in the very same way she was criticized. Since her defenses protect her sensitivity so well, nothing new can get through and there is very low potential for growth. She cannot face the vulnerability of letting go that is required to try something new. There is also a strong element of compulsion. A significant amount of energy is used in the effort to keep the persona in place, which makes it unavailable for use in developing other parts of the personality.

Often there is a high degree of achievement of specific goals based on following the rules and living up to others people's expectations, which comes at the expense of significant underachievement in creative potentials. The writing has an underdeveloped feminine identity. The good girl loses a part of herself as she attempts to conform because her deepest fear is to be abandoned. She would rather deny the person she is inside so that she can feel connected with another and she achieves this by being good.

Some of this is visible in the signature (Figure 8) which is larger than the text, highlighting the writer's need for recognition. She connects the two letters with significantly more fluidity than we see in the writing, revealing her unrealized desire to be connected to others. At the same time, she hides behind her initials. There is no sense of feminine or masculine in the name, no clues as to the individuality of the writer. She remains anonymous behind her shield of conformity where she feels safe. The insecurity of the writer is caused by a lack of self-confidence. She seems to make up for this with her compulsive pattern of behavior.

Figure 8

Motivating forces

Healthy guilt is the emotional core of our conscience. Fear, anxiety, and insecurity can be used as a motivator. A depressive character has a deep need for closeness, and they will use that as a motivator by being caring, helpful and endearing. Compulsive characters have a deep need for security so that they do not control. They are, therefore, sticklers for rules, traditions and keeping things in order to minimize change.

Anxiety can be positive or negative. It can mobilize our energies, push us to take risks and learn something new or it can cause us to withdraw, avoid or repress and stop us in our tracks. This is a person with a desire to be more that what she is today. Her growth potential is limited because her defense is so rigid. Change will be slow because with each new challenge she will battle the fear of being abandoned. Again. She is working with both a coach and a therapist to help reduce her rigidity, and that requires deep trust.

No person can fundamentally change the deeper parts of our character and personality but we can minimize our defenses, learn to feel more secure in ourselves, and embrace the humans we are capable of being. With the right encouragement, everyone is capable of evolving. By helping them navigate through their fears and anxieties, we can assist our clients to turn potential into performance and into a space of expansion and creative expression.

Most of us are not therapists, but what we do is therapeutic. Our work as graphologists can be so rewarding. However significant the knowledge we have, and however meaningful a contribution we can make, what we see in handwriting is but a small part of someone in a personal universe that is much bigger than any of us can ever truly see.

Graphology allows us the unique opportunity to observe the defense and resultant behaviors of the writer, and understand their deeper needs. After a session with this writer, she revealed her story to me. She validated the hypothesis tested in the analysis, and then sent this as her follow up when she thanked me for the session: "I thought the exercise was really interesting. Kind of mind blowing. I reflected this weekend on how much shame sits with me and how I can best let go of it. It's a steep hill to climb and I'm starting by just being mindful to notice and tell myself that shame is not serving me anymore and that I can leave it where I am in that moment in time. I'm ready to find myself. I mean not the person who everyone else wants me to be. But the person inside me that I need to get to know."

BIBLIOGRAPHY

Klein, Felix. "The Character Structure of Neurosis." *Gestalt Graphology,* 83-102. New York: IUniverse, 2007.

Rubin, Roger. *Character Structures and Defense Mechanisms.* Monograph.

Rubin, Roger. *The Uses and Abuses of Insecurity.* Monograph.

Shapiro, David. *Neurotic Styles.* New York: Basic Books, 1965.

Griffiths, Renate. *Tree Drawings: A Projective Technique to Assess Personality.* Monograph.

Griffiths, Renate. *Early Childhood Disturbances Reflected in Handwriting.* Monograph, 1991.

Stockholm, Emilie. *A Man is What Happened to the Boy.* Monograph.

BIOGRAPHICAL NOTES

Ashira Gobrin works with individuals to turn potential into performance through purpose, values, and great leadership. She is a certified graphologist, executive coach, and Brainspotting practitioner. She uses her skills to help people become the best version of themselves and perform to their maximum potential in whatever they choose. As an HR executive with over 25 years of experience, Ashira excels at simplifying the complex, removing roadblocks, and creative problem-solving, always focusing on the persona and turning great potential into measurable results.

ashira.lapin@gmail.com

Artfulness in Analysis

Lena Rivkin, MFA

Graphology is both science and art. Not the boldest assertion ever made about handwriting analysis, but allow me to explain.

When I was fourteen years old, my parents took me to the iconic Olvera Street in downtown Los Angeles. Amid the Mexican arts and crafts, we encountered a graphologist who analyzed my handwriting and swiftly interpreted my aptitudes for art and music. Not only was I surprised that she could elicit this information from my handwriting, I felt seen and validated in a way I had never experienced.

Inspired and determined to learn more, I asked my mother to take me to our local library for books on graphology. And one of my lifelong passions and professions was ignited.

Graphology refers to the scientific study of handwriting as it relates to personality. The science behind graphology is the study of letter size, structure, and movement as well as the degree and regularity of strokes, angles, slants, ornamentation, angularity, and curvature.

The psychological component of graphology is a gestalt form of analysis. In gestalt graphology, the handwriting sample is viewed in terms of the way the writing is arranged on the page (spatial arrangement), its form (style), and the way it "moves" across the page (movement). Gestalt graphology makes it possible to evaluate personality vis-à-vis the writing, regardless of style or language, and develop an accurate understanding of the writer's motives and behavior.

Neither graphology nor handwriting itself is linear, as is, say, chemistry, because human communication is never linear. Hence, graphology is also an art.

The gestalt of the handwriting sample should always be considered when interpreting the personality traits found in it.

Written words are powerful

Life is inherently personal. The overwhelming majority of my graphology clients, both business and personal, primarily want their private selves to be identified and recognized. Most, if not all, graphology clients are looking for guidance, direction, or clarity, either for hiring the right job candidate or for personal reasons.

A tremendous amount of information is provided in the way an individual communicates. When analyzing a handwriting sample, I strive to recognize and identify behavior in addition to patterns of behavior. A thorough graphologist also considers the reasons behind a personal or business request to analyze the handwriting of another individual.

I am neither a medical doctor nor a psychologist; thus, I never diagnose physical illness or mental health conditions. However, when I am given the opportunity to interpret handwriting, my personal credo is to remain open and teachable and follow the first law of medicine: do no harm.

As a graphologist practicing for thirty-five years, I see my job as to interpret the information present in a handwriting sample. So, I consider, *what is the best path for me to impart this information?*

Art can be created to be a shield, weapon, or mirror, depending on the artist's intent, technique, materials, and subject. As a professional artist and art educator, I am acutely interested in elucidating the handwriting of artists in relationship to their artistic output. Handwriting analysis shares the three major principles of art analysis: form, space, and movement. Sometimes the handwriting reveals more personal secrets than art does.

My graphology career has been a privilege and deeply rewarding due to having learned so much during my training, research, and ongoing practice. One unintended blessing of a graphology career is that a graphologist never stops learning. Rigidity and inflexibility in graphological interpretation can be quite limiting. Interpretation, by its very definition, is fluid, intimate, personal and a combination of fact as well as stimulating information shaped as opinion.

While it is also true that the personal psychology of each graphologist informs both their interpretation and analysis, the ultimate goal is to interpret a handwriting sample honestly and selflessly without injecting personal bias. All these disparate aspects of training, technique, and personality make for quite the balancing act a graphologist must perform when tendering an analysis.

Artfulness is a critical component of graphology in regards to the sensitivity necessary in relaying analyses to people. That said, as with all interpretational arts and sciences, it is nearly impossible to keep personal predispositions and prejudices from bleeding into analysis. Thus, in all things graphology (and art for that matter), I aim to bring my highest intention.

When a client asks me to analyze their handwriting, they are seeking confirmation and self-reflection. They are in search of an outsider's experience of themselves. I want to offer them insight and direction and to underline their strengths found in their writing. People are looking to me for clues and keys to their inner being, which requires delicacy and compassion.

Buddhism posits that there are only four situations: You can take a bad situation and make it better; you can take a bad situation and make it worse; you can take a good situation and make it better; you can take a good situation and make it worse.

My goal is to inspire and to open doors so that clients learn something tangible and positive with regard to their strengths, weaknesses, and challenges. In a related manner, my professional ethics include abstaining from judgment of a subject. Critical to my in-person analyses is that I strive to illuminate constructive implications and applications.

Intrinsic to upholding graphology as a respected art/science is a sense of personal responsibility, sensibility, respect, and most importantly, honoring our fellow humans. Therefore, all graphologists must recognize how their interpretations impact others.

My objective is to relay information as I see it with honest compassion, and without minimizing or embellishing what I have seen. When I work with a business client, my work differs from in-person analyses. The scope of my analysis depends upon the specific skills for the position under consideration. In other words, the candidates' aptitudes, communication styles, team playing abilities, work ethic, motivation, energy to complete projects, etc.

While my work for corporations covers less personal material than a personal analysis, I strive to be positive. Sometimes, if the prospect employee is a strong candidate but their skill set does not fully mesh with the position for which they are applying, I may suggest a more suitable position for the hopeful applicant.

There is obviously a major distinction between working with a flat sheet of paper and working with live people. I never downplay what I see in someone's handwriting and I remain mindful of the words I use to describe the behaviors I see. It is vital always be fully aware that this is someone's life I am discussing.

Form

The interpretation of personality through handwriting is tantamount to reading a body. The body does not lie, and graphology is body language on paper.

Body language, one shape of which is handwriting, reveals, in physical form, habitual behaviors and, unconscious tendencies. Additionally, it highlights how the writer may deviate from an archetype and where that deviation shows up in their behavior. We may study flat pieces of paper but we are dealing with human beings.

As the esteemed graphologist, Felix Klein, wrote in his essay, *The Power of Form in Art, Art Therapy, and Handwriting:* "Form is not only an integral part of life; it *is* life."

Further to Klein's comment, form is informative and it is information. Information is everything. Information can be deformed, malformed, misinformed, conformed, reformed, transformed. What we say holds power and careless language can burn down a house. Or tear a country apart!

Just as the body cannot lie, neither can handwriting. You cannot fake your IQ (intelligence quotient) or your EQ (emotional intelligence quotient). You don't know what you cannot see. One brilliant resource on the ways in which trauma lives in the body, is *The Body Keeps the Score* by Dr. Bessel van der Kolk. Recognizing the fragility of humans is merely one responsibility of all graphologists. I am committed to exploring the positive implications and applications of handwriting analysis. It is part of the professional ethics of my career and how it impacts others. Even a simple word, act, or gesture can be a force for good in the life of a person.

Much of my graphology ethos and education has been reinforced by virtue by my fellow graphologists. A wonderful resource, the AHAF (American

Handwriting Analysis Foundation) website, www.ahafhandwriting.org, is simultaneously exhaustive, magnanimous, and educational. Recommended texts cover graphology, psychology, typologies, drawing and projecting analysis.

Particularly rewarding are the recommended twenty hours of taped lectures on psychology by Yale professor Paul Bloom. One of the video lectures that resonated with me was one about suffering. Bloom states, "There is a deep insight here which is that the good things in life only make sense relative to the bad things." Chosen suffering (not accidents or tragedies) gives meaning to life.

Regarding how handwriting communicates the challenges and struggles that can impair our judgment and decisions, it is important for graphologists to balance this with helpful, constructive observations. According to Bloom, our lives must include some amount of suffering in order to be meaningful. "If you win every competition you engage in, there's no fun to it. You have to experience the possibility of loss. If all of your experiences are positive, they cease to become positive, you need a negative."

When I intuit something potentially hurtful or seemingly negative, I organize my comments according to what I find in the gestalt of the writing, striving to use language that describes challenges or limitations that hold the writer back in certain areas. I do this by using words that won't be uncomfortable to hear. I never judge, diagnose, offer advice, or try to 'fix' another person. My aim is to offer the people whose handwriting I assess honest insights about their stability, their mobility, their strengths, their potential, and their integrity.

Following are two handwriting samples and my observations about them.

Example A: Male, 81 years old

You must know that I appreciate
the very handsome exhibition of my work
and the fine catalogue that you have
arranged for the University of Arizona.
The quotations from, some of my writing
which were written many years ago, seem
still pertinent to much of the painting of
today. At least I still believe in what I
have said.

Although it cannot be detected in a copy, the intense pressure in the original sample conveys two equally powerful, albeit opposing, impulses: the writer's simultaneous compulsion to push people away and his craving to be among others. The gestalt of the handwriting is graphically strong and aggressive. It reflects his struggles in intimate relationships and/or deflecting others' struggles with him.

The pressure is muddy and sensual, revealing tremendous energy, drive, perseverance, and tenacity. Tight and cramped writing speaks to an inner tension. Also evident is his drive to be proactive and accurate (consistent rhythm, agile movement, and zonal balance).

The T-bars get progressively thicker, revealing a tendency towards bluntness and anger. Both the angles and the horizontal movement of the t-bars indicate controlling impulses. The spiked 'p' also demonstrates a need for control and a tendency to be argumentative. His tactlessness means that working for, or living with, this writer would require a thick skin.

The entanglement of the letters creates complications. He is likely to be emotionally intense, tightly wound, and a direct communicator. Self-confident, he prefers others to be equally direct in their communications. Angular letters, original formations, simplification, rhythm, fast strokes, and efficient connections all point to mental acumen.

The spatial relationship is crowded, showing that he needs to control his environment. He demonstrates a lack of perspective when interacting with others. The long and wide lower zone reveals a need for physical activity. He is focused, precise, and detail-oriented, valuing accuracy more than the average person. The speed is fast and assertive. The writing has flair and definition. You can count on the writer to be straightforward. This writer does not suffer fools gladly.

His work demands precision. There is a tremendous amount of energy here, indicating that he is authoritative in his approach and makes decisive creative decisions swiftly. Overpowering and demanding in personal as well as business relationships, he may not realize that he alienates others because of his need to do things his way. Chief among his many strengths are confidence, passionate productivity, and a need to achieve notable goals.

Example B: Male, 78 years old

There is a wide-stroked exuberance in the writing, which comes from his wrist. The consistent right trend indicates that he is action-oriented; certainly, this is a nimble thinker. The pressure appears to be medium and the letters present original and creative formations. Uniformly generous spacing between words illustrate that he needs elbow room and maintains personal boundaries. He eschews superfluous strokes, evidencing a high intelligence level and mental agility to think swiftly as well as an aversion to wasting time on unnecessary details. His writing is loose and thready. It is authentic, simplified, and unpretentious.

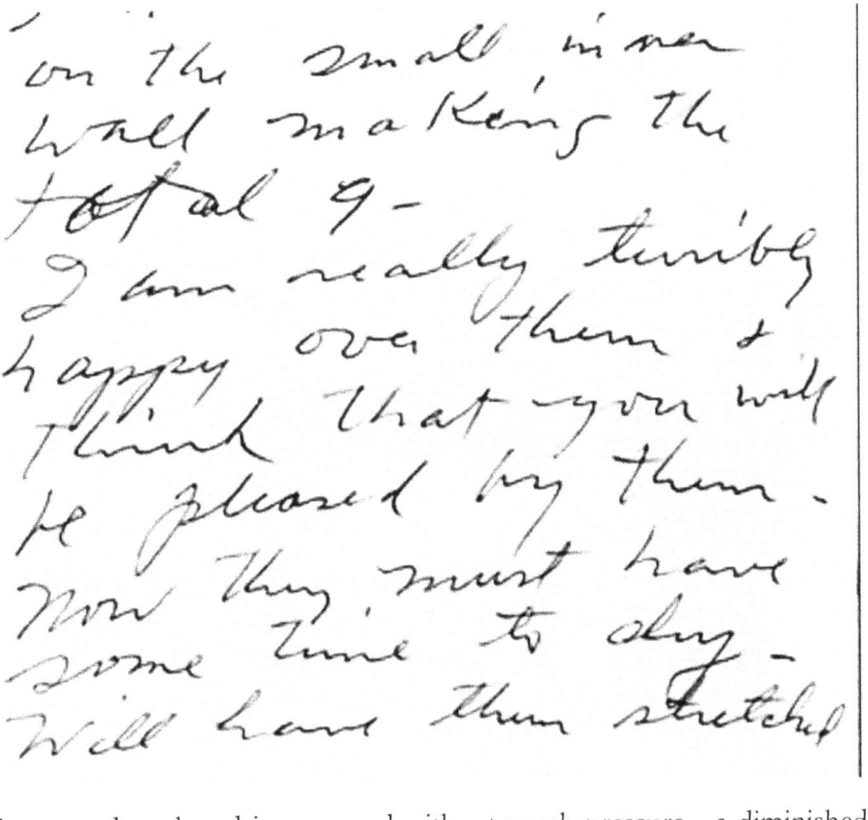
on the small inner
wall making the
total 9 -
I am really terribly
happy over them &
think that you will
be pleased by them.
Now they must have
some time to dry -
Will have them stretched

The secondary thread is conveyed without much pressure—a diminished formless scrawl that demonstrate evasiveness. He is conflict-avoidant and thrives in his active inner world. Strength is drawn from privacy, which also serves as a refuge from difficult issues. A limited number of lead-in strokes indicate a strong initiative to pursue goals. His personal pronoun 'I' is presented in different ways: one as a straight line, indicating independence and the other resembling the number 2, positioning himself in second place.

As the writing thins out in the middle zone, it further confirms the writer's lack of resilience and intermittent difficulty bouncing back from personal setbacks. He reads between the lines and prefers the company of others who possess a comparable capacity for inference. His connecting formations are a combination of threads and garlands indicating a gift with diplomacy, yet the frequent breaks within words and lack of extenders, with few exceptions, show a social awkwardness and tendency, at times, to exercise a great deal of restraint.

The rounded formations, disconnections in words and rightward slant reveal kindness, intuition, warmth, and sensitivity. Here is a writer who, although private, is comfortable among others. He prefers being his own boss; as his storied career has borne out.

Without revealing the identities behind these two samples, suffice it to say their respective levels of intensity, passion, drive, and intellect as well as their more challenging personality traits: impatience, tactlessness, and obstreperousness have all contributed to them being two of the most venerated, impactful, and influential painters of the twentieth century.

As graphologists, our choosing to frame descriptors in positive, affirming language illuminates an individual's secret ingredients. More importantly, it is our responsibility as graphologists to honor the whole truth with dignity regarding their equally flawed and fantastic humanity.

BIOGRAPHICAL NOTES

Lena Rivkin MFA, has been a handwriting expert for more than thirty-five years. She served as vice-president of the American Handwriting Analysis Foundation's Southern California chapter for a decade. She works with private investigators, mental health professionals, as well as forensic experts. Lena assists Fortune 500 companies, and government agencies in pre-employment evaluations. A Los Angeles-based painter and former art professor at Mount St. Mary's College, she offers graphology lectures and presentations nationally and abroad. Lena provides analyses of handwriting in a variety of contexts, including private consultations, conferences, and retreats.

lena@abouthandwriting.com

The Effect of Medication on Handwriting

Oladipupo Macjob, BPharm

I grew up learning about the seven wonders of the world. My excitement knew no bounds when I had the privilege of visiting one of these seven phenomenal works of art in Egypt, which continues to stun the minds of mankind generation after generation.

In my sojourn, I came across a body of knowledge which has never ceased to amaze me in the depth of scope it covers in terms of the solution it offers to humans with so much speed, accuracy and I dare say, cost-effectiveness. I am speaking about graphology, also known as Handwriting Analysis. In my opinion, graphology should be included in the list among the wonders of the world.

Definition

A simple definition of graphology is 'the personality assessment or profiling of an individual from the handwriting written on a document or surface e.g paper.' It is the behavioral traits of the writer crystallized on the page.

A unique aspect of handwriting is that no two are exactly the same, just as with DNA or fingerprints. This forms the basis for which graphology or handwriting analysis earns a place among personality profiling tools. This fact is responsible for the successes that have been recorded for decades in the area of personality profiling among other areas of benefits of graphology.

It is important to continue to validate the exactitude of graphological assessments, especially because decisions made from it can directly or indirectly affect lives. Therefore, we must also pay keen attention to factors that may influence this accuracy level or validity ratio of Graphological assessments.

There are several factors that are known to affect the handwriting; one is age. It's a no-brainer that the way someone wrote as a five-year-old would be different from the way the handwriting would appear at age forty-five. That is because with time, handwriting changes.

Other factors that could affect handwriting include the surface on which the writing was produced. Handwriting done on a rough surface is different from handwriting done on a smooth surface. For the purpose of this article, our focus shall be on drugs/medication as one of the factors that can affect the integrity of any handwriting.

Basic Facts about Drugs/medication

For the purpose of this article, the words 'drug' and 'medication' shall be used interchangeably. Having stated this, there are a number of facts that we need to understand in order to set the stage for the objective we have in mind. They are as follows:

- A drug or medication is any substance capable of altering the physiological or psychological functions of the body system systemically or topically is a drug.
- A drug or medication consists of two substances which includes the active ingredients and the excipients (coloring agents, preservatives, or fillers). Other names for excipients include adjuncts or adjuvants.
- Every drug is a poison, but not all drugs or medications are poisonous, provided the therapeutic window is not violated.
- The therapeutic window is all about the safety margin of a medication or drug.
- Not all drugs or medication affects the handwriting
- All drugs that affect the Central Nervous System (CNS) have an influence on the part of the brain that controls the handwriting
- Medications alter the space, form and movement of the handwriting
- All medications have duration of action (how long the effects last)

Basic Pharmacy Terminologies

Active Ingredient: the main chemical compound responsible for the activity of a medication though it does that with the assistance of other enablers.

Excipient: other ingredients besides the active ingredients that aids the drug to carry out its activity within the body system. For example, some aid faster absorption into the cells or dissolution within certain parts of the gastrointestinal tract.

Half Life: the amount required for half the concentration of a drug taken into the body to be excreted from the body system.

Pharmacokinetics: what the body does to a drug or medication. Better still, it is the effect of the body on the drug. They include the following: absorption, distribution, metabolism and excretion

Pharmacodynamics: the effect of the body on the drug or the medication. It is the study of the biochemical and physiologic effects of the drug especially at the molecular level.

Bioavailability: the amount of drug substance that goes into the circulation at a particular time.

Therapeutic margin: the dosage concentration of a drug that is safe on consumption without any incidence of adverse drug reactions. It should be noted that the undesirable effects observed from taking certain medications are as a result of the violation of the therapeutic margin rules of a drug.

Peak Plasma Concentration: the point at which the maximum effect of the drug must have been elicited before the concentration drops within the body system.

Drugs that affect the CNS and may ultimately affect handwriting

The Central Nervous System consists fundamentally of the brain and the spinal cord which play key roles in controlling handwriting. As commonly known to many graphologists or handwriting experts around the globe, what is considered as handwriting may actually be termed 'brain writing.' Writing impulse is generated from the brain and travels through the nerves to the muscles of the fingers before reaching the paper or document on which they are written.

The following medicinal substances can affect the handwriting of an individual especially when at certain dosage concentrations:

1. Amphetamines
2. Caffeine
3. Ephedrine
4. Methamphetamine
5. Nicotine
6. Pseudoephedrine
7. Alcohol
8. Flunitrazepam
9. Diazepam
10. Bromazepam
11. Alprazolam
12. Lorazepam
13. Cannabis
14. Opioids (Morphine, Codeine, Oxycodone)
15. Phenothiazines
16. Chlorpheniramine
17. Diphenhydramine
18. Orphenandrine Citrate
19. Tizanidine
20. Lysergic Acid Diethylamide
21. Propofol
22. Barbiturates
23. Ketamine

This list is not intended to be exhaustive. The chemical substances listed here are just some among the myriads of medications that affect the handwriting at certain dosage concentrations.

Effect of medication on handwriting

In 2017, I conducted a small but significant research project. Though the sample size was small, the results were statistically significant. Of twenty-five individuals who were placed on the medication, about seventeen of them had significant responses.

Sample size and type

Twenty-five males and females, none less than fifteen years of age, voluntarily participated in this research.

Methodology

This was a single blind research in that only the investigator (myself) knew about the medication that was being taken (Chlorpheniramine maleate 4mg). None of the study cohort had any prior knowledge of the chemical compound or the effect it was expected to elicit.

The basis for which chlorpheniramine maleate 4mg hereafter referred to as XT was used was because of its cost effectiveness, availability and efficacy.

Ordinarily, XT is an antihistamine drug/medication. However, one of its side effects is that it can sedate an individual even at 4mg dose, equivalent to one tablet. The side effect profile of XT was what was exploited in this study.

Each of these volunteers was given a plain sheet of paper to write about something of interest. They were to cover at least seventy-five percent of the page and sign twice on one side of the paper. After this writing exercise, a tablet of XT was given to each one of them to be taken with water. After about sixty minutes, a time at which the peak plasma concentration must have been attained, another handwriting sample was obtained from these volunteers, which was then analyzed and compared to the first handwriting samples obtained from each of them.

Prior to this, it was ensured that none of these volunteers were taking any regular drug medication or therapy such as antihypertensives or antidiabetics or any chemical substance capable of altering the pharmacodynamics of the drug substance.

Results

Signs in handwriting samples revealed that the writer was likely under the influence of a medication. However, I feel it is better to itemize the signs that a handwriting sample was *not* likely to be under the influence of a medication.

Again, as a reminder, its important to note that not all medications would affect handwriting. Even for the ones that do, they only influence the handwriting to the extent the therapeutic window or margin is exceeded. Also, the peak plasma concentration of the drug must have been reached to say the least, if not already exceeded at some instances.

Signs that a handwriting sample was likely *not* written under the influence of a medication or drug

- ☐ Good rhythm
- ☐ Good line and word spacing
- ☐ Small handwriting size throughout. It takes a level of concentration before many people can write in small sizes. The lesser the concentration the larger the writing size a lot of times
- ☐ Ruler writing

Signs that a handwriting sample *was* likely written under the influence of a medication or drug

- ☐ Distorted or clumsy baseline in the handwriting sample
- ☐ Erratic lines on some letters within the words that make up the write up. Example, from one of the samples of the volunteers I examined, I noticed that the tail of the upper zone letter 'd' was unusually extended beyond the level it should with a bit of tremor in the line quality which, of course, was very different from the comparison handwriting sample.
- ☐ Erratic line and word spacing
- ☐ Thready writing especially in the middle zone letters of the words
- ☐ Downward slope is common in the handwriting even though you may also find upward slopes
- ☐ Mixture of large and small letters which is different from the default handwriting sample or the baseline handwriting sample to be compared with.
- ☐ Increased breaks between letters different from the observed fluidity seen in the yardstick sample or comparison sample.
- ☐ Minor tremor between letters

- □ Reduction in the legibility of the write up
- □ Splotches in the handwriting sample at certain spots
- □ Mistakes in the handwriting and sloppiness
- □ Careless line drags on the pages of the handwriting
- □ Uncoordinated sentences or statement

Conclusion

It is important to state that the features captured here under the 'signs likely to show' a sample under the influence of a medication are not exhaustive and are a function of the kind of medication used. Of course, there are some that would have a class effect especially for medications under the same pharmacological class. Whereas some others would have a totally different dose response curve.

The basis and objective for which this study was embarked upon was for this piece of work to serve as a springboard for further studies and investigations as well as to serve as templates for peer reviews.

BIOGRAPHICAL NOTES

A graduate of Pharmacy studies from the University of Ibadan Oyo State Nigeria and former Brand Manager, Cardiometabolic Franchise, Novartis Pharma Services English West Africa, Oladipupo Macjob is a certified Body Language Coach and Deception Detection Expert. Oladipupo MacJob is Nigeria's foremost graphologist and a pundit of Non-Verbal Intelligence. He is an author, International speaker, coach and has facilitated trainings within his niche both within and outside the country. He was among the international speakers at the AHAF Conference in 2017 and has trained many public and private sector organizations, some of which include the AxaMansard Plc, Pricewaterhousecoopers (PwC), Lagos State Judiciary etc.

diptoy20m@yahoo.com

Graphological Types for Visionaries

Ruth Elliott Holmes, BA, CDE

When Marilyn Ferguson's book *The Aquarian Conspiracy* was published in 1980, it was hailed by the *Los Angeles Times* as "the watershed book of the New Age." It has been translated into ten languages and has sold 600,000 copies around the world. Acclaimed by the most influential thinkers and social planners of our time, this book describes the "conspiracy" in all areas of our lives, from politics, religion, economics, education and medicine to families and individuals. Marilyn Ferguson writes of the network of people "breathing together," who are quietly and powerfully changing the way consciousness is being raised as we move into the next century.

In 1989, Ferguson embarked on yet another seminal project. Her quest this time was to identify "natural visionary abilities" in individuals whose accomplishments were noteworthy in a variety of vocations from nationally-recognized leaders in business and industry to teachers, therapists, writers, scientists, artists, inventors, politicians and film makers. The "visions" of these people encompassed original products and services, art and films, scientific theories and books. Each of these individuals were successful in their own right. They had overcome obstacles, met personal and professional challenges and were prepared to share their experiences.

Approximately 100 individuals were carefully selected for their achievements. They agreed to participate in their own evaluations through eight forms of testing, which included the Herrmann Brain Dominance Instrument, the Birkman Method, the Gregorc Style Delineator, and birth, voice, body, handwriting and morphological analysis. In addition, the participants were asked to complete extensive six-page surveys. Questions ranged from asking for details on their earliest memories of "vision" to questions about their most valuable mistakes.

Method

In 1989, handwriting samples were requested, and handwriting analysis was added to the research design. The ground was laid for a comprehensive evaluation of a number of high level thinkers and achievers.

Participants in the Visionary Survey were asked to submit "a handwriting sample of several non-committal lines" with a signature on an 8 ½ x 11 paper. Not everyone followed these instructions, but profiles were constructed with whatever samples were submitted. The results were communicated to the participants individually in taped consultations or in person when 40 of these subjects met in Los Angeles.

At this meeting, the five members of the research team were asked to present their testing methods and the results of their evaluations on each of the participants as each visionary recounted his or her own life story. Researchers attending were psychologists Roy Mefferd, and Roger Birkman of Texas, whose psychological profile evaluation is used in management development; Sandra Seagal and David Horne of California, whose expertise is in voice and body dynamics, and myself, the handwriting examiner.

Through dialogue with the participants, in a number of instances, greater depth of understanding could be achieved. The goal was not to prove or disprove the merits of graphology, but rather to create in-depth profiles on each subject. Individual sessions with many of the participants also served to strengthen and/or challenge the veracity of the findings.

Discussion

In her upcoming text on visionaries Ferguson suggests that a new way of thinking and processing information is necessary if we are to meet the demands of the next century. A change in paradigm in our educational institutions, offices, factories, laboratories and political corridors is essential. Ferguson believes that if the common traits of the "visionaries" could be identified and quantified by various psychological, graphological and other tests, then information could be taught in our school systems to enhance these traits in upcoming generations.

One feature that appeared consistently was that these subjects tended to succeed in initiating and actualizing their original ideas in spite of all obstacles. Eager communicators, the study group willingly revealed their techniques of how, from diverse backgrounds, they reached the top in their respective fields of expertise.

Graphological Typology for Visionaries

Analysis

Despite large differences, many of the subjects shared the following characteristics:

CHARACTERS	GRAPHICS
An abundance of energy and good judgment	Good pressure and excellent line spacing
Intelligence coupled with common sense	Originality in letter forms and clarity
A powerful determination to overcome obstacles	Well-balanced writing (tri-zonal dynamics) and strong downstrokes.

Samples ranged from near copy book form to disjointed, unusual handwritings. Various ways of categorizing these writings were undertaken. The first stage was to use a six-tiered typology developed by Ruth Holmes and Marc Seifer. Ultimately, these six types were combined into the following four categories of creative types.

1. Conforming Creative
2. Conflicted/Compensated Creative
3. Versatile/Productive Creative
4. Empowered Creative

Some of the subjects succeeded and overcame obstacles by compensating for their own personal insecurities and early traumas. Other subjects, usually those less conflicted, achieved their success through a combination of intelligence, stamina and versatility.

When the results were summarized, the word "creative" was substituted for "visionary" because it was the process, as identified in the handwriting samples, that contributed to the evaluation of this select group. Different levels of self-actualization were observed graphologically in the original stroke formations. From a psychodynamic point of view, all the creative types found a belief in themselves to manifest their ideas or visions. Courage, hard work and positive attitudes guided their direction.

PERSONALTY TYPE	CHARACTER TRAITS	GRAPHICS
Conforming creative	Traditional, conventional Logical/methodological Reluctant to risk Internal & external control Need to belong Underachieving	Copybook style Connected letters Controlled writing Straight baseline Form conscious Subtle signs of originality
Compensated/conflicted creative	Early trauma Internal confusion Inconsistancy Variable self-image Escapist behavior Self-protective	Complex or distorted letter forms Variable slant Uneven middle zone Simplification Lower zone elaboration Extremes in shapes words, connections
Productive/versatile creative	Self-confident Motivated Mentally versatile Ambitious, bold Goal oriented Will power Initiative Resilient	Good zonal proportions Consistent middle zone Variety of forms & connections, Angular Rightward movement Powerful horizontals Rising baseline High Form Level Original style within traditional forms
Empowered creative	Self-actualized Good judgement Inner peace Spontaneous Authentic Autonomous, Independent Integrated Non-conforming	Simplified forms Ease of movement Original letters & Connections Uncomplicated spacing Balanced zones Excellent organization Highest Form Level

The following examples will illustrate the four types of creativity discerned in the Visionary Project. Case histories although of necessity shortened, still provide background information for better understanding why these individuals were chosen.

1. Conforming Creative (Examples 1 & 2)

Conventional, conservative forms, often school copy script, with subtle original forms and letters, reflect intense energy used to exert both inner and outer control of the individual's more innovative facets. Both are women raised with high standards and expectations made upon them to conform to narrow patterns of thinking and behavior. In spite of the traditional form, the writings are active and forward moving, showing the writer' strong determination and innate ability to achieve.

Example 1. The writing of the founder of the Giraffe Project, a non-profit organization which recognized people willing to stick their necks out for good causes. This project, named one of the 1,000 Points of Light during the Bush administration, was a way of giving recognition to those individuals who go out of their way to be helpful to others or their communities although they know there will not be any material reward.

Example 2. The writings of an art teacher and author of *Drawing with Children* and *Drawing with Adults*, who, without graphological training, teaches children to see everything in shapes: lines, circles, dots, curves and squares. The astounding results of her work would convince anyone that each of us has an artist within ourselves.

2. Compensated/Conflicted Creative (Examples 3 & 4)

Non-conforming, original and highly motivated. These individuals have achieved their goals thorough sheer determination and willpower, by overcoming enormous childhood trauma. Their perceptions of life are unusual because of the hardships they have endured, and yet with tremendous fortitude, and a sense of humor, they have seized opportunity to become very successful in their own fields of endeavor. Graphologically, there are long downstrokes, lateral movement and variable strokes in the vertical and horizontal axes.

Example 3. The compensated writing of a Greek hotel entrepreneur whose close early connection to his mother and domination by his father has led him to a lavish lifestyle of entertaining in his position as a hotel proprietor and proud owner of a priceless and provocative British art collection in New Mexico.

Example 4. The writing of a film producer and screenplay writer whose early childhood development was arrested by extraordinary emotional, physical and psychological damage from the time of conception. In spite of all odds, his courage, talents and innovative thinking found the creative outlet by reworking his own life on film. He became the hero of his own productions triumphing over tragedy. Earliest memory was being chained outside with a dog with whom he tangled in a dispute over eating a woodchuck.

3. Productive/Versatile Creative (Examples 5 & 6)

Astute, multifaceted, goal oriented and mentally flexible, these individuals have proven themselves in may areas of art, medicine, industry and education because of their ability to adapt, visualize with new perspectives and obtain results with enthusiasm and undaunted determination. The influence of their pasts seem to have been lessons more than traumas, so their powerful energies have been effectively captured and used productively. Their confidence has allowed them to use the resources available to them to become accomplished and well known.

Example 5. The writing of a New Age author and publisher whose books have been influential on a global level. Her mental alacrity and will power are sprinkled with her impatience with incompetence. Her considerable knowledge, wide network and activity have made her a major player in influencing personal and social transformation throughout the world.

Example 6. This hands-on, dynamic, practical, down-to-earth editor and writer has challenged political, medical and academic institutions in his extensive career of findings and reporting the truth. The ability to combine insight with common sense has made him a facile, outspoken master of multiple disciplines.

4. Empowered Creative (Examples 7 & 8)

Psychologically independent, resourceful, simplified and reserved, these individuals are the most self-actualized. They have dealt effectively with their pasts by comprehending and then clarifying their views of life. They are able to operate with directness, fluidity and keen intelligence to solve the most complex of human problems.

The integration of intellect and action has led them to paths of wide understanding and gives them an unusual perspective in helping other people. The highly refined and complex process by which they move from intellectual awareness to a plan of action is rarely understood and may be misinterpreted as emotional detachment or the quality of being remote or aloof. Their power rests in their insight and inexplicable ability to "know without knowing" (intuition) as well as the way in which they serve selflessly. They epitomize the timely statement: "the more you are, the less you need."

Example 7. This is the sample of a European-born therapist, writer and lecturer gifted with words, research ability and dedication to her field. Her personal experiences have made her an effective counselor and advocate of comprehensive therapy beginning with the earliest childhood trauma through the effects of the social consciousness and the environment on personality.

Example 8. The beautifully simplified writing of an innovative primal therapist who endured many years of childhood abuse. Her talent and insight, extraordinary intelligence and ability to see to the core of her patients has provided her a platform on which to base her lectures and the material from which to write a book.

As different and distinct as were the writings reviewed in the visionary research project, they all shared several identifiable features, including: vitality, keen intelligence, imagination, intuition, positive attitude and powerful inner strength. Graphologically, they tended to display good pressure, original letter forms and excellent spacing.

In short, each 'visionary' on some level knew of their talents; they felt what it meant to have the ability and they owned or took responsibility for their lives by using their gifts to achieve and then shared their insights with others. Perhaps this is the secret of the form levels!

Ed note: *Graphological Typology for Visionaries* Reprinted by permission of *Journal of the American Society of Professional Graphologists*

1) All I remember of what you said to me are the words "converted introvert" (which I don't remember you saying to anyone else so they were all our extroverts and "perfectionism" (and I don't know if you said I had had one or needed one!).

CONFORMING CREATIVE

2) Clouds are peachy pink and white against a beautiful baby blue. It rained last night and every is very clean and clear.

3) Were you aware when you wrote in the "Guest Book" "The best is yet to come"! What is to come or you just simply said it in gesture? [illegible] I tell you whenever you want to come [illegible] for your [illegible].

COMPENSATED/CONFLICTED CREATIVE

4) separation with God. The key with the question of death is to return to a world of spirit where we remember who we are.

5) Most of my handwriting is notetaking, with a lot of shorthand mixed in. — This is a sloppy version

PRODUCTIVE/VERSATILE CREATIVE

6) this exasperation ought to be reflected in today's hand/brain/arm wrestling with this ball point.

7) I do hope you will get a break when you go all go home to Boston – You have truly deserved it! Give my love to your parents too.

EMPOWERED CREATIVE

8) My day has been a pretty easy one without too many alarms and excursions. Phillip wants my undivided attention which of course he's not receiving at this moment.

Note: The author wishes to express her appreciation to Marilyn Ferguson and her staff, as well as Marc Seifer and Roger Rubin for their insights and assistance.

BIOGRAPHICAL NOTES

Ruth Holmes, CDE, is a professional handwriting and document examiner whose forensic, personnel and jury consulting firm, Pentec, Inc., in Bloomfield Hills, Michigan, advises individual, legal and corporate clients in the U.S., Canada and Mexico. Pentec often works for the Oakland County Sheriff's Department and Office of the Prosecutor, serving as an expert witness in major trials. One of those cases will be the subject of an upcoming program on HLN's *Forensic Files.* Ruth, who lived for eleven years in Brussels, Belgium and in Abidjan in the Ivory Coast, West Africa is former President of the International Women's Forum, Michigan. She was named one of Michigan's Top 10 Women Business Owners. *Corp!* magazine listed her among Michigan's 95 Most Powerful Women and in 2018 she was named Diversity Champion by the Race Relations Task Force.

pentecinc@aol.com

Passion for a Lifetime

Jane O'Brien, CG

How in the world does one become impassioned by a discipline or a field of study after graduating from college, helping running a catering business for 37 years as well as raising a family of four boys? My curiosity was tapped ten years before I finally found someone to teach me graphology when I attended a party where only the host knew any of us before that evening. One person in attendance announced that since we didn't know one another, she would introduce us if we were willing to just write a few sentences about anything and then sign our statements. She said she was a graphologist from Portland, Oregon.

As that evening turned out, the twelve of us were amazed what we learned about one another, not from what we wrote, but from what the graphologist reported about us from our handwriting. Because of what she saw in my script, I was told that this was a field of study that I would probably enjoy. I had interest in others, I was logical, reasonable, a communicator, organized and disciplined. And now, I was hooked!

When I finally had more time on my hands, I searched for a school or a person who taught graphology. With no luck finding a class in universities or community colleges in my area, I decided to randomly call a lawyer's office since document examiners sometimes know graphology too. The very first lawyer I called had just received a resume from Virginia Ryder who was both an expert handwriting witness and taught graphology. I called her that day and was invited to take a Psychogram class she would be teaching soon. Within a week, I started learning handwriting analysis with a fascination that has never left me.

Because Virginia had been in the field for many years before I took her class, she was part of several handwriting analysis organizations who offered conventions in cities throughout the United States. She not only sold me on joining AHAF (American Handwriting Analysis Foundation) and AAHA (American Association of Handwriting Analysis), she introduced me to many of the people I join today in handwriting analysis Zoom classes.

One wonderful benefit for me in taking up graphology was being invited to accompany Virginia on an all-expenses paid three-week Mediterranean Cruise, as she gave presentations on handwriting analysis to guests of the cruise. We were at sea, traveling to seven different countries. The audience were thrilled with her fun and interesting classes. She piqued the curiosity of her audience about the field of graphology.

At one of the handwriting analysis conferences I've attended, Felix Klein spoke about graphology as being "so important, it could save your life." Near the end of the Second World War he was imprisoned in Dachau Prison Camp. When an officer asked for a graphologist to step forward (graphology was a highly used field of study in Germany at that time), Felix feared for his life.

The officer wanted to know whether by looking at his handwriting, he could tell whether he would be a good Nazi soldier. Felix told him that he would be able to answer if he were given time to study the writing. The officer's warm office was like heaven to cold, thin Felix, so he took as much time as he was allowed. Because of the warm, caring, and humane signs in his script, he knew this man would not be comfortable fulfilling the demands made of the Nazi soldiers. When Felix told him, "You will never be a good Nazi soldier. You should be a farmer," he was sent back to his barracks.

The next day, when his name was called to step forward toward the fence, Felix was sure he was going to be shot. Instead, hanging from the end of the bayonet a soldier was pointing at him was a cheese sandwich. His life was saved. The officer, it turned out, wanted to be a farmer!

After finishing the first Psychogram course, I took Felix Klein's three courses in handwriting analysis from his wife, Janice Klein. Along the way, I practiced doing analysis of handwriting in those classes and made sure I understood this science and art. Continuing to attend meetings and conferences throughout the following years, I used what I learned to analyze the scripts of people who were interested and willing to have their handwriting examined. It took a long time, discipline, and practice, for me to be able and confident enough to do this.

Being honest in reporting the findings of a sample of writing also includes being kind in phrasing the outcome of the analysis. The feedback I received from the analyses I did was encouraging and gave me more confidence to analyze more often.

The most interesting handwriting analysis I wrote recently was for a woman and her four grown daughters. The analysis of each of the five people were done separately as they found courage to having their scripts analyzed. This project took at least six months to complete. As one would imagine, each sample of handwriting was quite different from the others, even though one of the daughter's samples was similar in many ways to the mother's script. I wrote each person an analysis and sent it to them, offering to answer any question she would have about the findings. None of them responded other than "thank you so much" and expressing their surprise with the analysis.

About one month after the last daughter's analysis was delivered, the mother called and asked if I would be willing to have a Zoom meeting with all five of them so they could meet me. We had that meeting and I was happy to put a face to the personalities I found in their samples of writing. Each person introduced herself to me and told me what she did in life. The shyest, yet probably most successful in business told us that she wept at the compliments she read in her analysis. Her confidence was boosted.

The most social person was very much like her wonderful mother who I hike with and enjoy in a book club. The colorful, neat, and organized daughter whose writing showed a fine appreciation of things she experienced through her senses, was an interior designer. And the youngest, busy one enjoyed the outside world, but frequently returned to the past for security.

As the graphologist, I was aware of the importance of allowing each person reveal or not reveal what the analysis showed to the others. We enjoyed being together and showing our amazement of the art and the science of the field of graphology. It never ceases to amaze me. If I were asked what is the clincher for me in graphology, I would have a hard time easily summing it up. But in considering the movement, form, and space of a sample of handwriting, I am always excited about the symbolism of a writing when I start to put into words what I see in a script. I am so grateful for the knowledge that I have accumulated in this wonderful field.

Johnjaneob@aol.com

Pens and Pups: Using graphology in the placement of service dogs with veterans

Cynthia Crosson, LICSW, CGA, CG

Years ago, I would never have imagined that two of my passions—graphology and service dogs—would come together in such an interesting and beneficial way. Nor did I suspect that the marriage of these passions would give rise to the first program in the nation and even internationally to place specially trained service dogs with veterans with PTSD.

I was initially certified in Graphoanalysis by IGAS in the early 1990s but saw it as something I had undertaken for an enjoyable hobby not a skill to use professionally. (More recently I became certified as a graphologist by AHAF).

My knowledge as a handwriting analyst was helpful throughout my many years as a college professor because the courses I was teaching on trauma required that I be aware of how my students were feeling. The mandatory logs that the students kept often alerted me to the mental and emotional difficulties they were having with the material, often as a result of their own past trauma. My ability to use handwriting analysis was also useful in my psychotherapy practice which specialized in trauma.

Fast forward to 2005 when, having graduated from the seminary, I applied to a local service dog organization for a ministry dog to assist me in my new work as a minister. The placement of my assistance dog, Dandi, came at the time that I was still grieving the death of my 22-year-old son who took his own life– a result, perhaps, of his military based post-traumatic stress disorder (PTSD).

The impact of this small Shih Tzu on my life and my ways of thinking was profound, reminding me daily of the healing power of animals.

The service dog organization, NEADS, had recently begun placing trained service dogs with combat veterans who returned with physical disabilities. The staff of NEADS discovered that many of these veterans also had post-traumatic stress disorder (PTSD) resulting from what they had seen and/or done in combat. In most cases their PTSD felt more problematic to the veterans than their physical disability.

Knowing of my background in treating trauma, the director of NEADS asked if I could design a program for them to place specially trained dogs to help veterans cope with their PTSD. Considering whether I could create such a program and how we would measure the success was challenging. I developed several tools to assess the applicants' PTSD and suddenly realized that there was another valuable tool that I was forgetting–graphology.

I designed a pilot program to begin placing dogs with veterans as well as assessing the efficacy of using these dogs to help with PTSD. The dogs would not be the only healing tools as we also required that our veterans be in psychotherapy and continue whatever medication they had been prescribed for anxiety, depression and sleep disturbances, all common symptoms of PTSD.

As part of the application, each veteran was asked to complete a hand-written one-page sample saying why he would like a service dog. I reviewed each of these samples and enlisted the help of several other graphologists to do the same.

Initially, we were not sure what we were looking for in this screening process but even the gestalt impression was interesting. Some of the handwriting observations that we made were documented. Downward slant (depression) was prevalent. The often-seen wide to variable spacing between words told of the veterans' difficulty connecting and the need for space from others due mostly to a lack of trust of others and even potentially themselves.

The majority of the writings were small (some even extremely small) and compressed, an indicator of withdrawal, social isolation, and fear of expression. Baselines, representing the line of reality (the 'street' on which they live and try to survive) were almost always extremely variable.

In essence, these veterans with PTSD were continuously traveling on a rocky road filled with potential land mines that could go off sporadically and unexpectedly. The uneven margins were another indicator of their inner turmoil as these men tried to find their place and sense of purpose in their environment. Some writings had large margins all around, giving the impression that the person felt boxed in, possibly even trapped. The writing was rarely centered appropriately on the page; rather many clung to the past (the far left margin) with the right margin wide, attesting to their fear of the future.

Slants covered the gamut. Some were variable, most were either very emotional, impulsive (far forward) or self-protective, skeptical (backward), There were also a number of vertical slants, showing control, no doubt attesting to their military discipline. It was interesting to witness that the veteran's slant almost always became evident by their behaviors when we interviewed them in person.

As we saw more veterans' handwriting samples, we recognized many universally shared traits. These included extreme anxiety (patching, pressure variations, compression of letters); very low self-esteem (small capital letters or oversized capital letters); low self-confidence (t-bars placed low on the stem); lack of self-direction and drive (short and/or lightly drawn t-bars); defiance (oversized or buckle in loop of lower case k) which is a desire for autonomy due to being over controlled. The defiant person can also have trust issues and may take on an attitude of, "Prove to me that I can trust you to help me!"

Even though there was an occasional overall rigid looking style of writing which lacked movement, many of the letter formations in the samples were often malformed or loosely formed which contributed to a lack of consistency in regularity, rhythm and legibility, another indicator of the writer's inner turmoil.

While trying to decide on the most suitable candidates, one major initial challenge was to determine which of the seemingly negative or defensive traits could be addressed by the placement of a service dog and which traits should result in the screening out of the applicant.

Depression, anxiety and low self-esteem were universal, and we had to determine if these individuals could be helped. When aggressive traits were noted, we had to evaluate the ability for the veteran to be able to keep his aggression somewhat in check. Working with a service dog can be a tiring task as there is much to think about in terms of commands and the welfare of the dog as well as the veteran's own comfort and ability to follow through with the tasks at hand. Therefore, the veteran who lacked stamina, will power, or whose left margin slanted considerably inward going down the page might suggest someone who did not have the ability, or ego-strength to complete the program.

Screening of the applicants involved assessing the applications, evaluating their writing and the PTSD grid, on which they rated the degree of their symptoms, and interviews with several staff members including myself as the consulting psychological professional.

Sometimes our previous assessment of the handwriting bore out in the interviews. Other times, we were surprised when we met the veteran in person. It was in these interviews that we had to weigh the 'brain writing' against the picture the individual was presenting in person.

The parameters we had set for eligibility also influenced the screening and in some cases graphology was helpful even though it could not provide a final determination. We required that the veteran not be actively suicidal (though many did show some ideation), not abusing substances (alcohol or drugs) and not having any other major mental illness. The application process also included reports from both primary care physicians and mental health providers.

There were sixteen male veterans in our pilot study as our initial applicants were men. (The fact that men and women may process PTSD somewhat differently became evident but that would require an entirely new chapter.) We placed between three to five veterans in each group and the study spanned over a period of two years.

Once screened-in, a group of veterans was invited to a two-week residential training on the NEADS campus. During this time, they received their dogs and then participated in classes with them to learn their training and care. I schooled them in what can best be called mindfulness training to help them use their dogs to cope with anxiety, depression and other symptoms of their PTSD. At the end of the training, they wrote another sample on how they felt the training had gone.

Over the next year, the veterans returned with their dogs at three-month intervals to be interviewed as to their progress. During this time, they gave us another handwriting sample at each visit that I looked at to see if there was progress or red flags. There were several instances when something that I saw in their writing gave us concern and we were able to address it.

It was interesting to see how the veterans' writing changed over time. We learned that their bonding with their dogs increased exponentially between the six and nine-month interviews and their writing also changed in a positive way.

Many of the writings increased in size, moved more toward the right margin and showed less signs of stress, anxiety and depression as some of the variables previously noted transitioned into more of a steady consistency. The veterans' wives and families described them as much more relaxed, less anxious, more optimistic and more independent. Veterans who at one time would not leave home or were overly dependent on family members found more confidence to venture out with only their canine "battle buddy" accompanying them.

The specific improvements that we noted in the final analysis of the pilot program were that the majority of veterans were less anxious and better able to leave home, making them less isolated. The dog provided them with a "battle buddy" that increased their feelings of safety.

Most veterans have sleep issues—either difficulty falling or staying asleep or being awakened by nightmares. The comfort of having their service dog helped them to relax and sleep. In addition, dogs were able to awaken veterans from disturbing nightmares and seemed to sooth them as they recovered from the disturbing images.

We found that with the reduced anxiety, veterans were often able to decrease their anxiety medications and develop a more hopeful outlook. Two outcomes that we did not necessarily expect were decreased suicidal ideation and improved relationships. Thoughts of suicide decreased as the veterans worried who would care for their dogs if they were not living. While we cannot make the definite claim that dogs decrease the likelihood of suicide among veterans, this was our experience.

The difficulty that veterans had with trust made their relationships especially problematic. Some wives and girlfriends were considering leaving the veterans just because it seemed that there was no hope for their recovery. Those who stuck by their veterans were often exhausted by trying to help the veterans cope or by their intense dependence. The service dog helped with the veterans' trust and even their anger issues and gave them feelings of more independence taking pressure off their significant others. Although we cannot say that every relationship survived, the majority did and improved. We jokingly credited ourselves with several saved marriages and even a few engagements during the period of our study.

The success of the program to place service dogs with veterans with PTSD became apparent and we continued to place dogs with veterans as we fine-tuned the process. To date, the program has placed close to forty dogs with veterans with PTSD and most teams have been successful. The idea for the program was soon picked up by other service dog agencies both in the United States and across the world. Unfortunately, others do not use graphology as we did, despite my suggestions to several programs.

I would also like to report that my own agency uses the benefits of graphology more widely, but this was not always the case. Some staff members see the benefit of graphology as one tool that is invaluable in both assessing the veterans' readiness and motivation as well as measuring their progress. For other staff, the efficacy of our craft is a harder sell. Ironically, many of the veterans were anxious to know how their writing demonstrated improvement.

As a mental health professional I have seen the help that graphology provides and I am an advocate for making it one arrow in the quiver of service dog agency placement. I would like to see agencies integrate graphology more into practice. Perhaps it will happen someday. We have our work of making it a reality cut out for us.

Many thanks to Eileen Page who has acted as my 'graphology consultant' in screening the veterans and also to those who gave assistance in the earlier phases of the project: Bonnie Lee Nugent, Pat Carter and Barbara Donato. Thank, too, for others of my NESHA group for their support and encouragement.

BIOGRAPHICAL NOTES

Dr. Cynthia Crosson is a former college professor and psychotherapist specializing in trauma and child sexual abuse. She has authored numerous college and educational texts. After receiving her own service dog, Cynthia designed the first program to place service dogs with veterans with PTSD. Her recent memoir, *You Can Not Cage the Wolf: A Mother Struggles with the Suicide of her Soldier Son*, recounts the story of how her varied background and her son's death led her to work with veterans and trained service dogs. Currently, she continues to write and is the pastor of a church in western Massachusetts.

harvestco40@hotmail.com

Sample 1 and 2 were taken at the time of the application

Sample 1 - Uneven baseline, intense, with poorly formed letters

never judge you. With dogs words don't need to be exchanged, they
can sence your emotions and can communicate with bodylannguage.
Having a trauma assistance dog that could go with me anywhere I go
would be a tremendous relief for me. Knowing that wherever I go

Sample 2 - Light pressure, lacking in energy, extreme downward slant (depression)

Sample 3 - Same writer as sample 2 after one year with service dog

(dog)
The Best Part of Having [redacted] is he
every wave with me, The Bond Between
and gives me Assurance that I will alw
have a Battle Buddy, Best Freind By m

Why Do Handwriting Analysts Need a Basic Foundation in Psychology?

Marion Rollings, Ph.D, CG

Handwriting is human behavior and human behavior is the subject of the sciences of psychology, sociology, anthropology, and neurobiology. Graphology is the study of human personality and functioning as it appears or is represented in handwriting. Psychology is the study of human behavior and functioning that overarches all science disciplines concerning human and nonhuman behavior, both individually and in groups, societies, and cultures.

In a Venn Diagram (figure 1), we would have the grand disciplines of psychology, anthropology, sociology, neurobiology, and graphology intersecting with one another. Handwriting is a complex psychomotor activity that involves both psychological and neurophysiological processes (Keefe, Riley, Herbert, & Stirling, 2013).

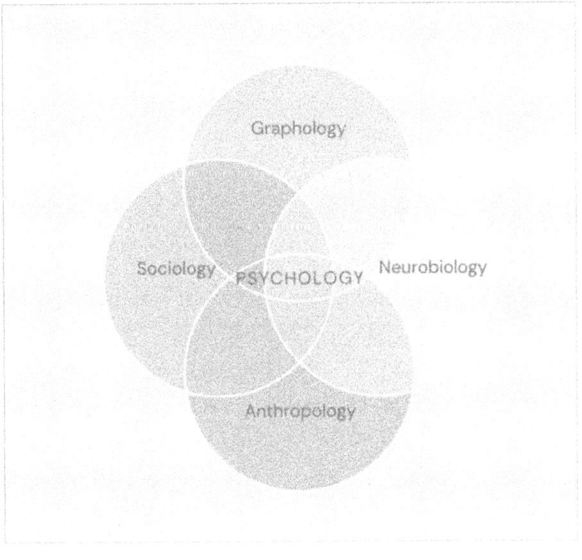

It is important that handwriting analysts have a basic understanding of psychology so that we are not just parroting the language we hear used in graphology groups or read in books, but rather know what is meant and whether we agree or disagree, based upon accurate knowledge of psychological principles.

The history of handwriting analysis has its roots in the scientific work of psychologists, philosophers, and many other scientists who were studying human perception, motivation, behavior, and personality. Organized handwriting analysis itself began with a scientific approach that Michon, Crepieux-Jamin, Klages, and others used to develop, test, and expand their theories (Lowe, 2018). An approach that historically is inextricably linked and intertwined with psychology.

Some History

Interest in handwriting and its relationship to an individual's personality go back to Aristotle (Lowe, 2018). In fact, all sciences have their historical roots in philosophy. It began when someone asked a question, which was followed by debate, discussion, and calculations that over time led to the models of scientific inquiry we use today to further our understanding of ourselves and the universe we live in.

Max Pulver (undated Klein translation, p. 1) stated "conscious writing is unconscious drawing." The term "unconscious" is a psychoanalytic concept that has become part of society's vernacular and the language of handwriting analysis. Having an understanding of how the unconscious works with other parts of the personality is invaluable information for the handwriting analyst to have.

Using a Freudian or Jungian approach provides further insight to the psychology of the writer. For example, we often see signs of anxiety in handwriting samples. But what kind of anxiety? There are many types: social, general, phobic, etc. When we know more about psychology, we expand our understanding of handwriting and the human being that wrote it.

Contemporary handwriting analysis has its foundation in historical psychology, especially Freud and the psychodynamic approaches to personality as well as the Gestalt and Humanistic schools of psychology, Trait-Stroke handwriting analysis has its roots in Michon's notion of isolated signs and fixed traits (Landau, 2007), but that school also has adapted Freudian and psychodynamic language in evaluating handwriting. The zeitgeist during Michon's time in France was focused on scientific inquiry. The French researchers Janet and Charcot were working on their notions of the unconscious which had a great impact on Freud who studied under Charcot. To this day, handwriting analysts use terminology and concepts that are derived from the early work of the psychologists and neurologists of the 19th century and onwards.

Although Freud (1933) himself did not "hold a high opinion" of graphology, his comments in many of his letters to friends and colleagues before 1933 show a different opinion. In Freud's (1928) account to his brother: "A graphologist would have to see from my handwriting that I have already lost several teeth." He seems to indicate that he believed at that time at least, that graphology had merit. Others in early psychology, psychiatry, and neurology saw the value in handwriting analysis, including many of Freud's followers, Alfred Adler, Carl Jung, and others.

Despite Freud's later views on graphology, his theory of personality remains important in handwriting analysis. The Id, Ego, and Superego are seen in how many view the Personal Pronoun I (Henley, undated monograph) lower zone (id), middle zone (ego), and upper zone (superego).

From Jung, who followed Freud but went on to develop an extended life span view of personality and psychological growth, came the Myers-Briggs typology that many handwriting analysts use today. Jung's notion of the shadow side of the human mind, the collective unconscious, and his (and Freud's) emphasis on symbolic representation have influenced graphology profoundly. For example, the way symbolism found in signatures is interpreted (Poizner, 2012).

Jung (1971, p. 917) himself believed that graphology was an external path that leads to internal psychic reality. Graphology belongs to the same class of interpretations from outward signs. As we can see, there are any number of paths leading from outside inwards, from the physical to the psychic, and it is necessary that research should follow this direction until the elementary psychic facts are established with sufficient certainty"

In the early twentieth century, Gestalt psychology came about through the work of Wertheimer, Koffka, and Kohler, in part as a reaction against Freud and psychoanalysis. In a similar way, in reaction to trait-stroke graphology, Klages and later on, Felix Klein, applied Gestalt psychology theory to handwriting analysis. (Lowe, 2018). They developed and expanded the field of Gestalt Graphology, as it is practiced today. Contemporary handwriting analysts like Roger Rubin and Sheila Lowe carry on the Gestalt tradition today through books, courses, lectures, and mentoring. So, the historical giants of psychology remain important in graphology today. We use their language and concepts in our interpretations of handwriting.

As psychology evolved, so did Graphology. The early founders of graphology recognized that an understanding of psychology is essential. It could be said that they did not see psychology and graphology as separate. In Felix Klein's collected works (2007), there are chapters on Neuroses (which we can also refer to as anxieties and phobias), the unconscious, a typology based on Alfred Adler's work, and the psychology of children's handwriting. Olyanova's *The Psychology of Handwriting,* Werner Wolff's *Diagrams of the Unconscious,* and Robert Saudek's *The Psychology of Handwriting* are other notable examples of early published works on handwriting analysis that are based in psychology. There are many, many more. Contemporary leaders in graphology also teach about the important role a solid foundation in psychology has in the understanding of the writer's personality as it is expressed in their handwriting. (e.g., Lowe & Bar-Av, 2018).

Graphology as Applied Psychology

We have established that the history of graphology is undeniably intertwined with psychology. We could say that graphology is actually applied psychology.

There are many similarities between the way a psychologist evaluates an individual and how a handwriting analyst evaluates a handwriting sample. When a psychologist assesses an individual, they observe their behavior (presentation), ask about the patient's age, cultural background, ethnicity, where they grew up, mental, medical (including medications), and family history. In a similar way, the handwriting analyst observes how the writing appears on the page by examining the space, form, and movement (the Gestalt or overall presentation), observes any peculiarities or idiosyncrasies of the writing, as well as the writer's handedness, age, health status, medications, disabilities, and place of birth, if known.

The handwriting analyst should try to gather as much information that is known about the writer at the time they wrote the sample as possible. There are some handwriting analysts who do not agree that the writer's history is so relevant, but the facts are that the writing is not a collection of traits we can simply extrapolate from; that is conjecture and reductionistic. We cannot reduce human beings to a few variables in the writing without consideration of the things that affect their writing. The writing is generated by a human being at a point in time where they are affected and influenced by any number of variables. To discount those variables is not scientific, but rather, pseudoscience.

Ethical Considerations

It is also important that we take into consideration what we don't know about the writer. For example, if the writer is European, their spacing and writing form may differ from someone from the United States. Knowing the writer's age is important as it will tell us the copybook they likely learned. It is also important to know if they have a disability, illness, wear glasses, or take medication.

The surface on which the person write, as well as the writing instrument can have a bearing upon the sample. Having more than one writing sample, from different times in the writer's life can give a stronger and more reliable picture of the writer's personality. In a perfect world, we would know those things and more, but it could be that we don't have any of that information. All we might have is a writing sample. Obviously, in practical terms, we have to base a handwriting analysis upon what is known, if anything, about the writer and what appears on the page. So, absent additional information, the handwriting analyst has to proceed with caution and restraint.

People are more than their symptoms and should not be defined by their illnesses. In psychology today, current practice is that we do not say a person *is* a schizophrenic, we say they *have* schizophrenia or they are schizophrenic (as a verb not a noun), they *have* anorexia instead of they are anorexic.

We should not pathologize individuals. So, when we perform a handwriting analysis, we must be careful in what we say about the writer. We have never met them and may have limited knowledge of their disposition at the time they wrote the sample. A superficial understanding of psychology leads to a handwriting analyst using the terminology of psychology in a superficial and limited way. If, for example, you are using Freud's theory of the id, ego, and superego, but are unfamiliar with his theory on motivation and instinctual drives, you are limiting your understanding of the writer's psychology and the handwriting sample.

Typologies

Many handwriting analysts use typologies as a framework for understanding the writer. These typologies are derived from psychological theories and research on human personalities. Familiarity with human lifespan development and psychological stage theories is essential for understanding human behavior. And having broad knowledge of personality theory and contemporary psychological thinking on human functioning is also important for the handwriting analyst to know.

The Myers-Briggs (which came out of Jung's work), and the Enneagram, as well as Maslow's Hierarchy of Needs, and The Big 5 in psychology offer us many ways to understand human personalities.

- For example, The Big 5 (acronym: OCEAN) stands for:
- openness to experience (inventive/curious vs. consistent/cautious)
- conscientiousness (efficient/organized vs. extravagant/careless)
- extraversion (outgoing/energetic vs. solitary/reserved)
- agreeableness (friendly/compassionate vs. critical/rational)
- neuroticism (sensitive/nervous vs. resilient/confident)

Although The Big 5 (as we refer to them in psychology) have been applied to handwriting analysis, it does not have widespread usage. The Big 5 come from decades of psychological research. One could correlate the Big 5 characteristics to handwriting features. (Malik & Balaji, 2021).

Maslow

Maslow's Hierarchy of Needs is a way of understanding basic human needs and is often discussed in graphology books. Many non-psychologists are unaware that Maslow (1943, 1954) expanded his hierarchy to include cognitive and aesthetic needs and transcendence needs (Maslow, 1970).

Critics of Maslow (see Liebermann, 2011), have argued that other needs are more important. Nonetheless, Maslow's Hierarchy is a useful, humanistic way to understand human functioning that does not pathologize the writer.

The Enneagram and tests

The Enneagram has its historical roots in Greek philosophy and the mystical spiritual traditions of the Middle East (Baron and Wagele, 1994). Some contemporary psychologists and psychiatrists have embraced the utility of the Enneagram (Alexander and Schnipke, 2020, and Hook, Hall, Davis, Van Tongeren, and Conner. 2021).

Occasionally, handwriting analysts use projective tests such as House, Tree, Person or drawing samples from the writer. Many tests require advanced degrees, professional licenses, and training in psychology. Although the tests may be available on the internet in pirated form, they should not be used by anyone unqualified. It would be unethical to do so and the test results might not be very accurate if administered by someone who was not properly trained in its use.

Humans have a level of complexity that is not readily deduced from a few sentences in a handwriting sample. Careful consideration of the gestalt–the space, form, and movement–will provide a great deal of information. Then working within the framework of a typology or personality theory allows us to expand upon what is seen in the writing and provide useful information about the writer's mental and physical disposition at the time they wrote the sample.

The handwriting analyst needs to know how to think critically, ethically and consistently within a framework of understanding that is firmly grounded in a clear methodology based upon psychology.

Critical Thinking

Two other areas that are worth highlighting are ethics and critical thinking. One thing a study in psychology provides is the ability to think critically and to know how to evaluate a source of information. That is, how to know when a source is reliable and trustworthy. When one speaks or writes about a topic, credible references should be listed that will allow the audience or reader to go back to the original sources themselves. If a speaker or writer makes statements about the psychology of handwriting without making reference to established sources, and does not have sufficient training and experience in psychology and handwriting analysis, then we have reason to question their credibility and should not rely upon what they are sharing as factual.

Therefore, we must always ask: What is the background of the speaker or writer? Do they possess some education and experience in graphology and psychology? Are they certified or licensed by a credible organization? Is their use of handwriting samples and tests ethical? This is not to say that everyone needs to have an advanced degree in psychology, but having a foundation in psychology, and providing appropriate references to credible texts and theory, provides some assurance that the writer or speaker are credible themselves.

Ethical Considerations

The words we use to think and describe what we do affect how we feel, as well as our actions. It is important that we do not judge the writer but rather assess the handwriting. Judging the writer can be subjective whereas assessment of their writing is objective. Assessment is based upon established standards and guidelines. Judging can lead to conjecture and often is more of a projection of the handwriting analyst's own issues and sensibilities. We must base our assessment upon what is found in the writing itself, which is neither subjective or a projection. From that, within a framework of understanding (such as a typology), we can provide an accurate portrayal of what the handwriting reveals about the writer.

Some Conclusions

It is fair to say that handwriting analysis is now in a critical period. If we want to move forward as a respected field of study in the United States, then it is absolutely essential that we hold ourselves to a high standard of professionalism, ethical comportment, and transparent, objective methodology based upon solid research.

As handwriting analysts, we have to be firmly rooted in ongoing education, practice through groups led by credible speakers, training from qualified teachers, and strict adherence to a model of handwriting analysis that is based upon our observations of the writing and not conjecture. In order for graphology to attain credibility, handwriting analysts must have a solid grounding in psychology. Without it, graphology will continue to be seen as pseudoscience practiced by charlatans who lack basic knowledge of personality theories and psychological principles.

Psychology provides us with an understanding of the whole person. With a basic understanding of personality theory, combined with advanced knowledge of graphology, the handwriting analyst can form an accurate understanding of the writer, as well as what makes them tick.

Psychology and organized handwriting analysis also provide the ethical framework within which we can professionally operate as handwriting analysts. A foundation in psychology allows us to understand the writer's personality in a structured and reliable manner.

As has been demonstrated, much of the language of graphology comes from psychology. Learning more about this history helps to shed light on why we employ the analysis methods we have today, where they came from, and how they have evolved over time.

We may conclude that graphology has always been a subdivision of psychology; an ignored and underestimated one at that. But as I have shown, early graphologists understood the need for a firm grounding in psychology and in fact, did not see what they were doing as separate from psychology. When we strip graphology of its psychological underpinnings, we are interpreting a collection of marks on the page with a shallow framework of 'this-means-that.'

The study of handwriting analysis is a lifelong occupation. One learns the basics in books and courses and builds upon that knowledge through mentoring, attending lectures and presentations, reading, and continued training. It is a challenging and enjoyable occupation that is helpful to others when practiced by a handwriting analyst who has a good foundation in psychology and ongoing training in graphology.

BIBLIOGRAPHY

Alexander, M. and Schnipke, B. (2020). *The Enneagram: A Primer for Psychiatry Residents.* American Journal of Psychiatry Residents Journal 15(3):2-5. Published Online:6 Mar 2020 https://doi.org/10.1176/appi.ajp-rj.2020.150301 retrieved 9/9/22

Baron and Wagele (1994) *The Enneagram Made Easy: Discover the 9 Types of People.* Harper SanFrancisco [sic]

Elngar, A., Jain, N., Sharma, D., Negi, H., Trehan, A.,j and Srivastava, A. (2020). A Deep Learning Based Analysis of the Big Five Personality Traits from Handwriting Samples Using Image Processing. *Journal of Information Technology Management,* Special Issue, 3-36.

Retrieved online from: https://jitm.ut.ac.ir/article_78884_2959805560be5b0bf7a105aad7477728.pdf 9/2/22

Freud, S. (1928) Letter from Sigmund Freud to Sándor Ferenczi, August 21, 1928. *The Correspondence of Sigmund Freud and Sándor Ferenczi,* Volume 3, 1920-1933 27:349.

Freud, S. (1933) New Introductory Lectures On Psycho-Analysis. *The Standard Edition of the Complete Psychological Works of Sigmund Freud* 22:1-182 p. 45.

Henley *The Freudian "I"* Vol. 1. Monograph available via AHAF library.

Hook, J., Hall, T., Davis D.,, Van Tongeren D., Conner M. (2021). The Enneagram: A systematic review of the literature and directions for future research. *Journal of Clinical Psychology,* 2021 Apr;77(4):865-883. doi: 10.1002/jclp.23097. Epub 2020 Dec 17. PMID: 33332604.

Jung, C. (1971). Psychological Types. From *The Collected Works of C.G. Jung, Volume 6.* Edited and translated by G. Adler and R.F.C. Hull.

Keefe, B., Riley, M., Herbert, L., and Stirling, M. (2013). International Manual of Graphology. *IGC Books.*

Klein, Felix (2007) *Gestalt Graphology.* iUniverse, Inc.

Landau, S (2007). Michon and the Birth of Scientific Graphology. *The Vanguard.* January-February, ed. Sheila Lowe. retrieved online at: https://www.britishgraphology.org/wp-content/uploads/2012/02/MichonAndTheBirthOfScientificGraphology.pdf

Lieberman, M. D. (2013). *Social: Why our brains are wired to connect.* New York, NY: Crown.

Lowe. S. (2018). *Reading Between the Lines: handwriting decoded.* Write Choice Ink

Lowe, S. and Bar-Av (2018) *Personality and Anxiety Disorders: How they may be reflected in handwriting.* Write Choice Ink.

Malik, N., Balaji, A. (2021). *Predicting the Big-Five Personality Traits from Handwriting.* In: Sharma, M.K., Dhaka, V.S., Perumal, T., Dey, N., Tavares, J.M.R.S. (eds) Innovations in *Computational Intelligence and Computer Vision. Advances in Intelligent Systems and Computing,* vol 1189. Springer, Singapore. Retrieved online at: https://doi.org/10.1007/978-981-15-6067-5_25

Maslow, A.H. (1943). *A Theory of Human Motivation.* In Psychological Review, 50 (4), 430-437.

Maslow, A. H. (1954, 1970). *Motivation and Personality.* New York, NY: Harper & Row Publishers.

Olyanova, Nadya (1960). *The Psychology of Handwriting.* Sterling

Poizner (2012) *Clinical Graphology: An Interpretative Manual for Mental Health Practitioners.* Springfield, IL: Charles Thomas.

Pulver, M. (undated monograph). *Symbolism of Handwriting.* Translation by Felix Klein.

Saudek, R. (1925) *The Psychology of Handwriting.* Allen and Unwin.

Wolff, W. (1948) *Diagrams of the Unconscious.* Grune and Stratton.

Recommended resources

For more on why handwriting analysts should have a foundation in psychology see:

Lowe, S. (2022). *Why do graphologists need to understand basic psychology?* The Vanguard. October-December. Published by Sheila Lowe. Available at https://sheila-lowe-store.square.site/ and AHAF Library (membership required)

Lowe, S. & Bar-Av, Z. (2018) *Personality and Anxiety Disorders: How they may be reflected in handwriting.* Write Choice Ink.

The Enneagram

Baron and Wagele (1994) *The Enneagram Made Easy: Discover the 9 Types of People.* HarperSan-Francisco [sic]

Baron and Wagele (1995) *Are You My Type, Am I Yours? Relationships Made Easy through the Enneagram.* HarperSanFranciso [sic]

History of Graphology

For an excellent history of graphology, see Lowe (2018) *Reading Between the Lines: handwriting decoded.* Write Choice Ink

Maslow

For the best explanation of Maslow and how it applies to handwriting analysis, see Sheila Lowe's (2018) *Advanced Studies in Handwriting Psychology.* Write Choice Ink.

Symbolic Representation

To learn more about symbolic representation from a clinical perspective, see Poizner's (2012) chapter on *Symbolism in Signatures.*

For Instruction in Psychology

Online Instruction: Coursera (https://www.coursera.org/), has basic and advanced courses in psychology from Yale, Penn State, University of Michigan, Wesleyan, Rutgers, and other well-respected universities, all for free. You won't get college credit unless you pay for them, but they are self-paced and excellent. Most are taught by prominent, respected psychologists. Local community colleges and universities offer courses in introductory and advanced psychology. I recommend taking a basic foundational course in psychology, then human development and theories of personality.

BIOGRAPHICAL NOTES

Dr. Marion Rollings is a licensed psychologist and certified graphologist. She is a volunteer on the AHAF Certification Committee and is the Director of Holistic Health Counseling Center in New Jersey. Her interests are in gestalt handwriting analysis, Jungian depth psychology, Freudian psychoanalysis, and dream interpretation. She lives with her husband, a house rabbit, two cats, tropical and pond fish, and a lot of birds near Princeton, NJ. Marion is an avid reader, philatelist, vegan home cook (especially of Asian cuisines), nature lover, and animal rights activist.

drmarion@drmarionrollings.com

Is Handwriting Genetic or Environmental?

Kathleen Dickinson, CG

This is a question that has intrigued many handwriting analysts, educators, and parents. When I was asked the question recently, I was led to take a look at handwritings of my own family members.

When babies are born, aspects of their personalities are often quickly evident. If you have had your DNA tested, you have learned that children of identical parents do not have identical DNA results. Siblings do not have similar personalities, inherited bone structures, physical maladies, or strengths, nor do they have identical writing styles

Do you write the way you were taught to write in grade school? Probably not. I was taught the Palmer method, which makes a fat capital F that I did not like. Nor did I like the Capital T. Although I write all the other letters in cursive, I use print forms for my F's and T's. That being said, my cursive lowercase f was the bane of my mother and Aunt Eileen Dickinson's existence because I write it in a forward direction, despite their insistence that I was writing it backward.

This article examines handwriting samples of several of my family members, along with some biographical information about them. The samples appear at the end of this article.

All four of my grandparents were born and raised in Ireland. They came to the United States in the 19teens. The samples are found on the pages following the text of the article.

My grandfather Dickinson's handwriting is from a note he wrote to his daughter, my Aunt Eileen. He had initially been trained as a typesetter in Limerick, Ireland. He joined the United States Army in World War I, where he lost two middle fingers. Later, he worked for the United State Post Office.

One of the things I appreciated about my grandfather was his enjoyment of reading mysteries. He introduced me to Agatha Christie when I was twelve. He had lovely handwriting with a sense of style, and dignity. He was in his 80s when he lost his legs to diabetes, which was unfortunate, as he played handball into his 70s and taught his sons, kids in the neighborhood, and grandchildren how to play. He loved to play the horses. His writing shows dignity and determination.

The 1962 note to my sister is from my grandmother, Eileen Hogan Dickinson. The bottom note to my father is written in 1930 from his grandmother, Ellen Guerin Hogan, my great-grandmother.

Ellen Hogan was born around 1864 and wrote this sample to my father on his first communion. It was in the prayer book she sent him and was signed, "Your fond grandmother Mrs. E Hogan." She had excellent attention to detail and strong determination. An optimist who had a strong interest in literature, culture, and the arts, she was very bright and had several types of thinking processes: analytical, cumulative, and keen comprehension. She also had good organizational skills.

The initial stroke on her capital M shows that she was always willing to take on more responsibility. She had a personal philosophy of life and kept her own counsel, intentionally keeping things to herself. I found it interesting that she did not capitalize the 'd' in Dickinson while she did capitalize the 'd' in Dear. Ellen had strong persistence, which is fine to a point, but if the person keeps *persistently* hitting their head against a brick wall because they think there is only one way to do something, the trait becomes a liability.

My grandmother, Eileen Hogan Dickinson, would have liked to accomplish more in her life. She was frustrated by her perception of the role of women. She always dressed elegantly in a skirt and blouse or suit, and often wore hats. She had excellent posture. During WWII she volunteered, rolling bandages. She was not warm or easy to know, yet she took the time to write in a prayer book for my sister for my sister's first communion.

In my father John Dickinson's, handwriting, the repeated signatures are from signing my report card in 1965-66 and the card to my mom is from June,

1978. He is the son of Eileen Hogan Dickinson and John Joseph Dickinson. My father was a sensitive man who worked his way up through the Post Office to become a Postmaster in the 70s.

He had strong integrity, was analytical, and had an excellent sense of humor. He had dignity and was a good listener.

His sister Eileen Dickinson's handwriting is interesting due to the compression of her upper loops, and to wonder about her spiritual philosophy. She was a member of the Sisters of Charity. She taught elementary school and painted landscapes, mostly ocean scenes. And, she took violin lessons for a while.

When Eileen's convent disbanded in the 1960s she continued teaching and, eventually retired with a fellow nun to North Carolina.

On the other side of the family, we have my grandfather O'Neill's handwriting, and his wife, my Nana O'Neill's. After fleeing political unrest in Ireland Grandpa worked very hard making his way in the United States. He initially ran a speakeasy, which he lost due to loaning money and not getting reimbursed. He worked at the Fulton Fish Market, and the A&P supermarket.

Grandpa had a way with words, and enjoyed listening to music. His rheumatoid arthritis was exacerbated by his early years at the Fish Market.

Nana was the very definition of resilient. She had a 6th grade education and came to the U. S. To work as a nanny at the age of sixteen. She worked her whole life, and was a charwoman for many years. Her last career job was in the kitchen at Columbia University, where she was forced to retire at 70, thanks to an age rule. She lived for more than 22 years after retirement. Nana cared about all 15 of her grandchildren and their children. She cared about her neighbors too.

My grandparents' daughters' handwriting can be seen next. Peggy O'Neill Clancy (born 1920). Her birth name was Kathleen, but once she heard the song *Peggy O'Neill*, she became Peggy. Eileen O'Neill Gonzalez was born in 1921, and Patricia O'Neill Dickinson was born in 1923.

Aunt Peggy gave birth to five boys and twin girls. She developed a phobia and refused to drive across bridges, which made it hard for her to forgive family members who moved away from the New York Metropolitan area. Yet, she was generous and cared about her children, grandchildren, nieces, nephews, and siblings. She always had large handwriting, while Aunt Eileen's handwriting was always small.

Aunt Eileen had one son and two grandsons. She was skilled at crafts such as sewing. Neither Aunt Eileen nor Aunt Peggy worked outside their homes after marriage. They were homemakers. Throughout my growing up years, my mother worked for companies such as Scholastic and Bell Labs as a switchboard operator. Like her father, she was quick with arithmetic. She had a beautiful singing voice, and was good at event coordinating.

My sister Patricia is my hero. She inherited A Quad Foot-Type (narrow feet) from Aunt Peggy; scoliosis, and stenosis from our father's brother, Peter. All of this was made worse in 1990 when a work colleague placed boxes behind her at work without telling her and she fell backward over them. Patricia inherited allergic reactions to all sorts of things like shellfish and medications from Aunt Eileen O'Neill. In 2015, the medications she has had to take as a result of two back surgeries caused her intestines to explode. She has a drop foot as a result of the back injury and surgeries, and is in constant pain with rheumatoid arthritis, (exacerbated by medications etc.). She has had to deal with a lot of bureaucracy. Yet, she keeps on going, helping neighbors and friends. She is amazing. There are many traits in her handwriting that show resilience. For example, defiance, persistence, and depth of feeling. She inherited creative skills from Aunt Eileen O'Neill, who inherited her creative skills from our maternal great-grandmother Kate Duffy.

And finally, my handwriting in 1972 and 2022. I found the changes in my handwriting startling. My natural skills have been as a coordinator. I probably inherited my coordinating skills from my mother. Currently, I coordinate trainings and events for K-12 teachers and students. In the past, I have coordinated recycling, environmental, prevention, and legislative conferences.

More research is needed in this area in the area of handwriting and genetics, but whatever the answer to this question turns out to be, and as a proponent of history, I think it is sad to lose the skill of reading cursive writing. There is an interesting article in the October 2022 issue of The Atlantic, titled "Gen Z Never Learned to Read Cursive. How will they interpret the past?" Author Drew Gilpin Faust writes:

> *Penmanship came to be seen as a marker dand expression of the self—of gender and class, to be sure, but also of deeper elements of character and soul. The notion of a signature as a unique representation of a particular individual gradually came to be enshrined in the law and accepted as legitimate legal evidence.*

https://www.theatlantic.com/magazine/archive/2022/10/gen-z-handwriting-teaching-cursive-history/671246/

In conclusion, It is my belief that handwriting is both genetic and environmental. We inherit certain personality traits, just as we inherit physical traits. We start off with qualities inherited from our parents. Personality traits are a foundation, and we develop them as we grow. How we use them, and how they evolve is an exciting part of our life process. They are reflected in our handwriting.

Great Grandma Ellen Guerin Hogan

Grandma Eileen Hogan Dickinson

John M. Dickinson, Kathleen's father

Grandpa John Joseph Dickinson, 1958

Dearest Girl:

Even in Limerick I can't forget my little girl. As I walk through the countryside picking black berries now & then, I seem to sense you by my side running wild along the country lanes & looking at the beauties of nature on every side. No more tenements but green fields with sheep and cows all over, bleating & mooing like they s
bees l
outside

Aunt Eileen O'Neill Gonzalez

Nov. 4, 1987

Dear Kathleen,

Surprise! Any excuse to write. I knew your mother made a mistake as soon as I saw the check.

Hope you are well! See you soon?

God bless,
love
Aunt Eileen

Great Nana Kathleen McCabe O'Neill

My Dear Kathleen
Please forgive me
for not writing to you more
often but my arthrites Pain I
just cant write, But I think
of you all they time and I
ask your mom about you
I hope you come east in
July so we can get towgether
for a day. You did not tell
me anything about Jim But
I will waite till I see you
your mom had a wanderfull
time on the Trip. Hoping
to Hear from you soon Love.
Great Great Nana O'Neill

Aunt Peggy (Kathleen) O'Neill Clancy

tract.
We are awaiting the birth
Kathleen's baby any day. I
be glad when it is over.
Joseph is getting married
January 31st. He didn't
but he was the marrying
but I guess when the right
comes along — that's it. She is
lovely girl.
Take care of yourself. Kathleen
Merry Christmas
Happy

Grandpa Arthur O'Neil

Just a line to wish you well
And Hope you never go to Hell
For although you were always
a little Brat
You are still my own my
darling Pat.

The old Bag.

Patricia O'Neill Dickinson (Kathleen's mother)

Michael O'Neill is getting married next Nov.

Thanks for info on the Govt. I will send a copy to Aunt Peg. she is having a bad time right now. (Cant walk)

Patricia Dickinson (Kathleen's sister)

Kathleen,

i circled a couple of #'s on the map. The more i kept reading the more confused i got & the picture of my #1 choice on page 14 doesn't look like beach front to me. #9 might be nice since its away from everything

I Don't know so have fun! i'm off from Sept 5th to the 20th but would like a couple of days here before i go back to work. Talk to you soon

PS your mother can't figure out how you got everything in by Birthday box she can't wait until i open it

Love
Me

Kathleen Dickinson

between the two countries, leads from the Great Lakes into the Atlantic Ocean.

The United States was interested in the development of iron ore in the Quebec-Labrador region as the U.S. doesnot have as much iron ore itself as it once did and iron ore is necessary for the production of steel which Pittsburgh is a major contributor of.

This is my writing NOW. It has evolved which may indicate writing can be influenced by work, circumstances, environment, health and all sorts of things. However, some of the personality traits remain.

BIOGRAPHICAL NOTES

Kathleen Dickinson has been a Nevada activist since 1986 in environmental issues, gun safety, and youth prevention issues for a variety of coalitions and organizations including the Nevada Coalition for Suicide Prevention (NCSP). She was President of Zonta (1998); the Nevada IGAS Chapter in Reno (1990s), and the League of Women Voters Las Vegas Valley (2005-2007). Kathleen has a bachelor's degree in Psychology from George Mason University and completed the American University Campaign Management Institute Program and the Washington Representative Program at George Washington University. She was certified by IGAS in June 1988 and by AHAF in 2013, and certified in Hypnotherapy in 1989.

kariedi@gmail.com

Gestalt Psychology and Graphology

Victor Clark, MSEd, CG

It was as my mother lay dying from a heart attack at 90 years old that I discovered the connection between graphology and gestalt psychology from William Stern. Only then were the perennial paradoxes of personality resolved for me.

On one hand, Stern originated reductionist concepts of individual differences according to positivist psychology for personality trait testing from critical review of Alfred Binet's intelligence testing of children. On the other hand, Stern developed holistic person-centered methods of character evaluation according to gestalt psychology from critical review of Ludwig Klages' handwriting analysis in graphology.

A full professor and department head at Hamburg University, William Stern was a world-famous psychologist during his career. But he was fired from his tenured position because he was a Jew in 1933 when German university psychology was Nazified and being Jewish was criminalized. Stern wrote his final book in German while hiding in the Netherlands, and eventually found employment at Duke University in North Carolina.

Since American psychology departments were already dominated by positivism, which remained antithetical to gestaltism, his favorite instructor assignments at Duke University were in the philosophy department.

A few months after meticulously completing the English translation of his last book, *General Psychology from the Personalistic Perspective* in 1937, Professor Stern died of a heart attack and was forgotten.

Gestalt Psychology versus Positivist Psychology

In the 1890s, both gestaltism and positivism developed contradictory philosophies of psychology. Gestalt holism contradicted positivist elementalism. Positivist sensationalism contradicted gestalt form quality. And gestalt configuration contradicted positivist associationism.

Gestalt Psychology Principles - Germany and Austria origin

1. Holism - Psychological phenomena is an organized, structured whole.
2. Form Quality - There is an extra-psychological experience not explained by the sensory elements.
3. Configuration - The different parts of an object are understood in relationship to the whole.

Positivist Psychology Principles - United Kingdom and United States origin

1. Elementalism - all knowledge (cognition) is built from simple elemental constituents
2. Sensationalism - the simplest constituents of thought are elementary sense impressions
3. Associationism - more complex ideas arise from the association of simple ideas

Controversy between the positivists and gestalts would turn brothers against their own brothers and psychologists against each other.

Sensationalism versus Form Quality

Music is a common example of gestaltism as it relates to perception. The gestaltism perception heard a melody as a unified suprasensory experience of intersensory perception, called form-quality, which is not explained by bottom-up addition of the individual sounds of musical notes.

Few besides William Stern's family knew that, like my mother, he was also an unsung classical pianist. My mother earned a music therapy and music education degree at sixty after raising six daughters and five sons. While sitting at her piano when I stayed with her in her last few years, she showed me the two different ways of listening to a musical melody.

You can listen to each musical note played individually, or to the whole melody played together, harmonized in time by rhythm. When individual musical notes are played simultaneously, as in chords, the reverberation of each note played together changes the sound of each individual note.

After several days of waiting for my siblings who were scattered across the country, to arrive, on 31 October 2013, the doctor told me my mother was dying. Trained to see the sound of her symptoms as "parts" of a mechanical clock, he said he could not explain why she was still alive and conscious.

At her request, we gathered around her bed in the Intensive Care Unit so she could easily see all of us. Although she could barely move her lips, her eyes were bright and expressive. Being at her feet, I saw how she unhurriedly rested her gaze on each of her adult children, moving from left to right, speaking to each one with her eyes. I prepared myself to look back into her eyes and see what she wanted to tell me. The moment was timeless. After she completed the circle, I saw her eyes grow brighter before gradually the light faded away like a flashlight that lost battery power at 8:11 PM, when I saw the inanimate body was deflated of personality.

In 1931, Charles Spearman of London College described in *Creative Mind* the positivism perception in which two musical notes played together could be analyzed by simple statistical correlation of two isolated sensations of sound occurring close to the same time. His statistical ideas are the basis for converting analog to digital sound recordings. But musicians can hear the difference between the harmonic depth of analog recordings compared to the thin and shallow sound in digital recordings.

"While elementaristic psychology attempted to explain intersensory perceptions by 'association' of the various specific sensations, personalistic principles [from gestalt psychology] impose a 'dissociation,' which is contrariwise the means of separating the special sensory components out of the non-specific total perception that is deeply embedded in the person. Only then may the liberated products of this dissociation, that is to say, specific items of experience, be united to form new intersensory perceptions" (Stern, 1938, *General psychology from the personalistic standpoint,* p.147).

The author & his mother at a 2013 Graphoanalysis study group

Positivist psychologists examine the sensation of music in isolated sounds as though they naively read sheet music one note at a time. Gestalt psychologists hear the harmonic symphony of all notes as they reverberate together, making a uniquely different sound than when played alone.

Character structure versus personality traits

Gestalt psychologists use a holistic approach in personality assessment. Allport (1937) gave a gestalt definition of personality as the character structure of an individual: "The dynamic organization within the individual of those psychophysical systems that determine his [particular] unique adjustment to his environment."

Gestaltism contradicts the reductionism of the positivist approach in personality testing, which defines personality to be constructed simply from elementary parts as personality traits.

Cattell (1945) gave a positivist definition of personality as predictive personality traits of individual differences, "which permits a prediction of what a person will do in a given situation. The goal of psychological research is to establish [general] laws about what different people will do in all kinds of social and general environmental situations."

Psychologists remain divided over whether personality should be defined according to general laws of personality traits or by particular psychophysical adaptations of character structure.

Gordon Allport is remembered for his influence in the development of personality psychology in America. He originally engaged in personality testing for classifying and measuring personality traits in his dissertation research, influenced by his older brother Floyd, who was a teacher at Harvard University.

Working with his brother was very gratifying for Gordon as a graduate student at Harvard and they were getting rapid results so that in 1921 they jointly published in the *Journal of Abnormal & Social Psychology,* where Floyd was an editor.

On a post-doctoral fellowship, the next year Gordon Allport listened to William Stern play classical music on the piano when staying with the Stern family in their home. After returning to America, he published another articlė that began:

"AN INCREASING number of investigators are engaging in the problem of classifying and measuring the traits of personality with the result that the advance in method is rapid and gratifying. But with analyzing, testing, and correlating most of these investigators become blind to the true nature of the problem before them. They lose sight of the forest in their preoccupation with individual trees." (Allport, 1924)

Gordon criticized, not only his own, but also his brother Floyd's previous research that focused only on analyzing, testing and correlating lists of personality traits. He also introduced the foreign German-Austrian derived gestalt psychology principle of form-quality using Klages' theory about form-level of handwriting.

"These form-qualities in script are irretrievably lost in any analytic system of graphology which concerns itself only with single strokes or letters. The essence of handwriting, says Klages, lies in the general form. It follows that the student must learn to interpret this Formniveau quite apart from the details." (Allport, 1924)

Although psychologists like Floyd believed positivist psychology was the only empirical psychology and condemned graphology as metaphysical, Klages developed dynamic graphology on empirical foundations of the gestalt psychology principle for form quality in handwriting. His theory formed the basis for diagnostic scales developed by Stein and Zubin, 1942, identifying specific contraction-and-release characteristics in handwriting for clinical and psychological assessment.

Personality trait testing, Jungian type diagnostics & gestalt handwriting evaluation

The onion of personality assessments–personality testing, Jungian type diagnostics and handwriting evaluation–can be unpeeled by the through-line of phlegmatic and sanguine temperaments.

While Jung (1919; 1921) in Switzerland–influenced by German and Austrian psychologists–followed a gestalt research tradition in character diagnostics, Eysenck and Eysenck, 1964, in the United Kingdom followed a positivist research tradition in personality trait testing.

Jung conducted word association experiments where he identified slow versus fast reaction times resulting in his theory of introversion and extroversion and leading to the robust theory of psychological types. Hans Eysenck's theory of personality traits borrowed Jung's ideas of introversion and extroversion from a gestalt view of character structure and reduced them into a positivist definition of generalized personality traits listed as trait-names amenable to statistical analysis for classification and comparison between groups of people.

Personality Trait Testing

An example of positivism in personality assessment is the personality testing approach of the Eysenck Personality Inventory, or EPI, represented by coordinate scales for the personality traits extroversion and neuroticism shown here.

Eysenck's theory was that individual differences in a personality trait should be placed on the normative scale of a bell curve, analogous to a classroom grade average. Two primary personality traits were extroversion and neuroticism.

The vertical scale measures the degree of extroversion from low to high (0 to 24) and the horizontal scale measures the degree of neuroticism from low to high (0 to 24). For example, the phlegmatic temperament is identified by low neuroticism and low extroversion, described as a stable introvert. The sanguine temperament is identified by low neuroticism and high extroversion, described as a stable extrovert.

Eysenck believed the four classic temperaments could thus be identified by relative scores on these two primary personality traits: neuroticism and extroversion. Other personality traits for each temperament are listed along the circumference of the circle. The sanguine temperament has these other personality traits: sociable, outgoing, talkative, responsive, easy going, lively, carefree, leadership. The phlegmatic temperament has these other personality traits: calm, even-tempered, reliable, controlled, peaceful, thoughtful, careful, passive.

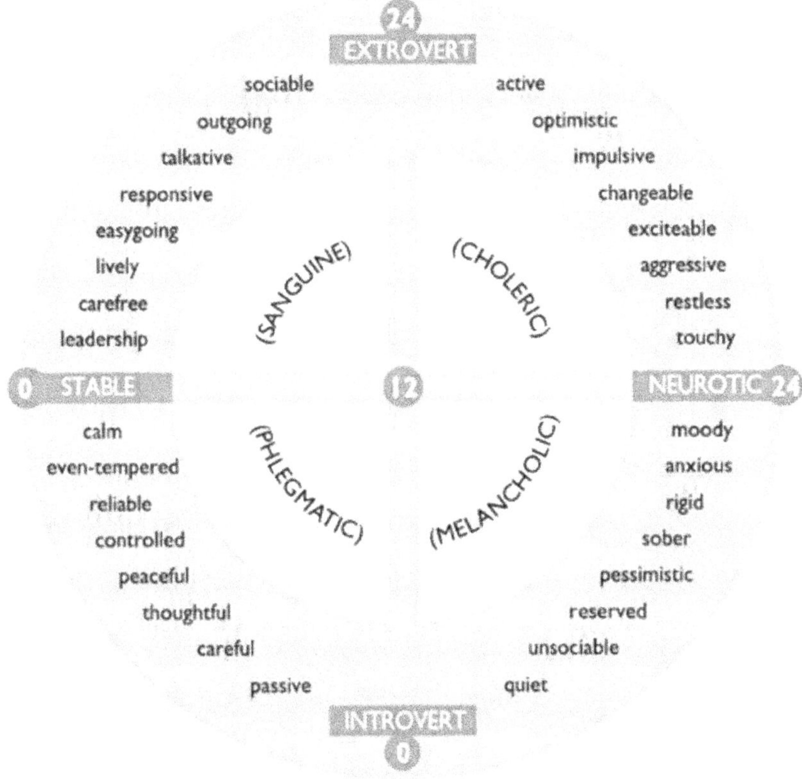

Personality trait testing examined statistical correlations in groups of people for their normal distribution in a bell curve of general characteristics as behavior traits. Character diagnostics examined reaction times one person at a time for their particular repeated patterns of expression revealing character structure as a psychological typology.

Jungian type diagnostics

An example of gestaltism in personality assessment is the psychodynamic analysis of reaction time in the Word Association projective test. Slow reaction times indicated introversion, while fast reaction times indicated extroversion.

But there was more to it because slower responses also expressed more feeling and produced more mental images than faster responses.

From these studies Jung developed his theory of psychological types concerning the relationship of psychological functions in orientations of extroversion and introversion. In Jung's theory extroversion and introversion are *orientations* of a psychological function, rather than stand-alone substantive characteristics or personality traits. The orientation indicates whether a function is energetically oriented outward towards the world, or inward towards the psyche.

Represented in the following diagram is a simplified version of this psychological type theory that focuses only on the dominant and inferior functions, represented as a vertical line (with the dominant function at the head and the inferior function at the bottom) described as a *spine*.

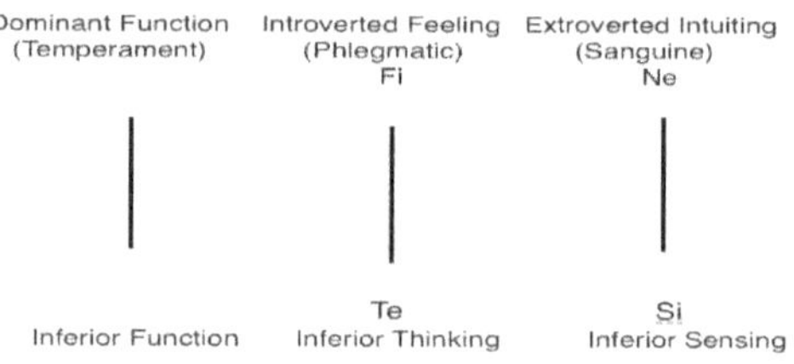

For this abbreviated explanation of psychological type theory, put aside for now the auxiliary and tertiary functions (usually described as *arms* and represented by a horizontal line centered as a cross at the middle of the spine),

In the diagram above, introverted feeling (Fi) indicates that the feeling function is oriented inward towards the psyche, while extroverted intuiting (Ne) indicates the intuiting function is oriented outward towards the world. According to this theory, development of the dominant function-orientation, Fi and Ne in this case, inhibits development of the opposite function-orientation, Te and Si respectively, called the inferior function for this very reason of being undeveloped.

In other words, a dominant introverted feeling type (Fi) is comfortable with introverted feeling but is unaware that they also have the potential for extroverted thinking (Te) that is unconscious and undeveloped. Dominant introverted-feeling psychological types (Fi) have characteristics of a phlegmatic temperament that is expressed by this adaptation of their character structure.

Likewise, a dominant extroverted intuiting type (Ne) is comfortable using their intuitive function in their attention outward on the world but unaware they have the potential for introverted sensing (Si) that is unconscious and undeveloped. Dominant extroverted intuiting psychological types (Ne) have characteristics of a sanguine temperament that is an expression of this adaptation of their character structure.

Analysis of psychological function-orientation maps configuration of a person's psyche concerning attention (inward and outward) and depth (conscious and unconscious) psychological character structure. Carl Jung's theory of psychological type was not comparing personality traits between people, but evaluated character dynamics within a single person.

The purpose of this psychological type analysis was to understand the individuated psychological structure between the person's conscious and unconscious functions in order to support their growth for well-being. Instead of judging people by the strength and weakness of their personality traits for employment placement purposes, for example, this gestalt approach helped to understand the dynamic relationship between what was conscious and developed and what was unconscious and undeveloped to guide the person's development of their total personality.

Gestalt handwriting evaluation

The gestalt theory of form quality in handwriting continues to be confirmed by psychophysiology research recently conducted by Professor Audrey Van der Meer's team at Norwegian University of Science and Technology. Van der Meer explained their conclusions why writing by hand makes kids smarter.

> *"The use of pen and paper gives the brain more 'hooks' to hang your memories on. Writing by hand creates much more activity in the sensorimotor parts of the brain. A lot of senses are activated by pressing the pen on paper, seeing the letters you write and hearing the sound you make while writing. These sense experiences create contact between different parts of the brain and open the brain up for learning. We both learn better and remember better."* [*Neuroscience News*, 1 October 2020, *Why writing by hand makes kids smarter.*]

The synthesis of sensory and thinking processes is the gestalt principle of form quality, transforming the writer's psychosensory processes to a higher level in functioning of imagination and insight with the development of fluency in handwriting. Unpracticed handwriters for example have stiff and heavy handwriting, while more fluent handwriters show rhythmic pressure and pace. These two aspects of handwriting movement create the quality of form, or line-value, in a hand printed line.

Form-level, or Formniveau, is this movement quality of pressure and speed which determine how expansion-and-contraction rhythm is expressed in the formation of handwriting. A continuum from extreme contraction on the left to extreme release on the right is represented in the cursive letter-f by their degrees of gradual expansion in loops.

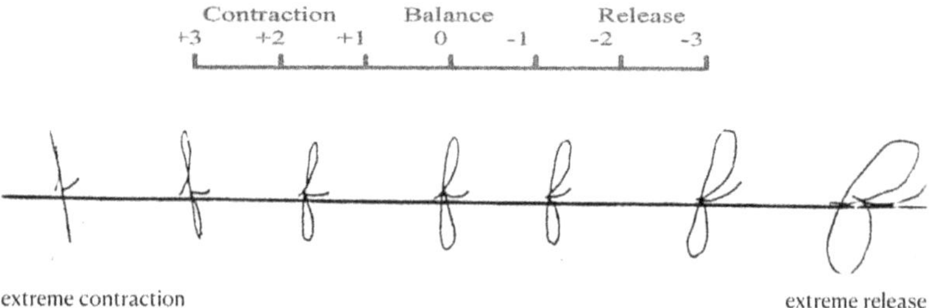

Simply put, the more restrained handwriting loops on the left express tendencies of psychological constriction and the more expansive handwriting loops on the right express tendencies of psychological release.

Gestalt graphology is based on the application of form quality in this fundamental concept of contraction-and-release rhythm of handwriting Klages called Formniveau, which is a result of psychophysical synthesis in tactile sensory awareness related to pressure and cognitive planning processes related to speed. In other words, sensory memory related to touch is synthesized with thought processes related to speed in handwriting.

The amount of pressure placed upon the page, is this not a tactile experience? You literally are touching the page with the extension of your pen.

But when you move the pen across the page what happens to pressure? Touching the page is forgotten as the pen is lifted—even off the page—with the rhythmic pace of your thoughts composing words and sentences, changing the surface shape of the page with pressure and movement.

Klages applied this theory related to pressure and speed in handwriting to identify classic temperaments. He considered that, contrasted with the heavier handwriting pressure of melancholic and choleric temperaments, both phlegmatic and sanguine temperaments had very light handwriting pressure.

Related to their very light handwriting pressure, both of these writers easily could forgive and forget, characteristics of both phlegmatic and sanguine temperaments. Since light handwriting pressure could be held as constant for both phlegmatic and sanguine temperaments, their differences would be determined only by the speed of their handwriting.

The lighter pressure, faster-paced writers were quick in thought but had a lower amount of feelings and images, characteristics of a sanguine temperament. While the light pressure, slower-paced writers had a much higher degree of feelings and images as they were more thoughtful in expressing themselves, characteristics of a phlegmatic temperament. Don't confuse these slower writers with being slow; rather, their feelings are easily stimulated and they are possibly overwhelmed with their abundance of feelings. While fast writers should not be confused with being fast, it is instead their thoughts that are easily stimulated even to the point of having racing thoughts, leading to confusion.

Klages concluded therefore that if handwriters had very light pressure, very slow writers would identify as phlegmatic while very fast writers would identify as sanguine. Klages' idea of slow versus fast handwriting and personality was probably communicated by his student, Max Pulver, to Carl Jung.

Pulver and Jung worked in the mental hospital together at the University of Zurich when Jung conducted word association experiments that led to his theory of introversion from slow reaction times and extroversion from fast reaction times to the stimulus words. But this is more than simply about slow versus fast handwriting or reaction time.

The gestalt concept of form quality is central to Klages' theory of form-level as the rhythmic integration of pressure and speed in the contraction-and-release of handwriting movement, which expresses the degree in psychophysical integration of the total personality.

Summary

For psychologists analyzing, testing and correlating lists of personality traits, the mind constructs perception and thought strictly from lower-level sensations that are related solely by being associated closely in space and time following the three principles of positivism: 1) Elementalism, 2) Sensationalism and 3) Associationism.

For psychologists who diagnose character structure, the psychophysical whole takes priority and the parts are defined in relationship to the structure and organization of the whole—rather than as isolated elements forming into a total composite—following the three principles of gestaltism: 1) Holism, 2) Form Quality and 3) Configuration.

Following Holism versus Elementalism, (1) above, Allport's holistic definition of character structure contrasted with Cattell's elementalism definition of statistical prediction for personality traits. And following Configuration versus Associationism, (3) above, Jung's configuration theory of psychological type contrasted with Eysenck's associationism theory of personality traits.

Following Sensationalism versus Form Quality, (2) above, the positivism principle that the simplest constituents of thought are elementary sense impressions in stimulus-response behavior conditioning contrasted with the gestalt principle that the extra-psychological experience of thought, imagination and insight cannot be explained simply by elementary sense impressions but are a psychologically transcendent form that is a different quality than the physical constituents from which they sprang.

BIBLIOGRAPHY

Allport FH, Allport GW (1921) Personality Traits: Their classification and measurement. *Journal of Abnormal and Social Psychology*. 16: 6-40.

Allport, G. (1924). The study of the undivided personality. *Journal of Abnormal & Social Psychology*, 19, 132-142.

Allport, G.W. (1937). Personality: A psychological interpretation. New York: Holt.

Cattell, R.B. (1945). The principal trait clusters for describing personality. *Psychological Bulletin*, 42(3), 129-161.

Clark, V. (2021, May) Psychologist, know thyself. *Theoretical and Philosophical Psychology Digest*. [https://www.apadivisions.org/division-24/publications/newsletters/theoretical-philosophical-digest/2021/05/updating-personality

Eysenck, H.J. and Eysenck, S.B.G. (1964). *Manual of Eysenck Personality Inventory*. Kent, England: Hodder and Stoughton [https://genepi.qimr.edu.au/contents/p/staff 1964_Eysenck_Manual.pdf]

Jung, CG (1919) Studies in word-association: experiments in the diagnosis of psychopathological conditions carried out at the psychiatric clinic of the University of Zurich. Under the direction of C.G. Jung. Trans by Dr. M. D. Eder NY: Moffat, Yard & Co.

Jung, Carl, Gustaf (1921). *Psychologische Typen* [Psychological Type]. First German edition, Zurich: Rascher Verlag

Klages, L. (1932). The Science of Character. (Trans. from 5th and 6th German ed. by W. H. Johnston). Cambridge, MA: Sci-Art Publishers.

Lewinson, Thea Stein and Joseph Zubin, 1942, *Handwriting analysis: a series of scales for evaluating the dynamic aspects of handwriting.* Kings Crown Press, Morning Heights, New York.

Spearman, C.E. (1931). Creative Mind. New York: D. Appleton & Company.

Stern, W. (1924) *Die Menschliche Personlichkeit* [The person as a multiform dynamic unity].

Stern, W. (1938). *General psychology from a personalistic standpoint* (trans: Spoerl, H. D.). New York: Macmillan. [https://archive.org/details/b29817067].

van der Meer, Audrey L.H., Askvik, E.O. and van der Weel, F.R. (2020, July 28) The Importance of Cursive Handwriting Over Typewriting for Learning in the Classroom: A High-Density EEG Study of 12-Year-Old Children and Young Adults. *Frontiers in Psychology.* [https://www.frontiersin.org/articles/10.3389/fpsyg.2020.01810/full]

BIOGRAPHICAL NOTES

Victor Clark MSEd, CG, has been studying research on handwriting and personality in peer-reviewed journals for over forty years and retired as clinical director of a psychotherapy clinic to start his Character Evaluation agency in 2010. He is a Certified Graphologist with a Master of Science in Education and Counseling Psychology, including liberal arts studies in history of biology and medicine, with membership in both the American Handwriting Analysis Foundation and the Society of Theoretical and Philosophical Psychology, Division 24 of the American Psychological Association.

victorgclark@gmail.com

Hiding in Plain Sight

Lauren Mooney Bear, CG

How long have we been hiding?

The first movements of a newborn infant are instinctive. The baby opens its eyes for orientation, raise its arms with tiny, folded fists towards its face, legs stretching out alternately, testing out the newly discovered space, then immediately curling back up into a more familiar fetal shape. Then, sometimes simultaneously, the baby lets out a cry. Not a howl of fear or pain–a baby knows relatively nothing of fear or pain. Instead, the cry is an instinct to clear the lungs of fluid and alert the parent that they need care, protection, and food. These reflexive actions are self-protective.

No one could reasonably argue that the reflexive and self-protective instincts of a newborn are based on hidden nefarious motives, past aggression, wrongs committed against others or even a horrible repressed memory deeply hidden within the subconscious. The self-protective reflex is an instinct with which all human beings, all sapient beings, are born as a means of survival.

This is what we had learned in science, biology 101 and in psychology 101. Those of us of a certain age (we'll call it retro) in the US grew up watching *'Mutual of Omaha's Wild Kingdom* on High Fidelity television on Sunday evenings.

You might recall hearing the voice of the host, American zoologist Marlin Perkins, as he spoke of one of his favorite animals, the chameleon, and the fascinating way it changed color in response to feelings or anxiety as it moved from one colored ground to the next. This ability to adapt and protect itself is a gift of instinct. The chameleon doesn't stop to analyze the best action for the changing situation, it simply reacts. The reaction is neither bad nor good, it just is.

Darwin called it survival of the fittest; Freud, self-preservation. In human beings, the self-protective instinct might be manifest in a thousand different ways, many times throughout the day. Most physical actions we take for self-protection are innocuous, harmless. Let's consider a few simple examples.

Imagine you work in a fast-paced noisy office. You take lunches alone, outside. Today, you are walking from your workplace down the block and across the street to a small park in town to enjoy your lunch. The breeze turns chilly, you pick up your pace, shiver, and pull on your coat. As you are walking toward your usual solitary place, the cloud above your block bursts open like a water balloon. You sprint to the shelter of the large tree and stand with several people talking about the odd downpour and how it has affected each of their days.

In this scenario, how many actions are relative to self-protection and boundaries?

1. Taking a solitary lunch sets a personal boundary and is perhaps compensatory for the over-stimulation of the office noise and hustle

2. You pick up your pace, pull in your coat and shiver as a reaction to protect yourself from the chill

3. Sprinting to the shelter of the tree is to protect yourself from the rain

4. Commiserating with others about the shared event is a way of adapting socially to the unusual situation

All of these actions are ways in which we adapt socially and to protect ourselves physically from the elements. In this case, there are also personal emotional boundaries for the person who tends toward introversion.

We use the word 'hideout' and 'hideaway' for describing both the good, such as a romantic interlude or rendezvous, and also as a place where the bad guys or criminals might go to get away. A tendency to protect ourselves or hide, so as to not reveal parts of ourselves, show up in our handwriting in multiple places.

How does this translate into handwriting and then into the analysis? Handwriting is 'brainwriting,' so it follows that everything that is a part of our psyche, our experience–that which makes us an individual–will appear in our script. Self -defenses, self-protective tactics, and the boundaries we set up, both physical and emotional, will also show up in multiple places in our handwriting.

While we may not literally be hiding fearfully in a closet or under the bed, in our handwriting we unconsciously cover the parts of ourselves that we do not wish to share with the world.

Note: illustrations of some of the following characteristics found in handwriting appear at the end of this article.

Hide and seek. Where are we hiding?

As children we played hide and seek in the twilight part of the day with the neighbor kids. There were many places to hide in our neighborhood. In our own yard we had the advantage because we knew every nook and cranny.

We know ourselves and our handwriting like we knew our backyards as kids. Tucked in every corner of our script are our secrets, boundaries, and our safe places, waiting like friends.

Let's explore a few of these nooks and crannies, beginning with a look at the space around our writing. According to Felix Klein in *The Unconscious and The Dynamics of Energy Distribution as Seen in Handwriting*, space is the most unconscious element in handwriting. The placement of the writing within the margins is an unconscious element that reveals our feelings about our past, present, and future. If there are unresolved emotions, the margins will show this. If we are uncomfortable about an ambiguous future and do not wish to venture forth, the margins will reveal this. If we are happier staying in a comfortable past, or long for the security the past held for us, along with other indicators, the margins will show this.

One of the places we 'hide' our insecurities regarding the past and the future is the margins. We generally begin to write at the top of a page and continue to the bottom. As the writing progresses, the top is quickly left behind, in the past. The bottom becomes the future. Similarly, as we write in English from left to right, the starting point on the left soon becomes the past as we move towards the future and the right side of the page.

These guidelines for interpretation would be adjusted for languages which are written in reverse, from right to left, as in Hebrew, or in any other order, such as Chinese, Japanese, Vietnamese and Korean which are traditionally written from top to bottom and ordered from right to left. The basic principles of margins apply, regardless of the language.

When the body of a writing has an extra wide left margin, the writer may want to leave behind unpleasant experiences and may not want to discuss these with others. Similar feelings might be present when the body of writing begins far down the page leaving and extra wide top margin.

A person may prefer to stay 'hidden' in a comfort zone or considering past and pleasant memories which represent safety and security rather than face the uncertainties of the future. This tendency might be seen in extra wide right or bottom margins.

Beyond the margins, other aspects of space in handwriting offer more places where we may unconsciously conceal personal insecurities. The primary space–the width of individual letters–gives clues as to fears or repressions.

When the letters are very narrow and retraced, the person is carting around a backpack full of unresolved emotions. This writing will appear brittle, with little room for flexibility. There is tension and slowness evident in the writing and in the intentions when the individual is faced with decisions regarding the future.

The secondary space–the space between the letters–is another clue. This space represents the emotional availability for the self and others in the immediate social circle. When the secondary space is compressed, the writer has allowed more space for the emotions of others than for their own; they have not allowed for release of their own feelings. They feel the need to be with others to fill up time and space so as not to have to confront their own feelings or thoughts. They are, in a manner of speaking, 'hiding in the crowd'. This is an indicator of fear, emotional self-neglect, and fragility.

The third space–space between words–indicates the writer's social adaptability and social preferences. One who prefers introspection has wider spaces. An extrovert writes with narrower spaces between words, generally speaking.

Do we hide in the element of movement?

Our best and worst impulses, motivations, and fears, are also revealed in the movement of the writing. Weak or disturbed movement leads us to assume compensation in the emotions and thought processes of the writer. So, next, we will look at the various aspects in movement.

What moves you? 'Different strokes for different folks,' so the saying goes. We are motivated by circumstances, impressions, experiences, all of which form our opinions and beliefs and thus show up in handwriting.

How slanted are your views?

The slant of the writing shows the writer's degree of emotional responsiveness. Far-left (moderate is 45°) is the most reserved of the slants. The far-left slant, also called reverse slant, and is misnamed left-handed slant, is used when the writer is least inclined to reveal their feelings outwardly to anyone. They may seem calm and cool but feel shattered inside. This writer is truly in the habit of hiding in plain sight. It is important to note that it was once commonly thought that left-handed persons wrote with a backhanded, left slant. Some do, most do not.

The upright, vertical (90°) slant can be described just as it sounds, it stays in the middle of the emotional responsiveness gauge. Those writing with this non-slant are also hiding in some ways. This writer tries to use reason before emotion when reacting and will be a good person to have around in difficult situations.

The vertical writer and the far-left slanted writer may have learned from past experiences to withhold emotional displays. They feel deeply and have emotional reactions, but will not display them. Both the vertical slanted and left slanted scripts might look as if they are stuck on the page, particularly when they are printed. The forward flow toward the right side of the page, to the future, is slowed by the slant.

The right-slanted writer is emotionally responsive and will more readily show emotions, but with some control. When the slant is so far right (moderate is 45°) as to be out of whack, the individual might be compensating with an overly dramatic display of emotions. Thus, they may lose touch with the core reasons for the feelings.

All about the zones

All three zones in handwriting hold keys to self-protection and boundaries when the person is hiding in plain sight. If something affects one zone it will have an effect also in the other zones, as there is overlap. "As above-so below" applies to handwriting. When part of a letter gets lost and wanders out of its zone, it needs to be noticed.

The upper zone contains the conceptual part of our selves. The spiritual, imagination, principles, intellectual and view of authority figures are in the upper zone loops. Compressed upper loops, especially where the loop is retraced, there are squeezed emotions and compressed feelings toward authority figures. Wherever there is a loop, or rounded form, there is emotion.

The middle zone is all about the daily focus, the self, the mundane, communications with others, emotional expressions, and adaptability. The middle zone letters are a, e, i, o, u, c, m, n, r, s, v, w, x. Note that these have no upper or lower loops. Other letters having parts passing through the middle zone, the part in the middle zone are considered in the middle zone.

Large middle zone writers, when one or both of the other zones are neglected, are unable or unwilling to face the subconscious or the unconscious. They hide in the mundane tasks and may keep themselves overly busy. Where there are stabbing strokes, broken lines, patched, muddiness, or other anomalies in the middle zone there are hidden emotions and fears.

The 'communication ovals,' letters 'a,' and 'o' are emotional vaults where we keep our secrets and the confidences of others. This is also where we hide things from ourselves.

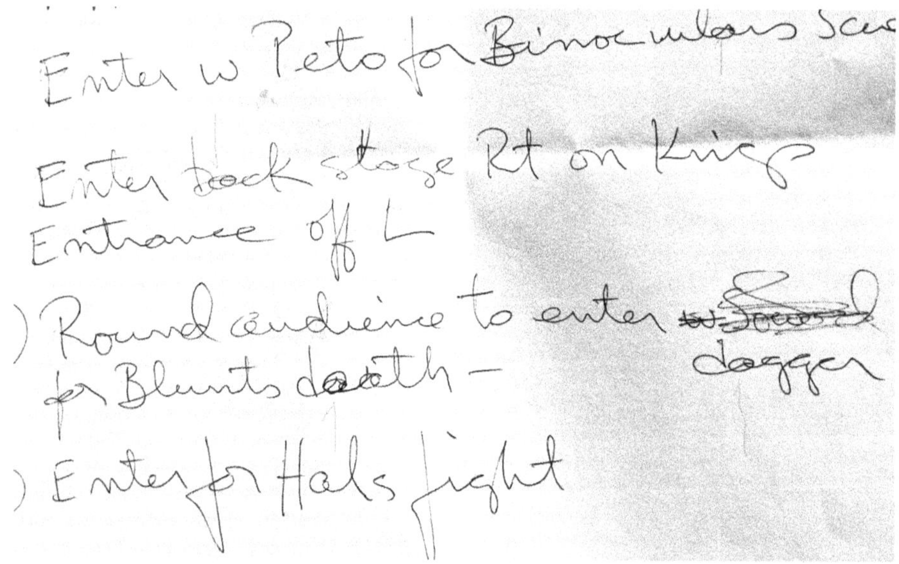
Enter w Peto for Binoculars Sce

Enter back stage Rt on King
Entrance off L
) Round audience to enter dagger
for Blunts death –
) Enter for Hals fight

Speaking of the lowercase o, the left side is for the self and the right side is for others. Loops or knots on either side show the writer is withholding, or capable of holding back information, particularly emotionally-charged information. The nature of the hidden emotion will reveal itself in the body of the writing with the combination of strokes, space, and movement.

In other words, in the gestalt–the whole picture. The lower zone contains the unconscious, hidden instincts, our need for activity, and variety. This is where biological, food, sex, and money needs are seen. Past memories and emotions may be hidden here. It is the perfect hiding place for our insecurities. Disturbances seen here reflect a need for keeping unpleasant unprocessed experiences and emotions below the surface–below the baseline.

When lower loops fail to return to the baseline they are avoiding or procrastinating painful feelings.

Hope this satifies your
letter writing it has been
many moons since I rote
a letter, I think it has
been since I was in the
Milary that I wrote letters
back home and to my girfrinds
Don't worry about the speling
not one of my strong points

Would Like To
Leave when Car
Done. No Later
Than 4? ← Thursday
Coming Home, End July
+ Weekend. Hopefully
Home By 8? 9?

Cradle-shapes show a need for nurturing.

I love camping reading & doing

Odd twists, and turns suggest distorted, out of the ordinary emotional processing. Overly wide loops are made by one who does a lot of unrealistic fantasizing and needs variety. Knotted forms are a way to avoid issues with persistence, defensiveness. Retraced lower zone letters reveal fears & inhibitions.

This is a cursory list. Each characteristic you identify needs to be verified and supported with the balance of the writing. These unconscious emotions must be supported and verified by looking at the gestalt of the writing: the spacing, pressure, slant.

Lower loop anomalies are most often due to childhood sexual abuse or emotional traumas. Each person experiences and processes trauma differently. Before making assumptions be sure to gather as much information as possible. Some anomalies may also be due to physiological causes. Lower zone letters are those below the baseline that have lower loops, f, g, j, p, q, y, and z.

When lower loops are disturbed, there is sure to be hidden emotion, shame or guilt and fear. When there is simply a straight line with no loops, you'll find avoidance of pain. Broken loops indicate uncertainty and anxiety. Triangles are made by critical people who are searching for sexual satisfaction. Lower zone strokes moving in the wrong direction indicate a brash and independent spirit.

Let's talk about strokes

First, beginning strokes or lead-in strokes. There is a term in sports from the mid 1920's called 'the running start.' Just as you might think, the athlete is already running before he or she hits the actual start line. In handwriting, it looks much the same, the writer begins writing the first stroke of the letter before the actual first letter of the word would normally begin.

This beginning stroke is most often used at the beginning of a new line of writing. When the stroke is too long, the writer is gathering steam. One reason can be a lack of confidence. When the running start stroke begins below the baseline, or line of consciousness, the writer is pulling back, drawing on past emotions for cues as to how to react to current situations. This is a disturbance in the elements of form and movement.

Ending strokes come in different forms. When they are helping us to hide, they are also helping to establish emotional boundaries with others. Extended, protective, strokes are seen most often at the end of a line of writing. They are used at the end of several words when a person is feeling particularly vulnerable or suspicious. These can be called 'keep-away' or 'stiff-arm' strokes because they look like a quarterback running with a stiff arm in front of him for protection.

When the ending stroke moves up above the middle zone, it has become even more protective and is now covering the body in an attempt to protect oneself from an expected tackle. These protective ending strokes will be supported by other parts of the writing.

Coverstrokes are some of the best places for us to play hide and seek in our script. Coverstrokes are used when the writer feels unworthiness, guilt or shame. This does not have to mean that the person has robbed a bank or committed a crime, but for whatever reason, they have some unresolved shame.

This may simply be a hangover from childhood experience or some unfortunate event or series of events which has not been processed yet.

What does a cover stroke look like? Any arcade, convex shape is a protective form. Picture an umbrella or arched walkway. In physical action, if someone throws or hits a ball in your direction and yells 'heads up!' or 'duck!,' you instinctively raise your arm and duck your head for protection. This is a means of self-preservation and independence.

I do not like passive aggressive behavior and perfer people to just "tell it like it is"!

Protective strokes

In handwriting, it can be found in extended ending strokes that circle back to cover the previous word. Many signatures end with or contain circular covering protective strokes, particularly among celebrities and those aspiring.

The covered, script like lower-case a, where the writer is protecting the verbal communication may indicate they are simply reticent, afraid to speak up. Again, this shape resembles the arm raised in self-protection. The person may experience feelings of guilt, but we cannot impute bad motives to them.

Hooded 'a'

Why are we hiding?

The answer to this last question, "why are we hiding?" is as simple and yet as complex as the human race itself. We are learning, growing, and we are all vulnerable, especially when we least want to be.

The beauty of this knowledge is that in understanding ourselves we can assist each other. We can give ourselves a break when we screw up, which, inevitably, all humans do. And in the end, before we pass through the veil, as have our friends and family before us have done, we can learn to have fewer regrets, use fewer protective strokes and stop judging ourselves harshly.

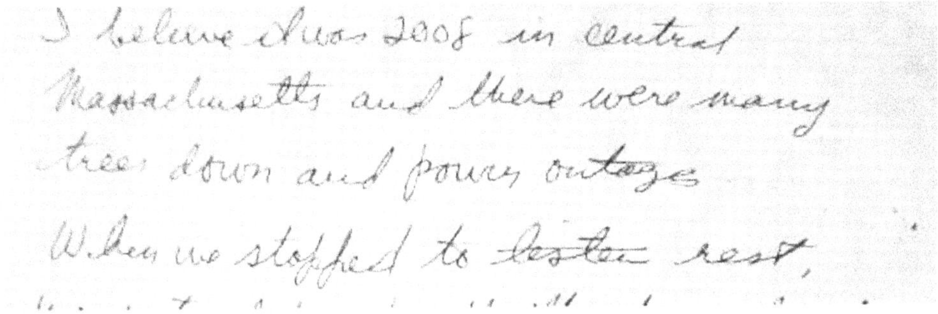

Various

Bibliography:

Amend, Stansbury Ruiz. *Handwriting Analysis: The Complete Basic Book.* Franklin Lakes, NJ. New Page Books

Brown, Brene PhD. *The Gifts of Imperfection.* Center City, MN. Hazelden

Brown, Brene PhD. *The Power of Vulnerability: Teachings on Authenticity, Connection and Courage.* 2012, Sounds True.

Chaney, Brandon. Sports terms and references.

Hayes, Reed. *Between the Lines: Understanding Yourself and Others Through Handwriting Analysis.* Rochester, VT. Destiny Books

Klein, Felix. Gestalt *Graphology: Exploring the Mystery and Complexity of Human Nature Through Handwriting Analysis.* Bloomington, IN. iUniverse

Klein, Felix. *The Unconscious in Handwriting: The Unconscious and the Dynamics of Energy Distribution as Seen in Handwriting.* Bloomington, IN. iUniverse

Lowe, Sheila. *Reading Between the Lines: Decoding Handwriting.* Ventura, CA. Write Choice Ink. 2018

O'Hare-Keeton, Monica. Graphology: A Guide to Health. London. Robert Hale Ltd.

Seifer, Marc PhD. *The Definitive Book of Handwriting Analysis: The Complete Guide to Interpreting Personalities, Detecting Forgeries, and Revealing, Brain Activity Through the Science of Graphology.* Franklin Lakes, NJ. Career Press, Inc.

BIOGRAPHICAL NOTES

Lauren Mooney Bear is the current president of the American Handwriting Analysis Foundation (2022). She began her studies in graphology in 1982 and has been practicing handwriting analysis for nearly 40 years. She has worked as a consultant for private investigators and the office of the District Attorney in the Seattle area. She has been interviewed by a variety of media including the *New York Times*. Lauren has taught and presented to national investigative corporations, service groups and at the AHAF conference. For the past five years, she has worked with the Campaign for Cursive initiative, serving as its chairperson for the last 3 years.

mooneybear19@gmail.com

The Mythological Types of St. Morand

John Beck

It has always been my belief that the psychological teachings of C.J. Jung are most appropriate for our work in graphology.

One of the central tenets of his teaching is that the human psyche is divided into two differing parts, that of the conscious and the *un*conscious. Both should act as a counter-balance one to another; a reaction in one half of the psyche has an equal and opposite reaction in the other half, and vice versa.

Put in a very simplified way, Jung believed that whilst our conscious minds are directly linked to personal individuality, our personal thoughts, motivations, drives, feelings, and our unconscious minds are directly linked to what Jung termed the 'Collective'. It is here that the universal memories and experiences gained in our m ill ions of years of evolution reside, and he taught that these collective memories are shared by the whole of mankind, and are the same for all mankind. The name he gave to these unconscious universal elements is 'Archetypes.'

Jung taught, therefore, that an understanding of a person must not only take into account their personal individuality and all of their individual and particular life circumstances, but also of the 'collective' elements that relate a person to their long history and origins in nature.

How can we do this in our graphological work?

Those familiar with Jung's teachings will know of the huge emphasis he laid upon myths and mythology as being vectors of universal experiences, conveyed from the unconscious in the form of symbolism. Therefore, to study classical western myths will in some way help us to understand the language of the unconscious, but how can we access this knowledge in our everyday work?

We can tum to the planetary myths that have been handed down to us from antiquity. These represent, as Jung said, the very first attempts of mankind to build the science of psychology.

It would seem that in some collective way in antiquity, certain people were able to isolate and identify a limited number of personality characteristics; they noted also that these were shared by everyone, and were present in everyone.

They noticed furthermore that these identified patterns of human experience and expression actually formed part of all people, and thus we may see them as 'Archetypal' (common to all mankind, in all places and in all periods).

Therefore, access to the knowledge contained in these myths can immediately put us in touch with the 'Collective' element of mankind that we need to embrace in equal measure to make our analyses whole. My general view is that we ought to embrace in equal measure the information we gain through standard worksheet breakdown of writing, which tends to delineate the conscious and everyday elements of human experience, with an underlying understanding of the unconscious or archetypal elements common to all.

This integration can be very easily achieved by the understanding and use of the "Mythological types" in handwriting as set forth by H. St. Morand. Let us return to the very early discoveries. The eight main functions of personality were set down as follows:

(I) Pride, individuality, and self-esteem.
(2) Imagination, reflectiveness, lack of structure.
(3) Speed of thought, communicativeness.
(4) Sociability, charm, and pleasantness.
(5) Practicality and dependability.
(6) Anger, drive, energy, and aggression.
(7) Wide expansiveness, broad horizons.
(8) Restrictiveness, withdrawal, seriousness.

These qualities were attributed to the planets that were seen moving above; thus, the eight planets they knew about actually took on each of these facets of personality. The connection they made is as follows:

(1) Pride, individuality, and self-esteem. SUN
(2) Imagination, reflectiveness, lack of structure. MOON
(3) Speed of thought, communicativeness. MERCURY
(4) Sociability, charm, and pleasantness. VENUS
(5) Practicality and dependability. EARTH
(6) Anger, drive, energy, and aggression. MARS
(7) Wide expansiveness, broad horizons. JUPITER
(8) Restrictiveness, withdrawal, seriousness. SATURN

These planetary types represent all that is connected with the immediate or foreground experience of humanity; the psychology of the outer planets of Uranus, Neptune and Pluto represent more the background of humanity's experience (not dealt with here).

This is now a vital point to bear in mind at this stage; these precisely defined human characteristics have their origin and their being within the human mind and the human psyche. They were effectively *projected upward* to the planets by the ancients, and their position in the sky was said to denote a particular change in a person's fortune according to the planet in question.

This is in fact a part of the study of astrology, and it is this link that has mainly caused graphologists to steer clear of its teachings. However, we can be confident that this typology has absolutely nothing to do with astrology for the following simple reason: these pre-existing human characteristics exist solely within man, and despite their having been projected upwards by him in antiquity, they still remain set human characteristics. In our contention there is no reverse influence from the planets above to ourselves below.

With this in mind, graphologists can be confident in using this archetypal typology, since it has been found by experience to be phenomenally useful in setting the background for the analysis, and providing that degree of 'Collective awareness' that is necessary in a Jungian sense for our analysis to bear the hallmarks of balance and wholeness.

There is at this point one particular good piece of news for graphologists who have not as yet used or considered this particular typology. The personality characteristics appertaining to each type actually do appear rather obligingly in handwriting, generally as a number of features appearing together. The graphic features relating to each type are given further on.

However, it is simply not enough for us to recognize the dominant type in a handwriting; we have to be able to set down a list in hierarchical order of the first type (the dominant), the second (sub-dominant) and then those that follow, similarly in order of their degree of presence in the writing.

Nonetheless, our task does not start and finish here. We must be able to note on our worksheet those types that either go well together (such as the Venus and Jupiter types) and those that do not go well together (e.g., Mars and Moon). A most important point to realize is that for any planetary types which clash with one another, what is expressed here is a central core of conflict within the wrier in question.

Finally, and for this we turn again to the work of Jung, we note those planetary types that appear to be absent (known in French as *en carence* meaning 'deficient.' Jung stated, of course, that it is not enough just for us to know what we are, but also to know what we are not.

Thus, those elements which are missing roughly represent the area of human experience that either eludes the writer or is unconsciously rejected by him or her. In the analysis, this can be of enormous interest; the non-presence or absence of any Mercurial indications, for example, may indicate that the writer does not lay emphasis upon the communicative aspects of existence. This finding on its own can be a vital piece in the emerging jigsaw of the personality portrait.

Earth

The first planetary type is Earth. For those used to the Jungian typologies, this is the Introverted Sensation type.

The keywords in this sense are stability, continuity, and a sense of down-to-earth simplicity. It also denotes all that is solid and precise, relating to the world of the real. There is concretist thinking, and a strong element of practical awareness and common sense. A fondness for order and routine actions can be found in people of this type, who often can tolerate repetitive work situations.

One of the main problems (especially if Mercury is absent or weak) is that they are famous for expressing themselves bluntly and directly with no frills or delicacy. Sensitivity does not appear to abound with this type, but it is present, even if very well hidden.

There is a fondness for material things, food, with bodily and sexual pleasures strongly indicated. Obsessions with physical well-being, or the lack of it, are very common.

Earth types are often solid and reliable, not making much of a show in relation to their social contacts. They are reliable and dependable.

Fig 1 Earth

spectacular
intriguing names from Hollybush Spout –
most waterfalls are 'Forces' or Spouts in
this part of Yorkshire – to Cat Leap Falls.
The curious thing about both of these
delightful valleys is that they were virtually
unknown until the latter half of the last
century when the railway reached Ingleton.

Earth – female, aged 58

In graphic form:

There is often a compact appearance to the text as a whole.

The rhythm is often of the constrained or stilted type.

The forms are often close to, or manifest the standard copybook.

Very common is the so-called "hugging of the baseline."

The speed, rarely fast, shows slow but deliberate progress across the page.

The pressure portrays heaviness, with a pastose or thick stroke quality.

Moon

In the Jungian types, this represents the intuitive introvert type. The moon represents dreams, the unconscious, imprecision, interior reflection, often upon aspects of life that have not actually come about. It represents all that is without form, but assumes form upon a whim or fantasy. The Moon has the quality of losing itself in the depths of the unconscious, and redefining itself in a quasi-magical way in real life.

As the Jungian type suggests, it is the intuitive thinking type and thus not bound by anything logical, reacting instead to ambience and external stimulation.

The classic Moon type is not flustered by great matters of principle and obligations, but favors a more unstructured and even amoral attitude to life. There is often a taste for the mystic, and a dream world which cannot be expressed. There is the love of fantasy and the irrational of course.

In their character there often exists a nonchalance, and little firm structure of rules and regulations; there is a preference for evading difficulties rather than facing them.

The Moon type does not possess great amounts of energy in the physical sense, and likes to show a softness and an accommodation to all passing events. There is an imprecision and a tendency towards moodiness. The Moon is malleable, full of non-structured possibilities, and more likely to be influenced by the presence of other stronger planetary types being revealed in the same writing. The combinations with other sub-dominant planetary types is therefore rather important.

Fig 2 Moon

Moon

Could you write to us and let us know what you think of the different handwritings or whatever, or if you can give us further advice about getting help.

Moon – age and sex unknown

In graphic form:

Wide-open spaces between words and lines.
Absence of rigidity in the movement.
Round letter forms and thread are usual connective forms

Unusual forms in the lower zone (normal for the intuitive introverted type).
Imprecision in letter formation.
A lack of energy and bounce in the rhythm. Often 'rivers' in word space.
Inequality of letter height, and much inconsistency.
Rising and falling lines.
Letter forms in curves, semi-circles and crescents.
Neglect; thready, often absence of any form at all.

Here, the keywords are emotion, affectivity, and balance. The Jungian type here is often the Feeling type, introverted or extroverted as the case may be.

Venus

Venus represents the female principle (therefore, often an anima factor in male writing). It is also the symbol of conciliation and gentleness, of tenderness, gracefulness, and charm. There is usually very good adaptability, and underlying all this there is usually a strongly seductive sexual characteristic. Venus type persons use feminine charm in order to combat any form of aggression

.Fig 3 Venus

Venus

school. I seem to recall that I was
required to attend extra classes in
an endeavour to make my writing
more legible. While one obviously
adapts over the years to speed of
thought and writing I would think that
many of the original forms survive –
but that is probably why I work in
a bank and don't make my
living analysing other people's writing!

Venus – male, aged 56

The judgment of Venus is greatly influenced by feelings of huge sentimentality, therefore by the strong factors of the Jungian feeling dominance. In view of this, it comes as no surprise to realize that the intellectual field in the case of the Venus person, is not usually developed at all. They seek for a suppleness and an ease of dealing with people, that makes for smooth adaptation to all circumstances. In character, Venus is receptive and very feeling. Also, she is sensual, with a desire to please very often, and even to seduce at times.

They are possessive, jealous at times, but are capable too of acts of great self-sacrifice.

Most importantly, Venus has a love of beauty and charm, and all that is beautiful (a nice face, for example) is all they need to fall in love. So, too, do they enjoy pleasure, and giving pleasure to others.

In graphic form:

Emphasis on a strong middle zone, combined with garland connection
A warm, pasty stroke quality.
Garlands often leftward, enrolled (gives one to believe the common trait of the Venus type is their charming selfishness.)
Planet of balance and harmony - zonal balance.
Balance and harmony affects the whole impression of the writing.
Rhythm is pleasing and progressive.
Connected (adaption)
"Pleasing" warm garlands
Warm and moderately pastose stroke.

Jupiter

The keywords here are powerful social desires and physical desires. The other important keyword is that of expansion; this latter word sums up this type very well. This type is hard to ignore. They enjoy a high profile with a taste for social acceptability and position. Jupiter represents authority, a strong social sense, self-assurance, and altruistic motives.

They often display strong humanitarian feelings and plenty of *savoir-faire.* They are fond of titles being bestowed upon them, and like to be successful and to achieve positions that will give them acknowledgment.

In character, they want to appear kind and warm, generous, proud or vain, often impulsive and going well over the top.

Jupiter types are often portrayed as larger-than-life characters and are dynamic businessmen. It is important for them to see concrete results for their efforts, and they have a strong desire to succeed.

Usually well organized, they tend to be highly sociable and very demonstrative, having a strong liking for life in general.

They have a love for themselves which borders upon vanity and self-satisfaction. They are incurable optimists, taking life as it comes.

Fig 4 Jupiter

a fairly horrendous journey
nowadays, as the people
who run the show seem
to have dreamed up an
unbelieveable array of fabulous
excuses to explain the delays
b-lls-ups and problems which
beset this service

Jupiter – female, aged 38

In graphic form

We see Jupiter as: large and dynamic writing.
Firm pressure, a robust sort of stroke.
Rhythm dynamic and moving all over the page.
The writing gestures are large and grand.
Capital letters are large and pronounced.
Middle zone well developed.
Letter forms are large and often curved.
Expansiveness, likes to spread itself about with grand gestures.

There is often quite a large amount of space used in the written text, and the letter forms may often be slightly ornate. Jupiter writing does not incline to simplicity or sober letter forms.

Sun

Although technically the Sun is not a planet, it is treated here as though it were. In the Jungian typology, this is the Intuitive/Thinking type.

Sun writers have a tendency to see themselves as rather special persons. Sun represents beauty, pride, idealism, artistic sense and aesthetics, and correct appearances.

Fig 5 Sun

Newcastle United are away at Middlesbrough
this weekend while Sunderland entertain
Leeds United.

In the Rugby... the big cup clash is Newcastle
versus Leicester Tigers.

Meanwhile, Alan Shearer has joined Bradford

Sun – male, aged 25

The Sun likes to hold himself up high and hold others at a distance.

In character, the Sun is typified by a strong sense of self, with strong pride, often resulting in idealism, nobleness of opinions, in arrogance and in haughtiness. There is often a sense of correct values, and a respect for hierarchies.

Selective in contacts, haughty attitudes, ambitious, independent. Searches for esteem and for power in his or her world. Good taste, boldness.

There is a liking for power and for domination over others. They may create quite a following for themselves, with admirers of various sorts. There can be a strong aesthetic appreciation, as well as a strong sense of self-pride.

In graphic form

Essentially, refinement of letter forms.
A strong tendency towards uprightness in the writing.
Straight up and down forms with elegant execution.
The forms are sober, typographic, or aesthetic.
The capital letters are large but not over-adorned (as Jupiter).
Combination of elegant vertical strokes with bold stroke quality.
Letter forms tend to rise up, and this affects the direction of lines (rising).
Stylized forms, and even at times an element of stylized artificiality.
By contrast, there may also be a strong emphasis upon simplification, but always combined with elegance of form.

Mars

This is by nature the toughest element of the planetary types, The Thinking type in Jungian typology. Mars represents action, conquest, boldness, willpower, the struggle, and business enterprise. Needs to subjugate and to transform all beings and entities by the use of force. It draws in its strength so to better strike out, to act and to impose. In character we see absolute authoritarianism, courage and ardor, either strongly for or against. Constructive or destructive, powerful, acting as protector or seeking to impose their will. Brutality is by no means unknown with Mars.

Energetic, proud, exclusive, they like to command, direct and decide: they are direct, frank and resistant. A great deal of willpower, tenacity, and physical strength with a tendency towards rashness and impulsivity. They think they are always right, even when they know they are in the wrong. The letter forms are not stylized at all, nor do they show much refinement. The writing shows a lot of energy and dynamism.

Fig 6 Mars

walks with Mabel is an experience. She pulls relentlessly at the leash and makes a loud, throaty, panting noise which some people mistake for growling. She frequently evokes a reaction from passers-by – amusement, fear, pity – it seems to be difficult to be neutral about her. To me she gives absolute love and loyalty which I sometimes return to her.

Mars – aged approx. 60

In graphic form

The pressure is strong and firm.
Nearly always strong angles.
Rigidity; lacks any smooth softness or curves.
Speed quite fast.
Slant is either left or right.
Sharp strokes, particularly end strokes and 't' bars.
May have excessive pressure that cuts into the page.
Angularity in the lower zone.
Strongly connected with fast speed.

Mercury

The keywords here are mental activity, intellectuality, vivacity, and emotional instability. There is also enormous curiosity for knowledge and learning in general. This is the symbol of the Introverted Thinking type of Jung.

Mercury is astute, clever, brilliant and multi-faceted. Quick to comprehend and react, he matches up well to any intellectual game set out for him. Also superficial and subversive, he lacks rigorous principles, but his faculty for articulateness is quite astonishing.

He loves to make intellectual connections between all things, and is fascinated by complicated concepts; the easy to access in mental terms bores him very quickly indeed.

Mercury is famous for being little interested in the feeling aspects of life, and is for the main part a very nervous and jumpy creature who lives on the edge of nervous collapse. He is highly mentally active and unstable at the same time.

Despite his usual mental brilliance, he often has difficulty in concentrating. There is a tendency to flit quickly from one idea to another upon a whim. He can, quite simply, show a complete lack of any common sense whatsoever.

Mercury does not follow anyone else's rules; he does as he wishes and has a talent for justifying all that he does.

He can also be a rather vulnerable person and often lacks confidence in himself His emotional stability is often very uncertain.

He is a brilliant communicator and is immediately at ease with people in all walks of life.

Fig 7 Mercury

Mercury

I am submitting this sample of handwriting for analysis. I presume you do not need any personal details as these can probably be revealed by your analysis? I shall be very interested to hear his comments and findings.

Thank you for the offer of this service – I have never had my

Mercury – male, age 60s

In graphic form

Small letter size executed very rapidly.
Irregularity of letter height.
Thread forms due to high speed.
Simplified forms in a very high form level.
Exceptional layout emphasizing a very well-developed mental nature.
The slant writing is upright or near upright.
The stroke quality is sharp and the pressure light.

The movement seems to glide swiftly across the page as if hastily making the smallest impression as it goes along.
The middle zone is the smallest zone and shows great irregularity.
The lower zone is often quite small.
The rhythm is very jittery.
Disconnected writing.

Saturn

Saturn's character is that of the abstract thinker and often a profound thinker. Saturn is a solitary type, who, above all else, sees the priority of his internal mental life. He is not greatly sociable, but is serious, scrupulous, a worker, conscientious and rigid in his principles, morals, and ideas. He does not always portray much in the way of levity or youthfulness, and nearly always is an old head on young shoulders.

He likes abstraction and deep thoughts, and can suffer from feelings of inner isolation and sadness. He is often serious and reflective; he is a distant and cerebral type.

He is capable of great concentration of mind, and demands perfection around him. He is often a disciplinarian. He is cautious and careful and does not usually take too many chances.

He can be devoted to his profession or an ideal, and he can organize well. However, he does often lack the common touch, and therefore adaptation with others is often his sticking point.

He is socially reserved, perhaps cold, and reticent. As something of a loner, he prizes his independence too much to mix well with a group. This is the silent type that does not indulge greatly in hedonistic activity. His feelings tend to be kept very deep down indeed, and although they are hardly ever shown, are nonetheless there. He needs a lot of love and understanding, but rarely gives either. Despite being famous for showing hardly any warmth or feeling whatsoever, he can be loyal and devoted. He demands a great deal of perfection from others, and is often disappointed, both in personal and career terms. There is a certain severity about Saturn types as they discourage much interest in fun and often seem to lack humor.

Fig 8 Saturn

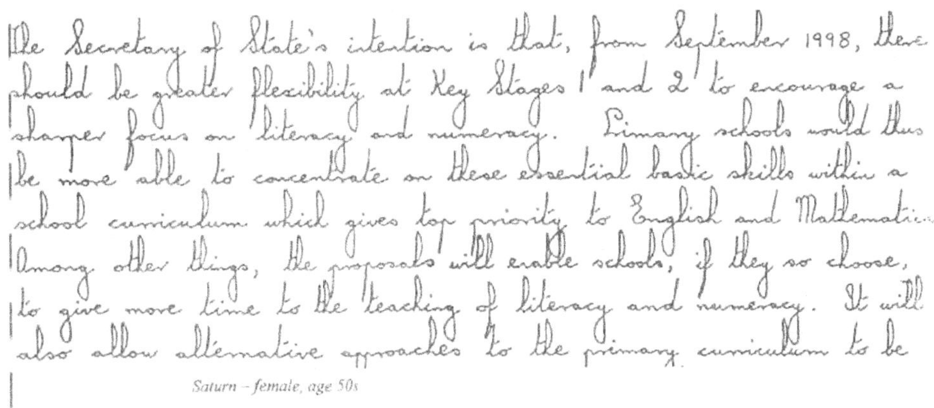

The Secretary of State's intention is that, from September 1998, there
should be greater flexibility at Key Stages 1 and 2 to encourage a
sharper focus on literacy and numeracy. Primary schools would thus
be more able to concentrate on these essential basic skills within a
school curriculum which gives top priority to English and Mathematics.
Among other things, the proposals will enable schools, if they so choose,
to give more time to the teaching of literacy and numeracy. It will
also allow alternative approaches to the primary curriculum to be

Saturn – female, age 50s

In graphic terms

Severe, narrow letter forms

Rigidity and some angularity.

The stroke quality is often sharp with sharpened ends to finals.

The letter forms themselves are often reduced in a simplified form, but show no warmth in the stroke.

The letter forms are often precise and unadorned, with the middle zone being the least well-formed zone. There is often a strong emphasis upon the linear nature of the text and little in the way of lateral expansion. The rigidity and severity of the appearance of the writing is often the clue in distinguishing this type.

There are frequent left tendencies, combined with a sharp and narrow script.

Conclusion

In conclusion, the St. Morand typology represents a very useful means for gaining fairly rapid knowledge of the archetypal bias within any individual; some people can be clearly defined by a small number of the types, others are very complicated balances of virtually all of them. It is only through skill in employing this system that the greatest results can be found.

In my experience, the combination of your findings for the Mythological types (representing the 'collective' in the writer) can easily be merged with your conventional findings with your normal worksheet (representing the personal particularities), to form a greatly augmented body of information about the writer, and thus a far more substantial and holistic analysis

Further reading:

Gille Maisani, (translated by Paul Ferguson) *The Planetary Types in Handwriting* (1990)
H. St. Morand (translated by Alex Tulloch) *The Mythological Types* (1994)

BIOGRAPHICAL NOTES

John Beck qualified in graphology in 1979. He works professionally, and is a senior member of the British Institute of Graphologists. He has studied extensively in French. As a teacher of graphology, John lectures widely and has written many papers.He performs research, and is a well known lecturer here in the UK. A tutor for the BIG, John runs very successful study groups for members online, spanning a number of continents. He is a specialist in combining the Archetypes of Jung and Jungian teaching into graphology, and have very written extensively on this subject.

jbeckgraphology@btinternet.com

Writing in Wood: Handwriting & puzzle pieces

Sarah Tucker, MA

As a third-generation graphologist I am intrigued by the many areas in which personality is reflected in human behavior. My grandmother, Rachel Page Elliott, who inspired my mother, Ruth Holmes, and me to study graphology was also the creator of hundreds of extraordinary wooden jigsaw puzzles. She cut for friends, family, art fairs and non-profits such as NPR Radio. Her enthusiastic fans supported her establishment of what is now a national association, called The Puzzle Parley, which hosts conferences in various parts of the country.

One of many recognitions my grandmother received over 96 years followed the donation of one of her hand-cut puzzles to an auction raising money for the non-profit organization, the Golden Retriever Foundation. The puzzle sold for $27,000 and shortly thereafter she was honored by the *Guinness Book of World Records* for creating "the most expensive jigsaw puzzle sold for a charitable art auction to benefit a non-profit organization."

As a tribute to her at what would be her final puzzle conference, 17 cutters were each given a section of a 24-inch x 36-inch print of a golden retriever (Shebell, 2005). Painted in the late 1800's by Maud Earl, it was one of her favorites.

On the following page is an example of her writing (at 93 years old) and the type of print my grandmother loved to transform into a puzzle. It had to "tell a story" she would say. We graphologists turn to the writing to understand the "story" of the writer.

We just can't tell
you how much you
all will be — and are
missed. Nor can we
thank you enough
for all you have done.
Where do you find the
energy?! Bless you,
dear daughter, and all
your wonderful family.

It was through a handwriting analysis back in the 50's when grandma was told "Pagey, you have writing, speaking and research ability."

This comment inspired her to follow her passion and she became a world authority on canine gait, structure, and movement. She traveled and lectured all over the world. Like handwriting, she traced the tracks of dogs and recorded them in her book and videos called 'Dogsteps.'

After attending a puzzle conference with her, I was eager to explore the relationship between a puzzle cutter's handwriting and their style of cutting. Forty jigsaw cutters were delighted to take part and each one submitted a writing sample as well as a sample of their cutting style. Some people traced or drew a few pieces, others photocopied an existing puzzle or donated puzzle pieces to aid in this research project. I am so very grateful to all of them for their interest and participation.

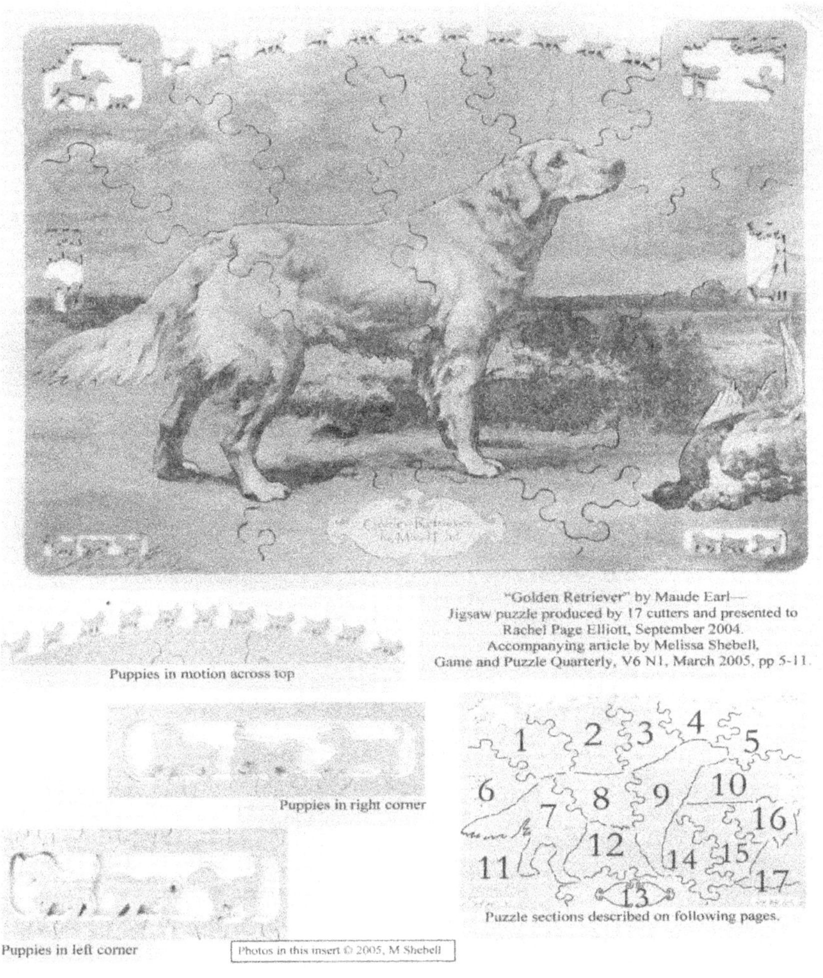

"Golden Retriever" by Maude Earl—
Jigsaw puzzle produced by 17 cutters and presented to
Rachel Page Elliott, September 2004.
Accompanying article by Melissa Shebell,
Game and Puzzle Quarterly, V6 N1, March 2005, pp 5-11.
Puppies in motion across top
Puppies in right corner
1 2 3 4 5 6 7 8 9 10 11 12 13 14 15 16 17
Puzzle sections described on following pages.
Puppies in left corner
Photos in this insert © 2005, M Shebell

Previous research into puzzle styles were identified and classified by Bob Armstrong (1997). He differentiated four styles with subcategories: Knob (round, square, curve, curl, earlet, foot, bulb, fantasy and random), Contour Lines (straight, crooked, crescent, jagged, one-by-one and angular,) Patterns (long/angular, long/round, long/jagged, long/wavy, long/bumpy, scroll, long/foot and random), and Strip Cuts (strip-grid, one-way strip-ribbon, strip cut with variety).

Jigsaw Puzzle Cutting Styles

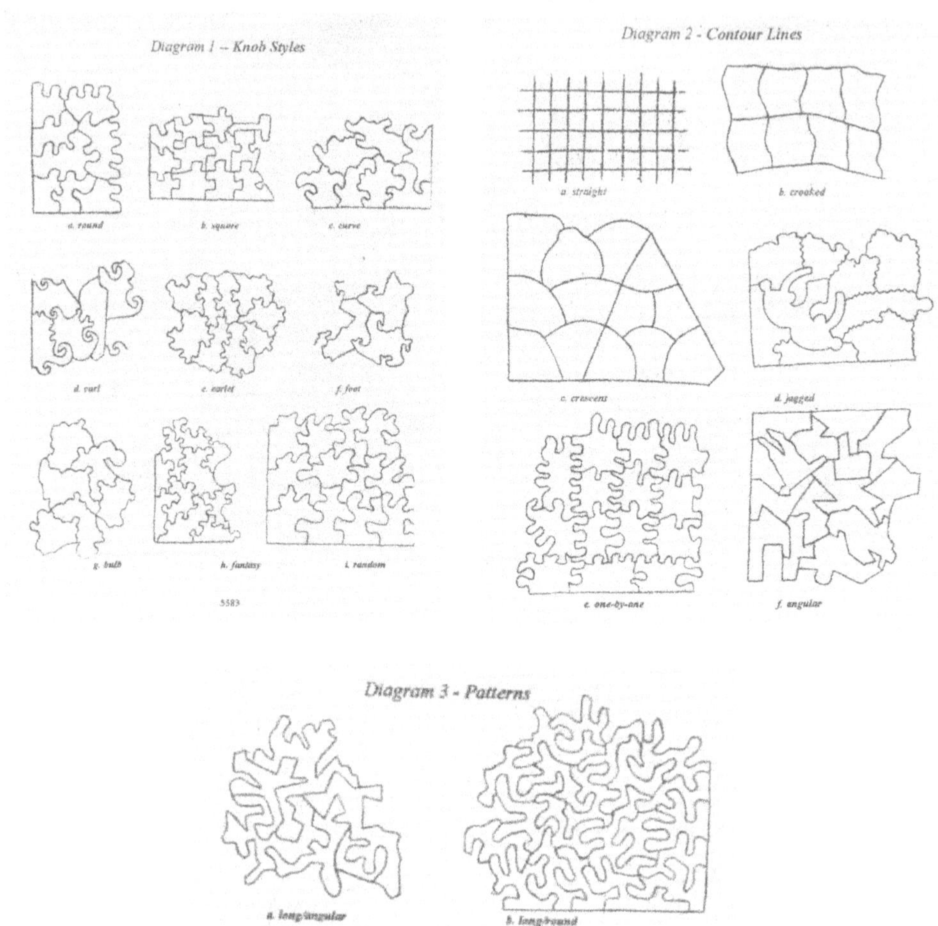

Following is a collection of some of the forty samples, photographs and my observations of how they reflect the character of the writer. Some writing and puzzle cutting styles were similar while others seemed to be inversely related. Like all handwritings, the puzzles vary in form, size, speed and movement. Many cutters add figurals related to the theme of the puzzle and a signature piece which is signed on the back as a form of identification. The age listed for each participants is from when the sample was taken in 2002.

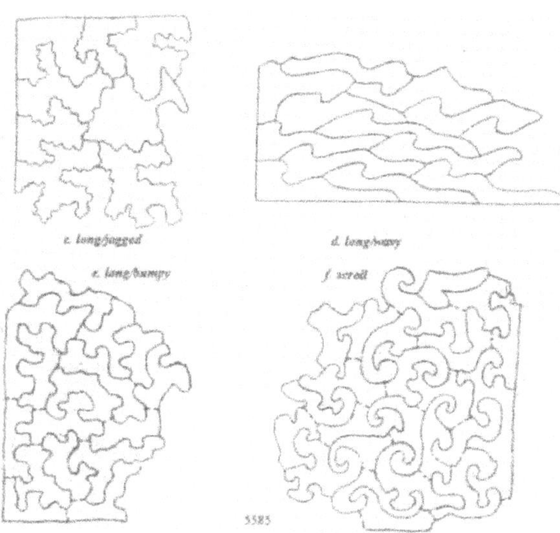

Sample #1. (54 years old, RH, female). An artist and puzzle cutter, it is clear to see how her original, dynamic and expressive style seen in the handwriting is echoed in these elaborate, flourished puzzle pieces.

Her high form level writing, both aesthetic and form-conscious, together with the curves, angles, rhythm and fluidity, indicates her mentally gymnastic, entrepreneurial style.

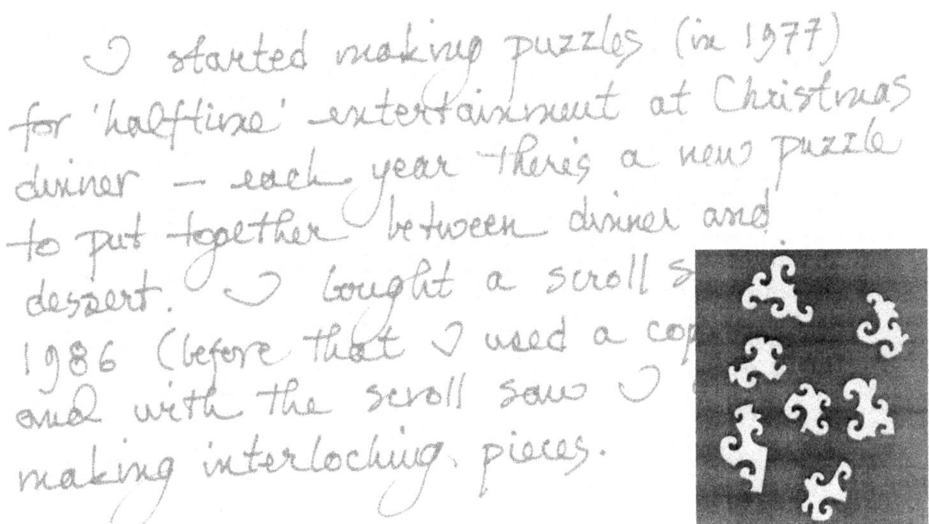

I started making puzzles (in 1977)
for 'halftime' entertainment at Christmas
dinner — each year there's a new puzzle
to put together between dinner and
dessert. I bought a scroll s
1986 (before that I used a cop
and with the scroll saw I
making interlocking pieces.

In contrast to the embellished handwriting and puzzle pieces in Sample #1, Sample #2 seems to have an inverse relationship. At 80 years of age, this woman is intelligent, capable and organized. Interestingly, while the writing is tight, narrow and angular with shapes that are almost formless perhaps representing the "rivers" in her writing. There is a freedom from control in the shape of her pieces while the writing itself is compressed, condensed and detail conscious.

Sample #2 (80 years old, RH female)

My cutting story must surely begin with my enjoyment of jigsaw-puzzles as a small child. This led to experimenting with a hand held fret saw and V notched table clamp in my teenage years. The next thirty years saw little cutting activity – perhaps five puzzles in that period. Then about thirty years ago I found an interest in cutting children's puzzles – people were happy to buy them, suitable pictures were obtainable. I bought a small scroll saw and with this mechanical aid I was on the road to a steady stream of puzzle production. I soon became aware that it was not a money-making project but this did not concern me. This was my hobby and a recreation – not to be governed by business pressures. I love the creativity of making puzzles and have enjoyed considerable satisfaction in producing the 1700 (approx) I have made to date.

In the space provide below please trace two or three pieces of your puzzle.

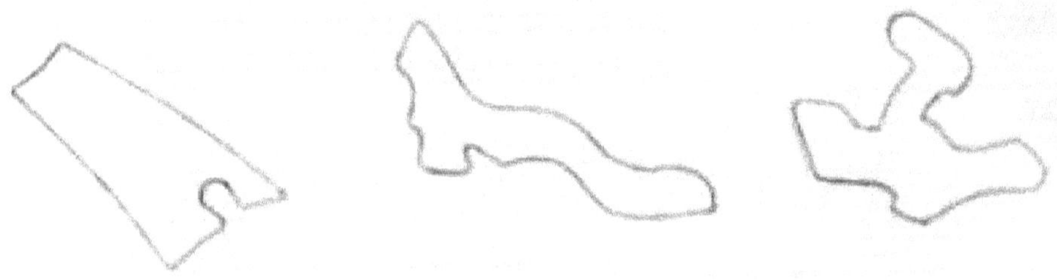

Sample #3 (64 years old, RH, Male).

Sarah — My handwriting has deteriorated quite a bit in the last few years. It used to be very legible. I hold a pen in an extremely cramping position and have to stop after 4-5 words.

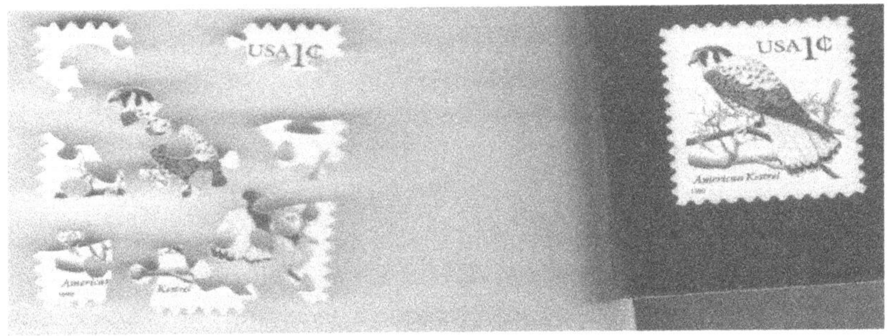

How interesting that this large, bold script is of a man who is able to cut a postage stamp into pieces that easily fit into a match box. Perhaps his confident, persuasive personality, as seen by his strong, forward writing, gives him the drive to create something unique and attention-getting which requires intensity, focus and control.

Sample #4 (65 years old, RH, Male)

Active, introspective, private and determined, this writer has chosen to create puzzles that are fairly complex with lots of pieces that are consistent among themselves. His figural pieces are a variety of wildlife (turtle, fox, rooster, squirrel, rabbit, geese, trotting horse & jumping deer). His puzzles seemed to get increasingly more developed and elaborate over time frame (see Sample # 4B).

I've been a wood-working hobbiest all my life. About ten years ago my wife, Judy, started collecting wooden jigsaw puzzles. We agreed from the start that we could make puzzles like these. In about 1999 we had the opportunity to visit with Bob Armstrong at his home. When he heard that we were interested in cutting puzzles - as well as collecting - he insisted that we visit Pagey Elliott. Pagey was very gracious, and showed me every step of the process. As soon as we returned home I traded a saw like Pagey's - and got started. Lots of fun! and some of the results are pretty good - Thanks for asking!

Sample #4A

Sample #4B (Three years after Sample #4A)

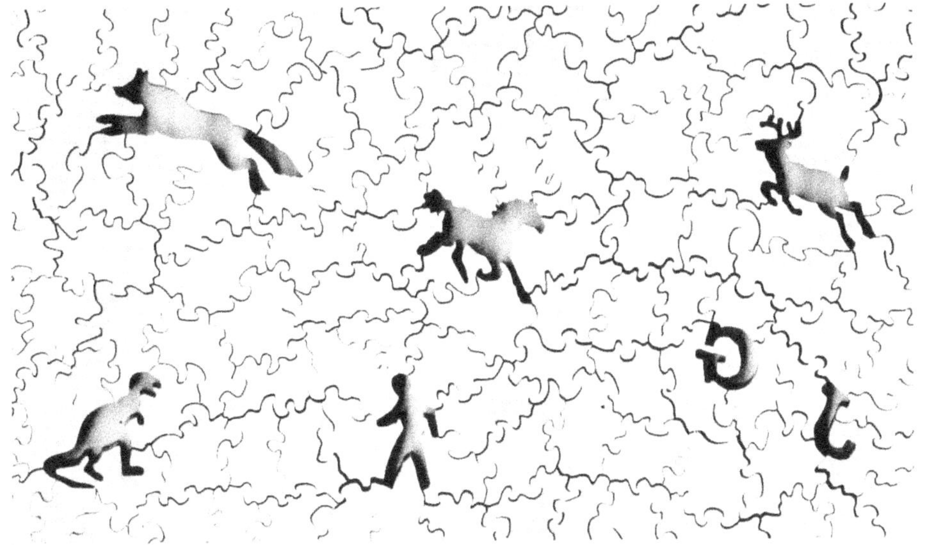

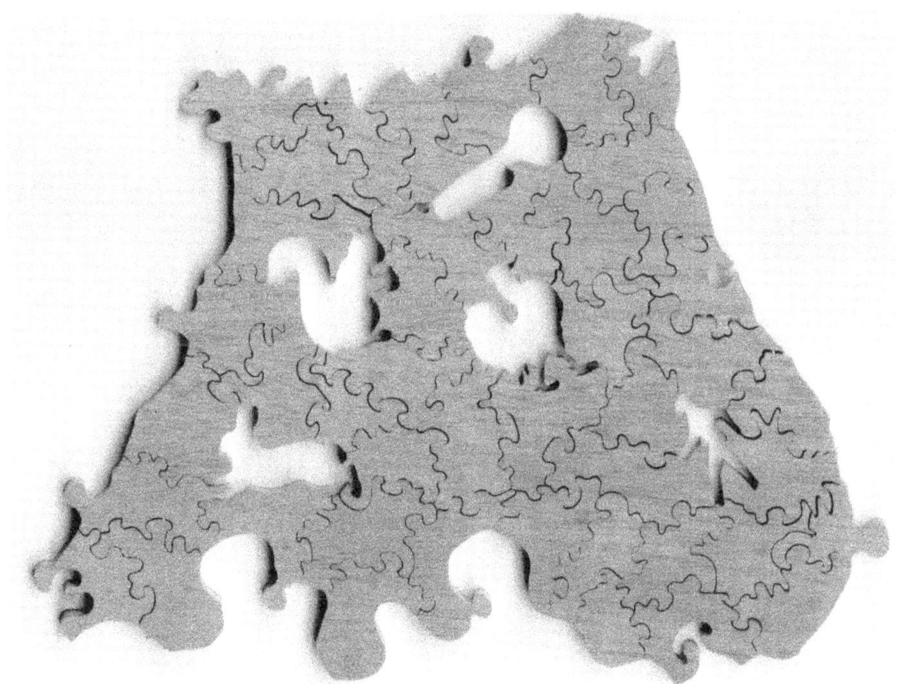

Sample #5 (34 years old, RH, Male)

My family always had a collection of wooden jigsaw puzzles, cut by different cutters from the 1920's to the 1970's. We always had puzzles out at holiday time and while away on vacation. In 1990 my father bought our first scroll saw, and we started experimenting with woods, blades, glue, techniques, etc. I really picked up on the concepts and techniques of wooden puzzle-cutting. I enjoy taking a print and somehow "changing" it to make it a more interesting and unusual puzzle. I also like watching people assemble my puzzles, to see how they (the puzzle) come together by someone who hasn't seen it before.

"Tough Play"
795 Pieces
December 2002

Perfectionistic, controlled and tenacious, this serious and purposeful man produces a fine, delicate cut. His writing is small, narrow and angular. Perhaps it is his tenacity and attention to detail that gives him the concentration to remain focused long enough to make puzzles ranging from 180-800 pieces.

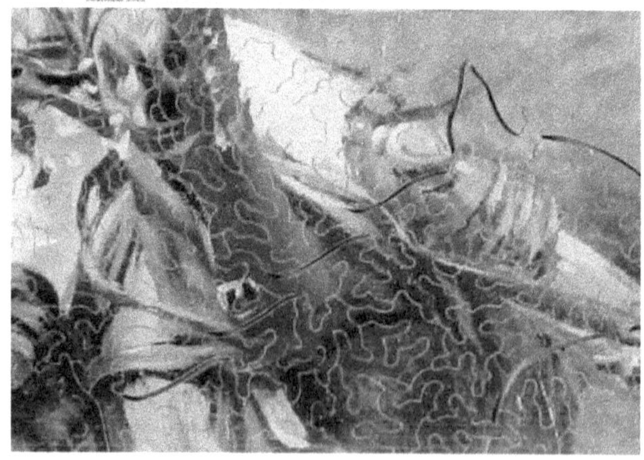

Sample #6 (Mother of Sample #7) (93 years old, RH, Female)

A friend of mine knew a Mr. James Browning who
cut puzzles (40 per month) to be delivered to Swartz, a well
known toy store on 5th Ave, N.Y.C. He was a great help
to me giving me wood, prints and saw blades. I am now
using a Stegner saw. The enclosed copy of enclosed
pieces enclosed.

Principled, conservative and disciplined, this competent woman is precise and focused. Her character is reflected in her small pieces which are a combination of round knobs and rounded square edges. Her quick, agile mind together with her physical ability to operate a jigsaw with such precision at this age is remarkable.

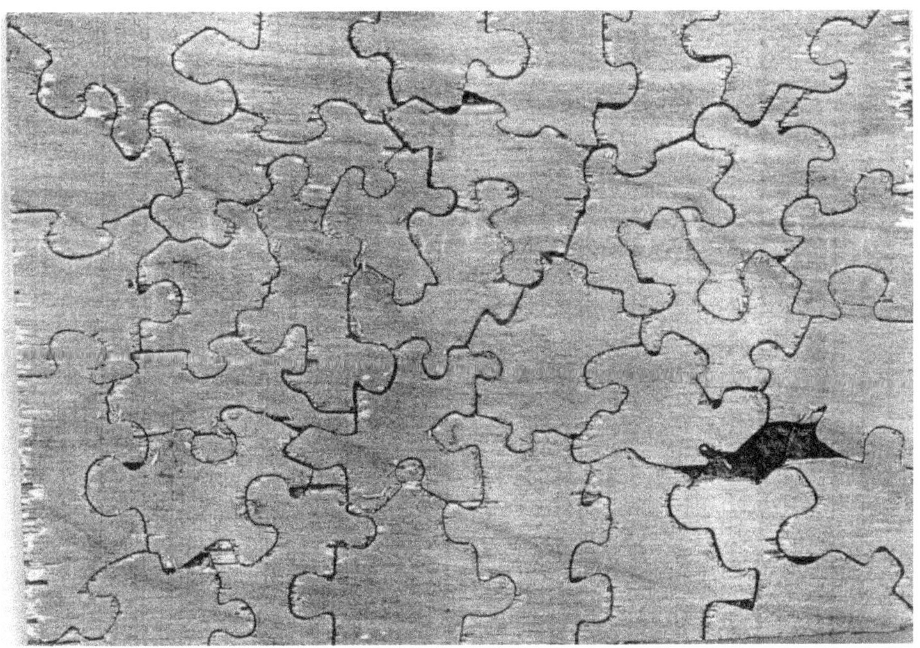

Sample #7 (Daughter of Sample #6) (63 years old, LH, Female)

I learned how to cut puzzles from my mother, Louise Barnard, who picked up her skills from the puzzle maker for FAO Schwarz, the New York toy store. I bought a used scroll saw back in the early 70s + still use it to cut 20 puzzles or so a year, ranging in size from 50 - 800 pieces. From seeing how cut style differs between my mother's cutting + mine, I'm well aware that no 2 people cut alike free-style but will be interested in your research + remarks.

Conventional and objective, this woman remains true to the high expectations with which she was raised. Principled and practical, she produces puzzle pieces that echo the smooth, fluid quality of her writing. There is a simplicity to her figurals in this sample but her persistence and groundedness makes it possible for her to create puzzles that range from 50-800 pieces.

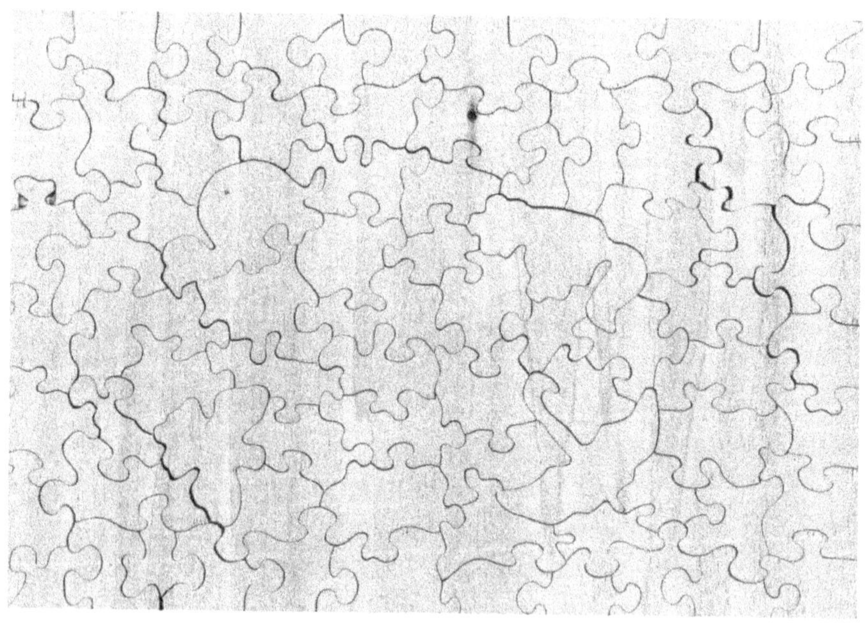

Sample #8 (66 years old, RH, Female)

I grew up doing wonderful wood puzzles
that my grandfather had made, and loved
them so much that – after years of being
without any new ones (he died in 1948) —
I got a small saw + began. Wore it out
in three months and got a proper good saw to
go on with.

Balanced, consistent and refined, this woman has elected a fluid, steady cutting style that is true to her character. The pieces are fairly long, with a narrow pattern that once established varies little from piece to piece. Tactful, poised and sincere, she has the discipline and determination to stay the course as she creates puzzles with hundreds of unique pieces.

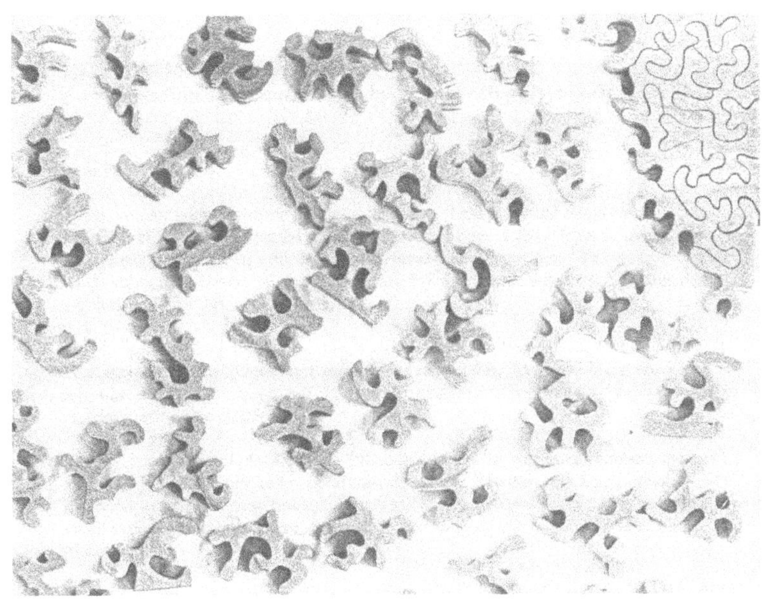

Sample #9 (49 years old, RH, Male)

I attended a Stave Puzzle party back in the mid-90s and was fascinated by what he had accomplished. I met Bob Armstrong there and he introduced me to one of his first Puzzle Parleys. I was hooked—I was in! I purchased a scroll saw and "learned" my way to the puzzles I offer today under "Fool's Gold."

Smart, dynamic and innovative, this entrepreneur knows his talent and has the charisma to show off his talent in a variety of puzzles. From those that are 3-D (with an accompanying teabag) to those with irregular edges, drop-outs, silhouettes and false edges, they are colorful, bold and challenging. His goal is simple "to create the finest jigsaw puzzles available anywhere." No two are alike and each one is custom-made with a jigsaw blade as fine as a whisker.

He takes great pride in packaging his puzzles in a gold pouch that sits inside a beautifully crafted black and crystal box. A sophisticated man with confidence and aesthetic awareness, it is no surprise that he is the engine behind these high-end puzzles which he describes as "true puzzler's puzzles."

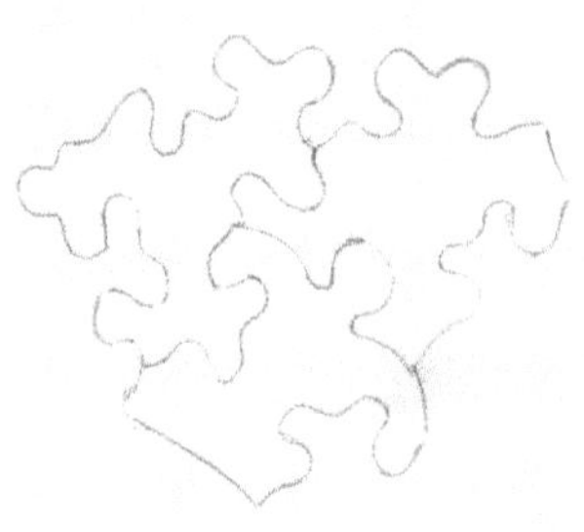

This was harder than cutting the puzzle!

Sample #10 (49 years old, RH, Male)

Well, here I am again.... on the east coast, visiting friends & family and for the 1st time in my 25 years of cutting puzzles I'm showing them to a puzzle audience instead of the art circuit.... Hmmm, do you think this is a paragraph's worth yet. Hope so! Oh yes... great smile you have, Sarah

****

In the space provide below please trace two or three pieces of your puzzle.

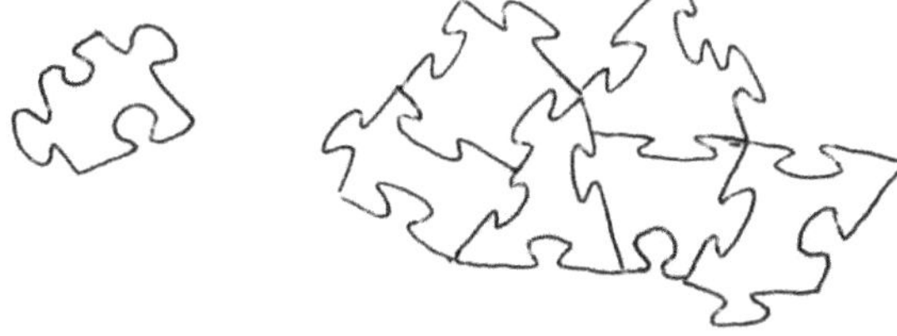

Angular and non-conforming, these pieces reflect the character of this original, unconventional man. He wants to stand out, be different and be recognized for his talent. The distinctive forms in the writing together with the heavy pressure and illegible signature makes it likely that his work in the arts gives him a place where he can expressive himself.

Sample #11 (36 years old, RH, Male)

Well, I was brought up around puzzles as a child and wanted to start doing wooden jigsaw puzzles again the price was too much and just then I came across an old scroll saw in a junk store. I bought it and away I went.

P.S. Sadly my writing style is sloppy to hide my misspell

****

In the space provide below please trace two or three pieces of your puzzle.

Small, fast and simplified, this writing is reflective of an original introvert who is intrinsically motivated. Private and intelligent, he has chosen puzzle pieces that have small, precise knobs and forms that require exactitude and precision.

Sample #12 (74 years old, RH, Male)

I wanted to cut custom-made puzzles for friends, sometimes erotic paintings, scenes with people, rich in figures, texture, color. While I would like to become a push-fit cutter I keep coming back to interlocking. My shapes are often determined by the subject matter.

****

In the space provide below please trace two or three pieces of your puzzle.

Figures are cut free hand

This accelerated writing stroke together with the refined forms indicates that this is a man with intelligence and vision. His space, style and movement are strong so he is driven, developed and confident. A predominantly angular writing with some garlands, his puzzle pieces are original and distinct.

Sample #13 (49 years old, RH, Male)

I got started cutting puzzles because I had purchased a scroll saw that I intended to use mainly for cutting replacement pieces for puzzles with lost pieces. Cutting new puzzles proved easier and more fun than attempting replacements. The puzzles with missing pieces remain incomplete.

I visited Bob Armstrong with my son. Bob demonstrated the relative ease and safety of the scroll saw and encouraged us to try it.

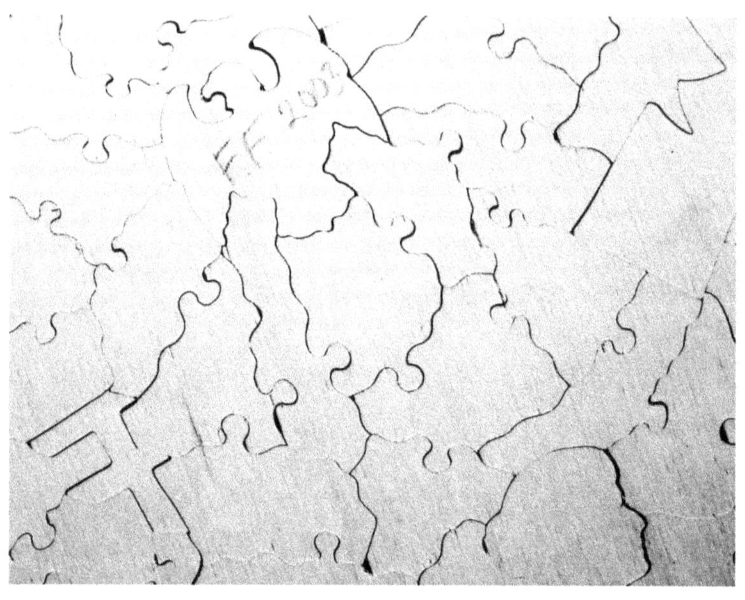

Authentic, novel and streamlined both the writing and puzzle pieces are made with speed and simplification. While the writing has more attention to form, the puzzle pieces have lost some detail as a result of the speed of the cutting process. His print-script combines angles, straight lines and some roundedness. This is a smart, competent man with energy and determination.

Sample #14 (63 years old, LH, Male)

After many years cutting shelves, plaques etc in fretwork (scroll saw),
I decided to try my hand at something a little different - yet
still within the sphere of craft-making in wood.
I scoured the Web and was inspired by the puzzles of several
US cutters, so started practicing, practicing, practicing - and here
I am, 3 years on, a cutter in my own right!

This connected, conservative and controlled cursive is complemented by a free, rhythmic, and consistent style of cutting. This angular/garland writing shows attention to detail and form. Likewise, the pieces are balanced and well-organized with a largely round, fluid line.

The opportunity to review this collection of handwriting and puzzle pieces has been informative and educational. These examples illustrate how space, form and movement can reflect personality and be observed in this form of creative expression. My appreciation goes to all of the participants in this study.

BIBLIOGRAPHY:

Armstrong, B. "Jigsaw Puzzle Cutting Styles: A New Method of Classification." *American Game Collectors Association- Game Researchers' Notes,* no. 25, 5583-5587, 1996.

Shebell, M. "A Puzzle for Pagey." *Game & Puzzle Collectors Quarterly*, 6, no. 1, 5-11, 2005.

BIOGRAPHICAL NOTES

Sarah Holmes Tucker, MA is a professional handwriting examiner who has traveled the country to conventions across the professional spectrum sharing the value of handwriting insights with clients ranging from small family-owned businesses to Fortune 500 corporations. She has also lectured on the subject of handwriting to local and national groups. Past President of the Great Lakes Association of Handwriting Examiners, she is a graduate of Colby College and received her Master's in Psychology from Boston University. She has been reported in the *Boston Globe, Pen World, DM News* and local papers.

sholmes@pentec.net

Squash/Ignore/Rescue

Adam Brand, MA (Cantab)

Psychologists and graphologists have outlined personality characteristics to distinguish various distinct groups. For example, Horney wrote about types who 'move towards, against and away from people' and Moretti discussed types who have the characteristics of 'assault, giving, resistance or waiting.' These headings allow graphologists to gain a broad understanding of a personality which can then be checked by examining interconnecting nuances and counter dominants.

English psychologist Dr Tony Lake also developed a scheme to place personalities in broad groups. He called his approach 'psychoeconomics' as it uses economics as a metaphor to describe behavior. Unfortunately, he died young and did not publish a number of these ideas, which are taken from a lecture he gave.

Deficit (crisis): If someone fails to replace or have enough key resources (energy, space, and time) he will go into deficit. At the bottom of the scale is one whose resources are less than his needs. When some moves into a deficit/crisis situation, he must control himself or he will be vulnerable to control by others. An example is a heavy drinker sliding into a stupor who is controlled and taken into hospital by others.

Break-even (coping): At this stage a person has enough resources to meet his needs and is able to defend himself and 'move up' in the economy with some choices, even though they may be limited.

Surplus (growth): This person has the resources he needs, so is able to manage and grow and have a wide range of choices.

Key Resources: Energy is produced by the body; space gives room to maneuver, and everything uses time and involves feelings.

Controls: Dr Lake considered the essence of his approach related to controls. He believed the impact of the environment was especially important between the ages of 0 and 3 years old. At this age a baby cannot control, defend, or manage himself, so his parents do it for him.

Those parents who want their children to fit into the family target controls on one or other of the key resources of energy, space, or time. The hypothesis is that if parental controls are heavy, the child may try these methods on other people.

The three major controls are: 'squash' controls that control energy and physical resources; 'ignore' controls that control space and material resources; 'rescue' controls that control time and feelings.

Depending on the extent to which the controls are absorbed, they may be turned outward or inward. The result is six stereotypes: squasher, ignorer, rescuer, squashed, ignored, rescued.

Types of parental control

Squash: there can be direct attack by the parent with threatening movements and shouting. The parent may break objects to intimidate the child, makes the child feel physically unsafe and will boast of using violence on others.

Ignore: banishment from attention and territory ('go to your room'). There are attempts to ridicule and make the child feel clumsy, so that he/she is not taken seriously as a person. A parent may be absent for long periods, too busy to notice the child, reject specific aspects of child's appearance, withhold promised rewards, tease the child publicly or is embarrassed to be seen with the child.

Rescue: the parent manipulates through activity or passively through words. The parent may train the child to be 'a good girl/boy,' give adult responsibilities too early (running errands), or try to make the child feel grateful or guilty. The parent may use the child to prop up their own ego, insist the child always says 'please', 'thank you', 'sorry' and will nag until guilt is felt by the child.

The parent may also give love on the condition that the child supports them in old age. They will make the child feel dependent, get into crises to make the child feel guilty or conspire with the child 'not to tell' in order to keep others happy.

The effect on personality as a result of these strong parental controls is Squasher (Sr)

Typical objectives: to be busy, to win, to achieve power, to lead and control, to avoid fuss, never to suffer fools, to avoid wasting time whatever the cost to self or others.

More likable characteristics: enjoys power and uses it effectively with common sense, a natural leader, physically competitive, practical, generous, likes to be seen as fair.

Less likable characteristics: roars with rage and blames others when threatened, impatient, ruthlessly competitive, can't sit still and be quiet, poor listener.

Squashed (Sd)

Typical objectives: to improve conditions, to curb the power of others, to fight hypocrisy, to realize ideals, always to try to do their best, to be at peace with oneself.

More likable characteristics: excellent as second-in-command, sets high standards for self, committed to practical methods of reform, friendly, sensitive, artistically creative.

Less likable characteristics: self-denigrates, lacks self-confidence, indecisive, over cautious, overreacts to criticism, tends to complain, depressing.

Ignorer (Ir)

Typical objectives: to be noticed, to gain recognition, fame/ applause/ popularity, to have lots of money to spend, to own impressive objects, to have lots of room to maneuver, to be free.

More likable characteristics: entertainer, a comedian or sophisticated 'man of the world', easy going, laid back, fun to be with, a salesman, a 'character'.

Less likable characteristics: refuses to take things seriously, avoids important issues or disappears when most needed, shows off, cynical, too laid back, jokes too much, has difficulty expressing emotion.

Ignored (Id)

Typical objectives: to be perfect at something, to analyze data, to know the facts, to be an expert, to own valuable or interesting objects, to find (and make) bargains, to stick to the rules, to construct rational arguments.

More likable characteristics: clever, imaginative, head full of valuable secrets, inventive or technically creative, meticulous, witty, detached observer.

Less likable characteristics: remote, cold, tends to be a loner, may be shy, easily embarrassed, miserly collector, socially inept, bad at own PR, hard to pin down, won't look or touch, may be a cauldron of anxiety inside and may want to escape into unrealistic dreams when under pressure.

Rescuer (Rr)

Typical objectives: to be useful, to help others, to avoid conflict, to show consideration, to be appreciative and thanked, to do some good in the world, to let nobody down, to be sympathetic.

More likable characteristics: people person, kind, helpful, caring, generous, self-sacrificing, considerate, good listener, comfortable to be with, supportive and sincere.

Less likable characteristics: takes responsibility unasked, too apologetic, and fussy, gets sidetracked very easily to help others, bad time keeper. Takes on others' problems and may come across as manipulative.

Rescued (Rd)

Typical objectives: to be a star, to be loved, admired, pampered, to stay young and beautiful, to avoid being bored, to have a full life starting now, to use whatever is going on, to be brilliant, to be helped along.

More likable characteristics: exciting, full of funny or dramatic anecdotes, looks attractive, often young for age, talented performer, generous to friends, impulsive, never boring to be with.

Less likable characteristics: drama king/queen who sulks to get own way or manipulates so others do the work, reckless, fickle, can be spiteful, jealous, bored and moody and may be highly dependent on inspiration.

Combination of types

(left column below shows the dominant type)

No person is likely to fit one type perfectly so combinations are possible.

Sr-Sd ineffective leader: tries to motivate others but often ends up as the victim.

Sr-Ir remote controller: energetic leader, ignores other people's feelings and is 'never there'.

Sr-Id hit and run merchant: effective, but devious and hard to pin down.

Sr-Rr nice guy really: wants to be liked and didn't mean to hurt you but did anyway.

Sr-Rd petty tyrant or super-brat: opportunistic, manipulative, controls by having tantrums.

Sd-Sr chip-on-shoulder type: miserable but effective; company politi cian.

Sd-Ir the sad clown or cynical old-stager: does little as possible and makes the most of it.

Sd-Id the hidden victim: quietly embittered but soldiers on regardless.

Sd-Rr the worrier, or likeable victim: a peace-keeper who hates others to get hurt.

Sd-Rd poor thing; the one everybody tries to help or cover-up for.

Ir-Sr the charming slob: who makes you laugh while putting the boot in.

Ir-Sd puppet on a string type: often the hatchet-man for somebody else.

Ir-Id blow hot, blow cold: loner, starts things and can't finish them but never asks for help.

Ir-Rr the patron or squire: kindly, but remote; charming but self-contained.

Ir-Rd the life and soul of the party, always getting baled out, a gambler.

Id-Sr the data miser: controls others by not releasing key information.

Id-Sd missing victim: always getting hurt and being forgotten; may be a Walter Mitty type.

Id-Ir light under a bushel type: beavers away quietly with the occasional flash of brilliance.

Id-Rr Titanic bandleader or perfect servant: kindly self-effacing administrator or secretary.

Id-Rd little boy lost type or shy little girl type: earnest but inefficient yet loved like a mascot.

Rr-Sr the arch manipulator or Machiavelli: helps you to help himself.

Rr-Sd wants to help but lacks the confidence: means well but often fails to deliver.

Rr-Ir the do-gooder who promises, but isn't there when needed.

Rr-Id the do-gooder by stealth type: hidden benefactor who abhors publicity.

Rr-Rd kindly but manipulative: helps you, but really wants you to help him/her.

Rd-Sr the boss you bail out: often needs help and asks favors, but then takes all the credit.

Rd-Sd the perpetually needy type: help all you want; this type will still be miserable.

Rd-Ir the poser: in a mess, but never stops joking about it.

Rd-Id mad inventor type: eccentric, unpredictable, but with flashes of pure genius.

Rd-Rr the 'one good turn deserves another' type: always passing on favors.

Possible uses for 'squash/ignore/rescue'

When counseling.

Counselors can help the various types below by ensuring: Sr types are less harsh with other people

Sd reduce harshness on themselves

Ir show off less

Id get pleasure from their lives more often (by reducing tendency to be 'quiet')

Rr are more selfish more often (and less manipulative)

Rd take the risk of self-sufficiency more often.

Counselors can help by achieving a switch in behavior.

Sr to Sd instead of directing anger outwards acknowledge others may have a point.

Sd to Sr express anger with those who provoke self-anger. Instead of hurting themselves, learn to control other people who hurt them.

Ir to Id learn how to strengthen quality, which is often sacrificed for quantity. Help their serious side to grow so they can be taken seriously again.

Id to Ir learn how to take a higher profile, so that they do not hide their light under a bushel. They can be helped to exercise their repressed wish to show off, to dress well, to be attractive and enjoy company.

Rr to Rd apply to themselves solutions they offer to others and learn to look after themselves first.

Rd to Rr help them to become more aware of responsibilities towards other people and less afraid of failing. Help them to learn to do things for themselves that others have always done for them.

When motivating

Squash types are about doing so give them something to do.
Ignore types are about having so give them information/ attention.
Rescue types are about feeling so give them a chance to help you.

When negotiating

Squash types need action so don't waste their time talking about yourself or family

Ignore types need information so come well prepared and don't use words such as 'trust me, everything will be all right.'

Rescue types are about time and feelings. They need time to decide whether you are the sort of person they want to deal with. They should not be rushed to a decision so don't expect to go home early.

When trying to cope with the difficult types.

Squasher. This type must be squashed first. In other words, you need to 'biff' them first which will get a look of surprise. This then needs to be followed up with a 'trade' which is a give and take contract. Finally, empathy should be used by suggesting a 'get to know you session.'

Ignorer. Don't get sidetracked listening to long funny stories; insist in knowing about the other person's feelings but don't try to get too close too soon - expect shyness - and acknowledge the person's cleverness.

Rescued. 'Rescueds' are all about feelings; they attempt to get their own way by being grown up babies. They can turn from a caress to a whine in a split second. You are supposed to feel bad whenever you refuse to rescue them. So, the tactic is confrontation.

That may result in an overreaction (you will be expected to feel ashamed for showing anger). Then you should offer to do a deal, which duties you will do and which you won't. Don't apologize and don't let them apologize ('sorry' is the magic word for this type). The rule is never attempt to rescue a 'rescued.' The words to use are 'I am sure you will manage' and not 'if you need any more help you only have to ask.' Never apologize, always explain.

When managing

The key is for a team to be in 'surplus' where they have choice and can grow. So, a manager will get the best out of a team by giving energy, space (freedom) and time (by listening) and by encouraging team members to 'subsidize' one another.Dr Lake said he was mainly indebted to Freud and Jung. Freud's phallic, anal, oral classification are the closest to squash/ignore/rescue.

Handwriting characteristics

Squasher – angles, pen pressure above average, military style and rhythm, narrow space between words, straight downstrokes, overall feeling of vigor.

Squashed – angles, overall feeling that aggression has been turned against the person himself, narrow, rigid, possible upper zone emphasis, variable middle zone height, trait suspendu.

Ignorer - wide spacing, not rigid or cramped but fluid and simplified. See sample of Oscar Wilde

Oscar Wilde

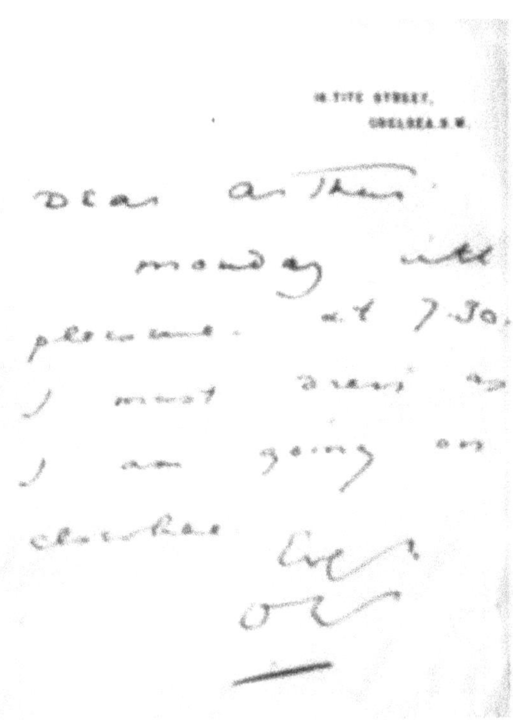
16, TITE STREET,
CHELSEA. S.W.

Ignored – cramped and small. The movement is stiff, subdued with some jerks. The rhythm is disturbed. Left margin is narrowing, descending lines, arcades, letters, and words closely spaced.

Ignored

A significant benefit has been my Chairmanship of SCIP (Europe). This has introduced me to my professional peers in other corporations, as well as exposing me to leading edge thinking in competitor analysis and business intelligence techniques. It has also brought me into contact with globally recognised authorities in the subject and provided considerable scope for developing own intelligence network.

So far as the production side of intelligence work is concerned, I get the greatest satisfaction from producing challenging in depth assessments, especially when it exposes a good opportunity or makes a critical contribution to policy decisions.

Elizabeth Fry – prison reformer Rescuer – right slant, garlands, some long generous word endings.

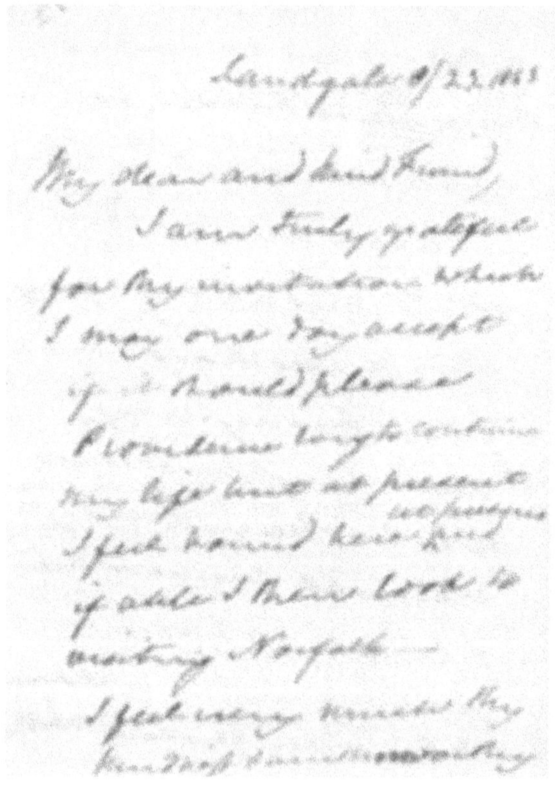

Sandgate 8/22 1843

My dear and kind Friend,

I am truly grateful for thy invitation which I may one day accept if it should please Providence to continue my life but at present I feel bound ... if able I have look to visiting Norfolk —

I feel very much thy kindness ...

Rescued – dominant middle zone, irregular slant, irregular letter and word spacing, convex baselines, overlapping lines, disturbed pressure, sudden angles in round writing.

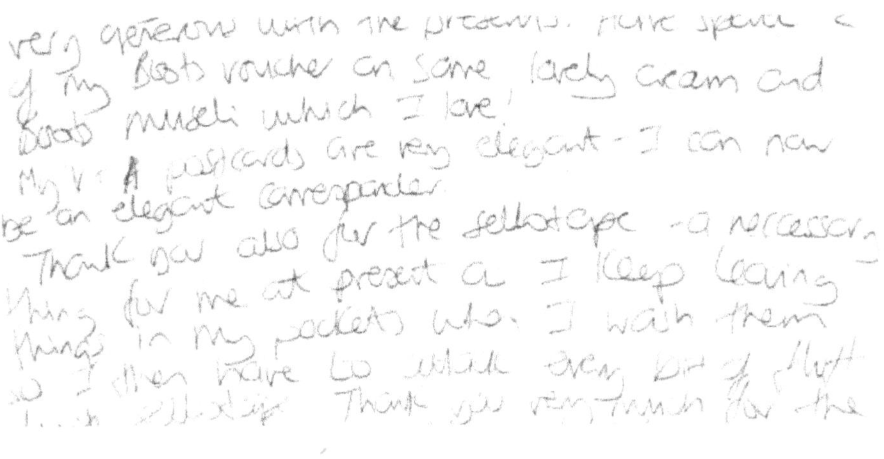

BIOGRAPHICAL NOTES

Adam Brand is a member of the British Institute of Graphologists of which he is a past Chairman. He uses graphology to help companies with recruitment and uses judicial graphology (when, of course, no personality issues are mentioned) for court work. He has appeared on BBC radio and television to promote the value of handwriting analysis.

adam.brand@virgin.net

Your Signature and Your Personal Pronoun 'I'

Linda Larson, MA, CG

You may have been taught cursive or printing during your elementary school education, but your signature is uniquely your own. It is something you created, probably around the age of thirteen, and have likely redesigned several times.

Many factors affect handwriting and signatures, such as alterations in your employment or marital status, physical /psychological health, or trauma, so yours may have changed over the years due to situations. It is not uncommon to have more than one style of signature to represent who you are on paper–one for business, another for personal interactions. This is especially common for entertainers or others in public life.

Most people choose to include their first and last name, or first, middle, and last name, or initials, to represent themselves. Some people are comfortable with a straightforward, legible signature, while others enjoy creating a more elaborate version. Some protect themselves with illegibility, and some use their own version of their initials as a personal representation of self. If the writer is illiterate, the use of an X or a thumbprint is acceptable as an identifier in lieu of signing their name.

To American graphologists, a signature has long been considered as 'just' an expression of the ego. However, we are now learning from our colleagues in other countries that the signature can teach us a great deal more about the writer than just the image he wants to show to the world.

Neither the signature nor the text can be fully interpreted in isolation. One may be in conflict with the other, offering more complexities to the writer.

When there is a difference between the style of the text and the style of the signature, it raises a significant question about the writer's disclosure of his or her self and inner life.

In his course, *Advanced Graphology*, Andre Lecerf wrote that the signature is the most intimate (personal, secret, innermost, unspoken, or undisclosed, profound) aspect of the personality. "The conscious dictates, the unconscious writes." The text, therefore, is a direct message from our conscious self, premeditated to project a socially acceptable image of the writer. Lecerf also wrote that it is the text of the writing that is the public image, whereas the signature is the intimate or innermost representation of the writer.

Children start experimenting with their signature around the age of ten or eleven, and often imitate the signature of a parent. Around the age of twelve to fourteen, they begin searching for a style to suit their own personality. It is at this time when the signature begins to give some important information about the writer.

As with adults, the signature of an adolescent will reveal how he feels about his position in his family, as well as his intimate circle; the relationship between his personal name and his family name. If the surname is larger than the first, it shows inadequate self-confidence and dependence. Should the child (or adult) cross through their signature at any point, there may be a significant issue, signaling a potential destructive self-sabotage, or the personal experience of someone close to them dying.

Analyzing the signature

What the writer reveals about himself in his choice of signature is particularly significant. While the text is written for the reader, the signature is written to express the writer's image and current feelings. Text is about others; signature is about self and one's desires for the future. What the writer makes clear or illegible in his name is notable. And what the writer adds to his signature is also significant.

The writing aspects

Size: as the writer becomes an adult, signature size is about how the writer sees himself in the world and assesses his own importance. This may be related to a high-ranking job and a belief (or reality) that the writer is an influential person.

Style: is about form or letter design. The form may be consciously chosen to initially impress or deliberately make clear about who the writer is.

Legibility: is about clear communication. Handwriting is communication, so if one's writing is illegible there is a lack of communication.

Embellishment: what is added to the signature. Where the intention is for the reader to focus on the image and not the substance, extra loops, exaggerated extensions, or oddly shaped letters may be a distraction.

Location: may be affected by culture. Americans tend to sign on the left side of the page in business correspondence. European sign on the right. If placed in the middle, assuming it is not a business style, there may be a hesitancy of commitment.

Size: (how the writer sees himself in the world and assess his own importance). Self-importance/self-esteem. This may relate to a high-status job and/or a belief that the writer is in a non-influential position.

Style: attitudes and feelings on a wide range of subject

Legibility: clear communication, revealing self-protecting motives; sense of superiority; speed of work.

Embellishments: what is added

Pressure: vitality, emotional memory

Location: (on the page) attitude about past/present/future.

The four telling elements of the signature

1. The writer's vitality.

2. The writer's evaluation of himself—sincerity and honesty, or otherwise.

3. The degree of reliability and morality.

4. The writer's family history: the summation of his childhood, personal history, situation. His experience in the family home and how he felt about it; the degree of attachment to a memory— past happiness or misery; all reflected in his future, direction.

The signature may suggest the most significant pain, or ultimate desire of what we hope to become, or the reality of who we are right now.

In *Reading Between the Lines,* Sheila Lowe, states:

> *"Developing a signature is a highly individual and personal matter, like choosing clothing. Someone whose body is covered with terrible blemishes might select a heavy overcoat as a covering. Or perhaps he feels the need for a suit of armor as protection from a world that seems threatening. On the other hand, maybe the writer is a nudist who isn't bothered if others see all."*

There are hundreds of variations of signatures: legible, rounded, angular, thready, arcade, embellished, covering, extended, severally simplified.

When the signature and the text are entirely different there is a duality of personality.

(1) When a signature is ascending the writer may be ambitious, optimistic, and motivated. The writer may also be battling depression.

(2) The crossed-out signature: disappointed in what the writer has not accomplished; concealment; anxiety; self-destructive; places self in harm's way.

(3) If the signature is the same form and style but is larger than the text, there is a discrepancy between who the writer is and how he prefers to appear. This may (with supporting signs) indicate an inferiority complex compensated by arrogance and pride. (Renna Nezos, page 198, *Graphology*)

(4) If the signature is embellished with elaborations and the writer is not from a Latin country, the writer may use charm; humor; flirtatiousness and playfulness to persuade. There may be a self-confidence and striving for position; scheming and even hypocrisy.

(5) In order to fully analyze a handwriting, understanding the role of the signature is important and significant. It is also the symbolic version of the writer, on many levels.

Dismissing analysis of the signature is a mistake. I posit that it is as significant as the text, and consciously, and unconsciously represents the writer and their past, present, and future lives.

Analyzing a signature

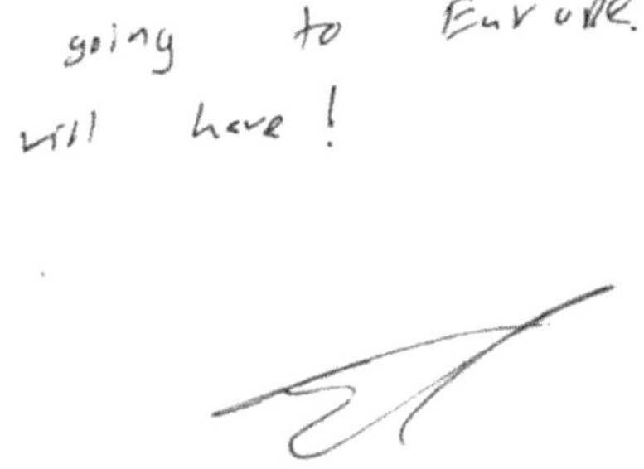

1) A full signature is preferred (not initials only).
2) The analyst needs the exact name spelled as the writer spells it.
3) It can be deceptive to analyze an autograph or signature belonging to the famous or infamous, as such signatures are often a stylized public image.
4) Remember, there are limitations to what graphology can do.
5) An analysis of the three zones and right and left movement is necessary.

Rising signature

Signature represents the image (and personal belief) that no matter what, she always sees "the sunny side." It is difficult for her to reveal what is really going on with her before someone has earned her trust. Dolly Parton is known for her upbeat attitude. The rising signature can indicate the ambitious; optimistic; go-getter; hopeful; activity. It may also be a person battling depression, depend on the other aspects of the writing.

Illegible signature

Male/30+/-, design engineer/ Rt handed/ light pressure. The writer is very private and highly ambitious, but with little energy to support his ambition. His attitude toward other people is seen in the way he carelessly tosses off his signature.

Far right slant

Male/60+/-Pressure unknown. The writing is has a far right, emotional slant and suggests the writer is demanding, vibrant and volatile. The signature is illegible and squeezed which makes him tense, reactive as well as private. Loops in the signature indicate creativeness. It is a writing that says 'do-as-I-say-and-not-as-I-do.'

Signature that does not conform to the text

Male/45+/-, right-handed, heavy pressure. The text suggests emotional distance (spacing between words). Signature is illegible and ambitious. Going through a divorce and custody battle for four children.

Lasso

Male / 36.

A protective leftward loop over and through his signature. The signature is printed, interpreted as a need for control and emotional distancing. The leftward loop is often called a lasso, a protective stroke that moves towards the self. It ends with a small, tight loop ending to the left in the lower zone, the area of subconscious **activity**.

Self-destructive

Male / 25 +/- unknown pressure (courtesy of Kathleen Dickinson)
A hostile form of downstrokes and angles.
A stroke move through the entire 'signature,' which is initials only. The writer wrote a book about his experience of jumping off the Golden Gate Bridge in San Francisco and living through the experience. The signature is still highly self-destructive.

Crossing out

Female / 32 +/-
The confusion and crossing out suggest a habit of giving misleading double messages. She is self-destructive in all zones, intellect, emotion, subconscious. Feels undeserving, acts out on that belief in various ways.

The personal pronoun I

While languages other than English use a whole word to represent the personal pronoun (e.g., moi in French, ich in German), in American cursive, the self is identified by a single letter, the letter 'I' (PPI). The fact is, though, this single letter represents a great deal more than just the self.

Handwriting is filled with symbolism and the PPI is one element that reflects this. It is an aspect of handwriting that symbolizes the nurturing and the authority experienced by the writer from his mother and/or father. Experienced analysts understand that the symbolism does not literally stand for mother/father, but the mother-figure and father-figure, which may be a grandparent, neighbor, teacher, counselor, or even a mythical parental person.

In the gestalt system of graphology, no meaning is ascribed to any one aspect of handwriting; every part must be considered. With that in mind, the PPI is connected to the signature in its ability to identify ego strength. Still, other elements must also be considered, such as the height of the lower-case i, spacing between letters and words; margins, the lower zone (which may pull to the left or right, may have incomplete or odd formations), the connective forms, and the signature, which we discussed in the previous section of this article.

What the writer wants in life (ego needs) may be indicated in the signature, but on its own, the signature does not reveal the ability to manifest his desires. If, for example, the writer uses a lower-case PPI to represent himself, there may be an issue with ego strength.

Personal Pronoun I samples

Sample 1

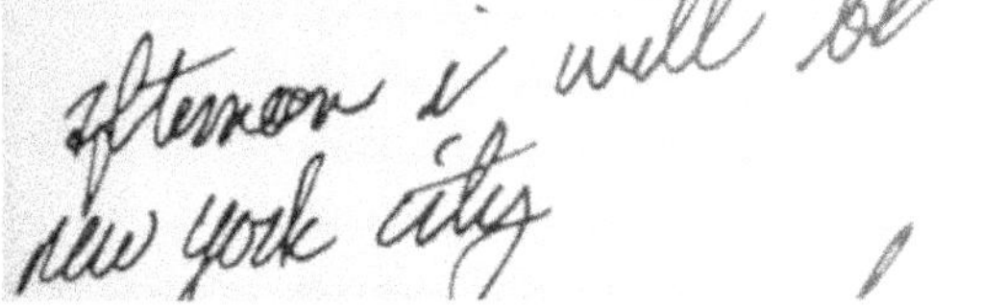

A PPI written as a lower-case letter—especially with a circular i dot—represents a writer who is hiding from his abilities. This has been called an indicator for the "shrinking violet." More than just the small height of the letter, it is a way of ignoring the power of the form altogether.

Sample 2 & 3 Palmer & D'nealian copybook

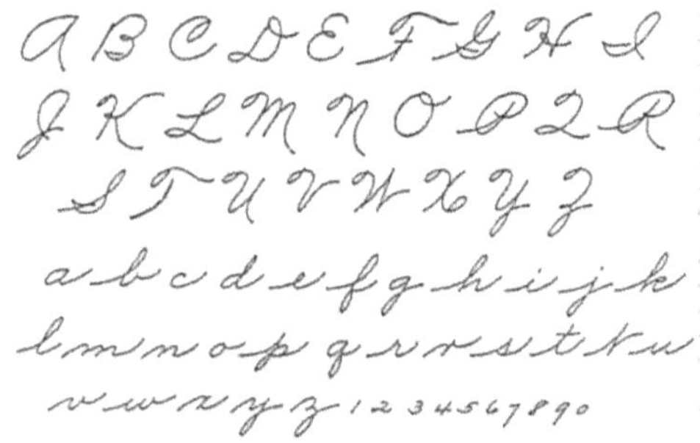

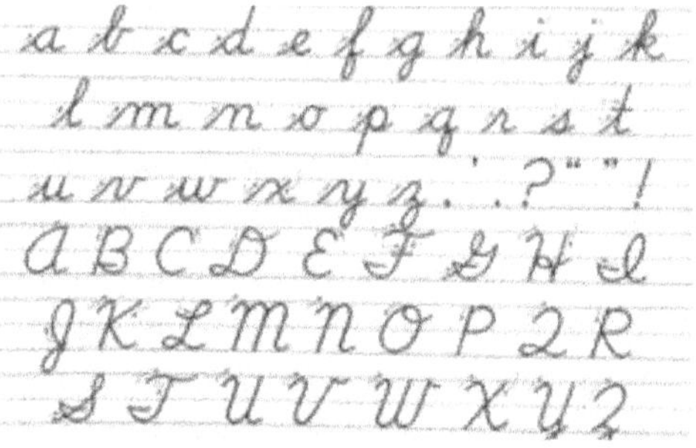

A distorted copybook PPI indicates an unresolved issue in the relationship with the authority figure or the nurturing figure. The type and location of the distortion will provide information about the unresolved issue. This may be seen when the middle zone crosses through loops, or the lower zone does not return to the baseline, or the margins grow wider. Why the margins? Because margins also speak to the relationship of the writer to the mother (or nurturing figure) and father (or authority figure). A wide right margin indicates issues with moving out into the world. A wide left margin suggests a need to move quickly away from the nurturing figure.

Of twenty writings from people in their 20-40's living in Silicon Valley, California, eighteen were a printed style with printed PPI's—either a single stroke or a Roman numeral form. The other two were written in cursive in the D'Nealian form. A printed PPI can still disclose information about the writer's family relationships. In this group, the PPIs in the printers' handwritings showed subtle variations.

Sample 4

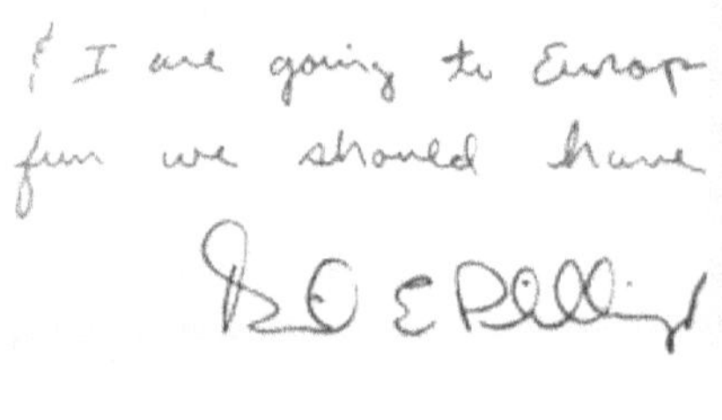

If the surname in the signature is made smaller, the lower zone and margins are often more hesitantly written, or if the spacing is wide between names there is distancing. Check who the last names represents to the writer—the father-figure, ex-husband of a divorced person.

A PPI made in the Roman numeral fashion or is a simple stick form shows independence from the influence of the person who is represented by the last name.

With the first name of the signature written larger than the last name, and depending on other aspects of the handwriting, the writer may be proud for having achieved independence.

The PPI is related to the signature in terms of its ability to identify ego strength. Elements to consider in this regard include the height of the lower-case i, the margins and the lower zone letters (whether they are completed or not, or otherwise distorted).

When one name in the signature is smaller or illegible but the PPI is strongly formed, it may point to the writer's ability to overcome the issues of the family-figures at one level, but not at a deeper level.

A Roman Numeral I with extended horizontal strokes suggests that the writer wants distance from the parental figures. When the upper stroke is disconnected from the stem it typically represents the distancing from the nurturing figure, and the lower stroke the authority figure (it is unwise to assume which part is the female and which is the male. Remember, the forms are symbolic, not gender-specific.)

The stick form of the PPI, when written perpendicular to the baseline is, in general, about aspiration, firmness of attitude and self-control, sometimes, depending on other elements, coldness.

If the two names of the signature do not agree, with a smaller first or last name, consider the rest of the writing to confirm your conclusions.

Summary

The signature, the PPI, the lower-case I, the lower zone and the margins are all interconnected, as are all the elements of handwriting.

People are complicated and graphology is complicated, too. To understand the depth of graphology and apply it takes serious study, kindness, and wisdom. It also takes great commitment to continue learning about the intricacies of personality and handwriting. If you undertake this study, you will find that graphology gives so much back for the work you do.

BIBLIOGRAPHY

Brooks, C. Harry, *Your Character From Your Handwriting, Guide to the New Graphology,* 1930, London. Reprint, Hervey Press, 2011

Green, Jane and David Lewis, *(?)* 1990, London.

Hearns, Rudolph, *Handwriting Analysis Through its Symbolism*, Vantage Press, Inc., NY, 1966.

Koren, Anna, *The Secret Self, a Comprehensive Guide to Handwriting Analysis,* Bravo Limited, 1988.

Lowe, Sheila, *The Complete Idiot's Guide to Handwriting Analysis*, 2nd Edition, Alpha, 2007

Lowe, Sheila. *Reading Between the Lines: Decoding Handwriting.* Ventura, California: Write Choice Ink. 2018.

Marcuse, Irene, Ph.D., *The Key to Handwriting Analysis*, Rolton House, 3rd Edition, 1962.

Nezos, Renna. *Graphology*, London: Rider & Co ., LTD, 1986, 196-197.

Peterson, Pat, *Fast Facts Two* (2 volumes), Self-published, 1995, Naperville, Illinois.

Pulver, Max, *The Symbolism of Handwriting*, (translated from the German; Zurich, 1940), Scriptor Books, London.

Roman, Klara, *Handwriting, a Key to Personality,* Noonday Press, University of Michigan, 1962.

Saudek, Robert, *What Your Handwriting Shows*, T. Werner Laurie LT, 1932.

BIOGRAPHICAL NOTES

Linda Larson has been a member of the American Handwriting Foundation for more than 40 years and was certified as a graphologist in 1984. She has lectured throughout the US and has analyzed writings for Adobe Corp, Target (at the TED Conference in Vancouver, B.C.) and for computer corporations in NYC and Silicon Valley. Linda has written monographs on self-destructiveness, children's writing, and eating disorders seen in handwriting. She has lectured on suicide, signatures, memories seen in handwriting, left and right trend, and motivations. A lifelong student in graphology, she lives in Santa Cruz, California.

lindalarson260@gmail.com

Unlocking Hidden Meanings in Signatures: An illustrated guide to symbol & self

Annette Poizner, MSW, Ed.D., RSW

"Sign here. Right here." Each time you sign a document, information about self and soul flows out of that pen, meaningful signs etched into the page, a fact of which you are usually oblivious. As you will come to see, handwriting, in general, and signatures, specifically, contain embedded images and symbols, relaying something unique about each writer's individuality. This is a book designed to help you learn how to see.

When I was a kid, comic books always had a page at the back to entice you with little purchases for a whole dollar. I never sent my dollar away but sure was tempted by those seahorses. Live seahorses? That come out of a package? How does that work? The product that I really lingered over was those x-ray glasses that let you see right to the bones of people! Wow! Awesome!

Alas, I was too skeptical and missed my window. Many years later I was in Israel and was told about the work of a most interesting clinician, a psychologist, an artist, a graphologist. Sounded fascinating! I wanted that experience, so I went for an assessment that was life altering!

The experience drew me back to Israel one year later to go into therapy with that psychologist. A few months into that process I sheepishly explained that I, too, would like to learn to read handwriting. And that was my beginning.

Throughout my Bachelor's degree at York University, my Master's degree at Columbia University, and my Doctorate at the University of Toronto, I've been studying graphology (handwriting analysis) and researching its use in the context of psychotherapy.

I wrote a 300-page doctoral dissertation on this topic, part of which became a book that was published by Charles C Thomas, a leading scholarly publishing house. The book, entitled, *Clinical Graphology: An Interpretive Manual for Mental Health Practitioners,* finds its place alongside others in the collection of a publisher who has brought out leading texts in the fields of psychiatry, psychological measurement, art therapy, forensic policing, and other interesting disciplines. This work has been featured in dailies across Canada, magazines across North America, in professional journals and at academic conferences.

I've been using graphology in my practice for almost 30 years. Graphology is a form of projective personality assessment, something that I have practiced over the years in the context of doing psychotherapy. Clients would bring in their dreams they woke up with, handwriting samples, drawings I had them make, stories I had them generate, a joke I asked them to remember, their ten earliest memories from long ago. I analyzed all that, a portal for understanding personality, personal psychology, and intra-psychic makeup/dynamics.

It's a look under the hood, you could say, and incredibly useful when dealing with health and mental health issues that have not responded to conventional psychotherapy. I like to think of myself as a complementary health care practitioner doing something akin to the psychological version of 'alternative medicine'.

As a general rule, when using these projections (as they are called because people are projecting or expressing their essential nature when they do whatever they do), I always use a scattering of behavior samples, never just one. In a clinical situation I would never look at a handwriting sample on its own and conjecture about personality on that basis alone. But for the sake of learning, in the interest of showing a fascinating phenomenon, I present here handwriting only– specifically signatures–so we can see what shines forth when people pick up a pen. You can bear in mind that, in so doing, I deviate from normal protocols, generating conjectures based on a very limited 'sample' of behavior, but I do so in order to share an area that is, frankly, fascinating.

We will be looking at handwriting of celebrities since I cannot bring you into the confidential materials of my psychotherapy clients. Nonetheless, we are going on an interesting journey. Here is what I'm trying to engineer for you. It's a moment that I myself had. It's a moment that is described beautifully by one particular graphologist, Max Pulver, who said: "The feeling for a love of handwriting are spontaneous happenings. At a precise moment of our life, their written form fall suddenly under the light of our consciousness."

What handwriting says about you

Junior is at sleepover camp and you are tracking his activities: a trickle of thumb written texts, a handful of acronyms and emoticons. Do you ever feel nostalgic, remembering handwritten letters from yesteryear? Or, like many, do you consider handwriting obsolete, preferring a clean, sharp font to Junior's illegible scrawl? Some think that when we gain new handheld technologies, nothing is lost. I'm not so sure.

Many experts claim that the process involved in acquiring fluent cursive handwriting is something like Pilates for the brain. According to handwriting expert Beryl Gilbertson, handwriting production uses at least 80 percent of the cerebral cortex and almost all of the deeper structures. If the act of handwriting engages a range of cognitive processes and underlying mechanisms; it means that the child who laboriously shapes the curves and lines of every 'p' and 'd' is getting a brain workout, well beyond the one we get when we perform a static, repetitive movement like keyboarding. Compare mastering the violin with playing the triangle. They are both expressive activities but one is that much more complex.

And then there is the function of handwriting as a form of expression. Do you remember being 13 or 15 years old and signing your name, again and again, on the back cover of your notebook, mastering the insignia which would ultimately be yours? As it turns out, clinicians in Israel and in Europe have been analyzing handwriting for decades now, systematically deciphering personality from chicken scratch. If personality is somehow encoded in handwriting, can we not assume that the act of handwriting, much like drawing or singing, promotes self-expression and is psychologically useful?

As a clinician who analyzes handwriting within the context of psychotherapy, people routinely ask me whether handwriting can be analyzed now that some writers, so acclimated to computers, have a script that is rough and unpracticed. I tell them that if handwriting goes the way of the dodo bird, I will still have a day job.

Trained clinicians can analyze virtually anything, from simple drawings, made-up stories or even memories from childhood. The greater concern, then, are the implications for a generation who have been unmoored from one of the 3R's. Most handwriting experts suggest that mastering penmanship facilitates a shift, moving children out of right brain processing, associated with imagination and emotion, into the detail-oriented, left-brain processing that we know as analytical thinking.

Flickering colorful screens are everywhere, seducing us all to right brain processing. Surely children, now, more than ever, need to master the written alphabet, to engage a sluggish left brain that so easily lags, developmentally speaking.

What does your handwriting reveal? A lot. It reveals unique facets of your personality, but more importantly, if you are of a certain age, its trace attests to the care and sustained efforts of those who taught you how to write. Though you may not give that fluency a second thought, I argue that you continue to accrue benefits from it to this day, an advantage that will likely be denied to many, moving into the future.

Learning to See

Learning to see the truth is important, but truly learning to see, that is much more to the point. In her TED Talk, Pamela Meyer demonstrates that we need training in order to identify the liar. Of course, nobody wants to fall prey to deceit. Still, her lecture raises an even more important question: do we actually know how to see? Can we detect the essential nature of people, events, or reality, more generally; Or are we rather blind to the way things are. Watching this lecture, don't you find yourself wondering, "what else am I missing?"

I think people are missing a lot. By way of example, look below at the signature of Karen Kain, former prima ballerina, current Artistic Director of the Canadian National Ballet. See what you see.

Signature of Karen Kain

Certainly, context informs what we see. If you noticed that signature on a check, you would see a consumer making good on the promise of payment. If you saw that signature on the playbill of an artistic production, you might see a treasured autograph. On an advertisement or a petition, you would see some kind of endorsement. Barring any additional context, though, take a moment and look carefully at nothing but the basic signature.

Graphology, or handwriting analysis, is a discipline which teaches practitioners how to really see. Graphologists study the psychological meaning of those quickly penned letters and symbols that routinely appear on the papers that clutter your desk. With this training, you look at Kain's signature and see an identity that is shaped by the majestic vision of performance and choreographed harmony.

Note how those two capital letters form little stick figures, arm in arm, performers taking their final bow after a successful performance. The graphologist finds within this signature an identity premised on the value of grace, cooperation, and teamwork. And being able to see the grander pattern within a simple signature is the domain of the person who can delve into what stands before us and perceive something of the inner nature. Did you see that grander pattern?

Most people have not honed their perceptual faculties and therefore don't see the bigger picture. Welcome to the limits of everyday perception, limits subtly alluded to in a quote attributed to Gertrude Stein: "I like museums. I like to look out of their windows." Perhaps we can see the world best when we activate the patient, probing eyes we use at the museum.

Some might argue, though, that we see in spite of our eyes and not because of them. Those greedy orbs dart around, hungry for fast-paced, colorful imagery. Zingrone, in his book *The Media Symplex*, cites research describing the effects of the explicit visual imagery we consume while relaxing in front of the television: the left brain, the intellectual mind, becomes dormant. We see but do not think. The eyes, so fascinated by all that glitters, actually blind us to reality. We don't know what we're seeing.

So, Meyer is trying to open our eyes to the fact that any number of times we are not seeing well. In pointing out meaningful patterns which we can interpret, she is activating the use of the inner eye, your inner eye, actually; a perceptual faculty that you have which, when trained, can identify those patterns that reveal the intrinsic nature of things. If we open that eye, if we train it by learning how to look in a more mindful and deliberate way, we derive more information about the world and the people around us.

Meyer starts a conversation, helping us realize that there is more to be seen than what meets the naked eye. Her talk stimulates many thoughts and questions. In a world that gives the impression that "what you see is what you get," how can we train ourselves to access more information? How can we — and our kids — actually learn how to see when we are all inundated by imagery that, on one level, is blinding? What kinds of practices can help us learn how to see properly? Or, more to the point, how can we encourage a daily dose of real vision, a.k.a. Vitamin See?

Now, let's look at the signature of former president Donald Trump on the next page.

What Donald Trump's signature says about him

Remember Donald Trump's hairdo from yesteryear? Freud said, "betrayal oozes out of the individual at every pore… If his lips are silent, he chatters with his fingertips."

If Freud was right, Trump's characteristic forward-thrusting comb-over would have been indicative of something. But what? I will assert that we can learn from what used to be a unique signature trait, and also from his signature.

Take a look at Trump's signature. In general, cursive handwriting is comprised of straight lines and loops. But Trump favors straight lines and does away with curves or loops. For the graphologist, roundedness implies emotionality and softer aspects of the personality. Harsh angles imply critical thinking and also a sharpness that will be expressed in word and deed.

But what is the meaning of the straight line? The straight line extends forward, intensely pursuing established goals in a linear and focused way. The straight line, whether in handwriting or expressed in a comb-over that thrusts forward, represents the capacity to be single-minded, undeterred by obstacles. The person with an affinity for the straight line is linear, analytical, driven, and focused.

Signature of Donald Trump

Signature of Former President Harry Truman

Look at the signature of former U.S. President Harry Truman. Here's a quote from Truman: "I don't give people hell. I tell them the truth and they think they are in hell." In their handwriting, straight lines balanced by ample roundedness implies the individual whose critical thinking skills are tempered by emotional sensitivity and emotional intelligence. Without enough roundedness, we may have a toughness that becomes a lead personality trait.

Alexandre Dumas pointed out that any virtue, in excess, becomes a crime. When straight lines have such a strong presence in a handwriting, the graphologist hypothesizes an individual who focuses intensely on achieving goals. Yet, we also identify that that very virtue, untempered by influences to soften it, fuels a personality that may be difficult, at times, resilient and impervious to distraction, at others.

What does all this have to do with you and me?

An individual walks into the psychotherapist's office, plagued by difficulties getting along with others. This is someone who has figured out that "my way doesn't work" and is hungry for feedback. "What am I doing wrong?" For this individual, it might be helpful to have a therapist who, early in treatment, can identify one or more underlying personality patterns that are exaggerated or imbalanced. Now we have a way of making the whole issue visible for the client, literally.

You know the expression, "seeing is believing?" Our society is so oriented towards the visual, even our language reflects it. The concept of "knowing" is represented by words like "illuminating," "insight," or "visionary." So sometimes therapists can show clients the metaphor embodied in their handwriting which might prompt a moment of self-recognition and trigger new intentions for changing behavior.

And that can be helpful.

What Osama Bin Laden's signature teaches about evil

A spate of murders leave us grappling to understand. So much ink is spilled as pundits and experts alike try to explain the unexplainable. A different type of ink trail can also inform our understanding of evil, a topic that surely defies an answer from any one source.

The field of graphology, or handwriting analysis, asserts that handwriting, in general, and signatures, specifically, relay information about the identity of the writer. The signature -- chosen as the writer's representative on the page -- often embeds symbols that may tell us about the writer's identifications.

Signature of movie star Jane Russell

For example, we find an important symbol in the signature of Jane Russell, a sex symbol who rose to fame in the 1940s. She built a career around her buxom figure and even embedded a symbol of that attribute in the first letter of her surname (a name which, graphologically speaking, provides information about the writer's professional or public self). Even once she retired from films, Russell appeared in TV commercials, modeling brassieres.

Signature of Filmmaker Alfred Hitchcock

Compare her graphic symbol with that of filmmaker Alfred Hitchcock, famous for his contribution to the genre of horror films. In his signature, we see a centrally placed sharp implement which stabs into the lower zone of the handwriting. Perhaps the underscore resembles a weapon of aggression, looking somewhat like a sword with a handle.

Looking at these signatures, we can note that their respective symbols do not dramatically distort the writings so as to render either signature completely illegible. In Russell's case, the symbol integrates comfortably into the handwriting, whereas the signature of Hitchcock only slightly distorts the 'd' and 'H' in his name. Still, in neither case is the signature - read 'the identity of the writer' - overwhelmed by a preoccupation that is so bloated that legibility is lost.

I present these two samples so that they can be compared to the final sample, an Arabic signature thought to be of Osama bin Laden. Take a close look at that signature before you read on. Look for symbols that would reveal important identifications.

Purported signature of Osama Bin Laden

In their book, *Sex, Lies, and Handwriting*, Dresbold and Kwalwasser point out that this signature is rife with symbols of violence. Starting at the right, we find a machine gun. In the middle, we see an image of a grenade with a pin, ready to be detonated. To the left, see a dead body with blood oozing out of the head. How does an identity become so completely saturated by violence?

My hunch tells me that when an identity becomes completely subsumed in this way, we are seeing not the mark of nature, not that of nurture, surely the influence of both. Beyond that, though, I suggest that the pronounced affinity for violence, to the extent that individuality is surrendered to an all-consuming preoccupation, is forged by a lifetime of choices.

There is a parable told by a Native American shaman in the 2003 film, *The Missing*. It goes something like this: there are two dogs that live in the heart. One is good and one is bad. Which one rules? Whichever one you feed. Sometimes the accumulation of choices is so powerful and indelible that it saturates not just a life, but even leaves its bloody imprint in the handwriting.

What an Athlete's Signature Teaches about Olympic Psychology

The Olympics are coming to a close and, once again, swimmer Michael Phelps leaves having set new world records. His recent performance takes me back 40 years. It was 1972 when his predecessor won seven gold medals, the most that had ever been won by an athlete over the course of one Olympiad. Mark Spitz retained that honor for many, many years.

What do we know about the psychology of an Olympic athlete? The signature of Mark Spitz is worth examining. We can learn something about what it takes to excel in sports; also, in life.

Signature of Mark Spitz

In earlier blog entries, I pointed out interesting symbols that we often find in handwriting. In the signature above, we notably find the image of the swimmer, arms outstretched as if executing the butterfly stroke, this embedded in the writer's first name. For graphologists, the first name informs us about the writer's personal self (compared to the professional self, represented in the last name).

I noted a symbol in the signature of movie star Jane Russell and reflected that that symbol was comfortably integrated within her signature. By comparison, in the above signature, the symbol overtakes or even consumes the personal name which then becomes illegible. What does this mean to the graphologist? The first name represents the part of the self that governs personal vested interests. This is exactly the part that so often must be compromised in the quest for greatness. Those who attain exquisite accomplishments are usually those who have negated the sovereignty of the personal self, at least in part, in order to either achieve a feat of significance or to align with higher values. It's a trade-off; would you prefer comfort, or kudos?

The Olympic athlete knows much about that sort of surrender. Interestingly, in an interview, Spitz told a reporter that he will never race his sons in their backyard swimming pool because, "when I swim against somebody, I don't care if you're my son, I'm going to kick your butt." In other words, the athletic response is so deeply ingrained it overwhelms the more personal dimension of self, even the parental response which might otherwise dominate the consciousness of a parent.

Signature of Tami Simon, Publisher of Sounds True

In another example, the signature of Tami Simon, a publisher of spiritual books, shows the inspiration she garners from Eastern philosophy. In her signature, we find a symbol reminiscent of the Chinese Tai Ji with its Yin and Yang facets, mirror images of each other. Showing her strong identification with a discipline that corresponds both to her personal lifestyle and her vocational calling, the symbol renders the signature illegible, as if the personal becomes less important given another priority: the desire to be an ambassador of a spiritual ideology.

In this day and age, when children and adults alike minister to their personal cravings in a myriad of ways; when life has become a veritable buffet of distractions, video games, television programming and access to large volumes of rich and sweet snack food, we would do well to remember a story told about violinist Fritz Kreisler. That famous violinist was supposedly approached after his performance, by a woman who exclaimed, "I would give my life to play the violin as beautifully as you do." Kreisler replied simply: "I did."

BIOGRAPHICAL NOTES

Annette Poizner, MSW, Ed.D., RSW, is a Columbia-trained clinical social worker, a published author, and a community educator. She is the author of *Clinical Graphology: An Interpretive Manual for Mental Health Practitioners,* as well as other graphology-oriented titles, including *Reading the Soul: Kabbalah, The Psychology of Handwriting,* and *Unlocking Hidden Meaning in Signatures: An Illustrated Guide to Symbol & Self.*

ap@annettepoizner.com

When First We Practice to Deceive

15 Signs of Deception

Teresa Abram

Dis-hon-es-ty (noun):

> Lack of honesty or integrity, disposition to defraud or deceive; a dishonest act. - *Merriam-Webster Dictionary*

Before diving into a discussion of deception in handwriting, we need to consider some of the fundamentals of handwriting and behavior.

Have you ever sat somewhere, watching people go by, and made up stories about them? Maybe you were in a busy shopping mall at Christmas time, sitting in the food court, recharging with a cup of coffee when your attention was drawn to someone. Something about their attitude and the long, quick steps they took to dodge around others let you know that they were in a rush. You felt a little sorry for them as Christmas crowds are the worst when you are in a hurry! Then you noticed someone limping and sympathized with their sore feet, glad that you were giving your own a rest.

Perhaps you also saw a child who was so excited about Christmas that they seemed to bounce rather than walk! It looked like they had too much energy to contain in their little body, especially compared to their parents, whose feet were dragging on the ground because it is tiring keeping track of excited children.

Then you notice someone who seems to be acting suspiciously, walking jittery and glancing over their shoulders anxiously as they leave a store. Suddenly they burst into a full-on run! Did they steal something? Should you take their photo? Call security?

What you may have noticed is that in all these scenarios, we automatically fill in the blanks about people based on the kaleidoscope of information we observe about them, how they dress, how they move their head, how they walk and for handwriting analysts, how they write. When someone is feeling upbeat and optimistic, we see a spring in their step and dynamic movement in their handwriting. When someone is feeling anxious, they shift their weight from side to side, unable to stand still. Their writing may be full of retouched letters. Our feelings show in our handwriting just as they show in our actions.

Actors tap into this inherent and silent way of communication whenever they play a role and viewers pick up on it. Think someone who is eavesdropping. How would you expect them to move? Would expect them to walk with large, confident steps, stopping to jump up and down occasionally? Or would you expect to see them hunched over, with an ear cocked to the side while carefully picking their steps so they don't make a sound?

One of these responses would be the accurate and believable body language of a person who is being stealthy and eavesdropping while the other one would be an unnatural, uncomfortable, and incongruent body language display for the person's emotional state. It would, in essence, be dishonest.

Consider the similarities between a person's gait and handwriting, which are unique to an individual and reveal tidbits about our inner workings.

A Comparison: walking and handwriting

The way we walk is usually an unconscious movement, allowing us to talk on the phone or search for our car keys at the same time. There are, of course, times when we consciously try to walk in a certain way. For example, trying to walk in a straight line for the nice police officer. Most of the time, however, once we have learned how to put one foot in front of the other, we tend to pay no attention. The brain monitors and adjusts according to our surroundings and how we are feeling. Thus, the brain ends up creating our own unique gait.

In a 2012 study of walking styles, individual gaits were matched successfully 99.6% of the time to the right individual. Researchers concluded that it "seems plausible [that] individuals move their bodies and limbs in highly unique and highly repeatable patterns." (https://www.ncbi.nlm.nih.gov/pmc/articles/PMC3284135/).

Handwriting is the same. Once we have committed the letter forms to memory, the actual formation of the letters is usually done automatically, leaving us to focus on spelling, punctuation, sentence structure and content. Ask a Grade 10 English teacher to match the student to the handwriting and most will match them up correctly. Even though most of us learn the same letter formation, our writing styles are unique. You could pick out your own handwriting from a group of others, and perhaps even that of a loved one. I can recognize my mom's, my dad's and my kids' just as easily as my own.

There are times when we deliberately make our handwriting look a certain way. For example, imagine writing a one-page letter to a handwriting analyst. There is a good chance that you will pay more attention to each letter formation and possibly even write it out a couple of times before sending it off, knowing that it is going to be examined.

Your handwriting can change, and not just depending on who will see it. It will also vary from day to day, year to year, much like how a person's walk changes. It is a river of ink that charts the writer's emotional state, fluctuating not just with the passing of years, but with the instantaneous change of emotions and intent.

Research shows that how we walk is influenced by our age, personality, sociocultural factors, mood, and health. And personal experience shows that it can change dramatically when a rock gets in your shoe.
(https://www.ncbi.nlm.nih.gov/pmc/articles/PMC5318488/)

An Experiment: Walk and Write

Try walking outside along a familiar sidewalk while writing a thank you note that could be read by another person.

What happened? Odds are you either had to stop walking to write the note or rewrite the thank you card as it was a complete mess. Since you can walk and talk on the phone, search for your car keys, and continue your train of thought simultaneously, this may be a surprise. But walking and writing at the same time is a difficult task. Even when jotting down a simple shopping list on paper various parts of your brain must work together, including the frontal lobe, basal ganglia, motor cortex, cerebellum, hippocampus, Wernicke's Area, the Visual Cortex, angular gyrus, and the insular cortex.

Why so many parts? Because, even though the letter formations are usually unconsciously created, writing by hand is one of the most complex brain activities. It combines all the intricacies of language with precise physical movements in real-time. Creating something as simple as a shopping list requires focus and intent and brain power that utilizes the same areas of the brain as walking, plus the parts of the brain that are used for speech, memory, and auditory information.

The benefits of writing by hand have been extensively researched over the past several decades. A summary of that research is presented in the updated 2021 White Paper prepared by Dr. Jane Yank for the American Handwriting Analysis Foundation. Many studies within that summary have shown that writing by hand, "…stimulates brain areas that focus attention. This stimulation activates and coordinates activity in the cognitive, visual, auditory, motor, and emotion centers in the brain, enabling knowledge to be more deeply embedded in memory for understanding and ease of recall."
(Pg4 https://docs.google.com/document/d/1zn5PCpxWue0SK38Yqpfty_MjkQTneiTKnijfhOoP-Un8/edit)

Now, let us take this experiment one step further. Try walking while writing a thank you card and include a lie in the written text. Imagine what that thank you card would look like. It sounds like a recipe for disaster and brain overload which could cause someone to exclaim, "Oh what a tangled web of ink we weave when first we practice to deceive" (with apologies to Sir Walter Scott).

Brainwriting

Handwriting is also known by the term 'brainwriting,' a term coined by Wilhelm Preyer (1841-1897). When you consider just how much of the brain is used to create a written note, 'brainwriting' is an appropriate expression. It is an intimate reflection of one's habits, thoughts, and emotions in the exact instant when paper and pen meet.

Handwriting can be used in the early detection of certain brain disorders. A recent study found a 97.5% accuracy for the early detection of Parkinson's

Disease through studying the handwriting of a patient and observing certain characteristics, such as variable pressure, micrographia (abnormally small or cramped writing), increased angularity and shakiness, as well as slower writing overall

(https://www.sciencedaily.com/releases/2013/09/130909105033.htm)

(https://link.springer.com/article/10.1007%2Fs00415-013-6996-x)

Furthermore, in a startling 2007 study, it was determined that psychopaths can pick the easy 'prey' just by observing the subject's walk. It turned out that they were assessing, correctly, the subject's vulnerability.

And much like how known psychopaths found their victims through the subtle signs in their walk, a skilled handwriting analyst can spot deception through subtle shifts in writing that indicate the brain's emotional response to the act of lying. With training, a skilled handwriting analyst can look for and find traits that are out of place in someone's brainwriting, indicating that they are intending to deceive.

Deception in Handwriting

To be very clear, a handwriting analyst does not claim to 'see dishonesty' in handwriting. As handwriting expert Reed Hayes writes, "Dishonesty is not a single trait, but any number of trait combinations added to the right circumstances." (Between the Lines)

As there is no one definitive stroke or magic combination of strokes that indicates dishonesty, we must instead look for multiple signs in the writing sample which could indicate any of the following:

1. A lack of honesty, integrity, spontaneity, clarity, reliability and regard for rules;

2. A change in the writer's emotional state; and/or

3. Guilt

Because we are looking in writing for signs that would indicate any of the above, it is important to remember that we can only see the deception if:

1. the person is intentionally trying to deceive;

2. the person feels guilty about what they are writing; or
3. the person has a habit of muddying the waters.

In other words, a person must have deception on the brain, whether consciously or unconsciously, for it to be visible in their handwriting. Thus, the behavior of a true sociopath may not manifest the same in handwriting as someone who experiences guilt.

It is important to remember that there is a big difference between labeling someone as dishonest and spotting deception in their handwriting. We do not, and can not, know why someone is not being entirely truthful. The handwriting analyst can see only what was happening in the instant pen and paper met, and certain emotions were present. Sometimes, the deception is deliberate and sometimes it is unconscious in the same way you might respond to the question, "How are you doing?" automatically by saying "I'm good," even if you are not.

In my practice, I ask every client to include a lie somewhere in the handwriting sample they provide. By finding their tell, it can provide a vital clue to their personality, and there is almost always a tell. One notable exception was when I received the handwriting of Jack Barsky, an ex-Russian spy. Jack was a master of deception in life and writing. He lived in the US under an assumed name for 16 years as a KGB spy until his cover was blown by the FBI. His writing sample showed no signs of deception but it did show high intelligence and creativity.

When you spot signs of deception, it is vital to remember that you do not know what may have prompted a person to be dishonest. Take, for example, my clients. They know that they wrote the lie because they were instructed to do so. They know that, and I know that, but anyone else reading their sample would not know that. To label them as dishonest or deceitful from that one sample, would be both unethical and irresponsible.

In other cases, the writer might have felt they had no other choice or that it was expected of them. Perhaps they were trying to protect their loved ones or themselves. Maybe they thought nothing of it, believing it to be a socially acceptable white lie, like the kind people might write in thank-you notes.

For example, I once received a note where the writer said they couldn't wait to have an analysis done, but the shifts in their handwriting said something else. When I mentioned that it appeared as though they were more anxious than excited, they freely admitted that while they were looking forward to the experience, they also regretted agreeing to it.

Now, let us look at some common signs of dishonesty. Keep in mind that in a real sample, you would look for at least three signs grouped together to spot a direct lie. Similar to how your normal walk looks markedly different when you get a rock in your shoe or you feel guilty about shoplifting, lies often look markedly different from the rest of the handwriting.

Remember, the writer may be experiencing an emotional response to what is being written, and that can affect the way they write. Apply common sense to the handwriting sample to determine if this is the case in the sample you are analyzing. If you see signs that could indicate dishonesty, a great first step is to say, "This subject seems to be important to you. Can you tell me more about what is going on here?"

While there are a multitude of different signs for dishonesty and deception detailed extensively in Kim Ianetta's book, *Danger Between the Lines*, the signs listed below are ones I have personally found to appear regularly in lies. In other words, they are real-life samples of lies that have been confirmed by the sample writer. They are all examples of dishonesty in action.

15 Signs of Dishonesty

1. Unclear, illegible writing: thats

2. Exceptionally thready writing

ars. I have seen his friend
he lives in Seattle Washington.

3. Sudden changes in slant, pressure and/or size

I moved to a new country all
have lived in more than 4 countries

4. Complicated or double-looped circle letters

even after another night
h we are all tired about
how we can pull through
we know that she will
n the weekend and we
en haha! How lucky.

5. Hooks inside circle letters

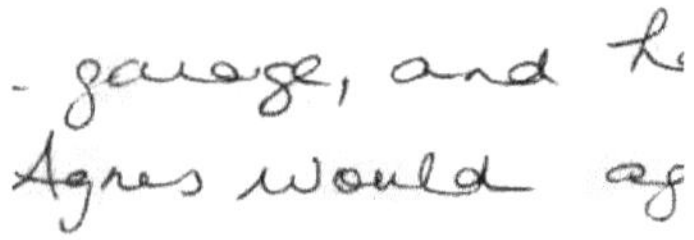

6. Fragmented letters (open at the bottom or segmented strokes that do not connect)

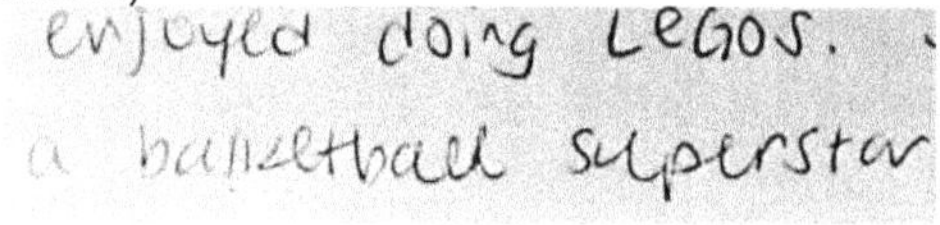

7. Tricksters (letters that are unrecognizable when taken out of context)

8. Frequently corrected or "soldered" letters

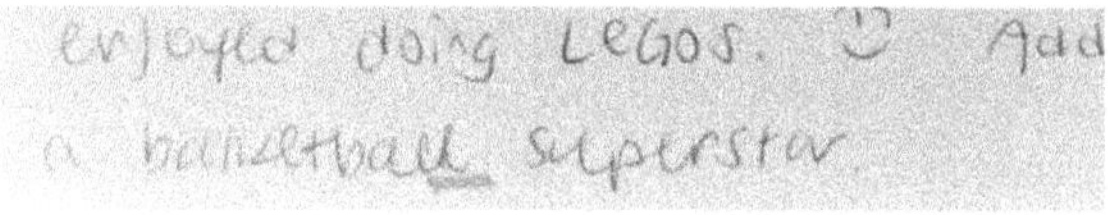

9. Omitted letters or parts of letters

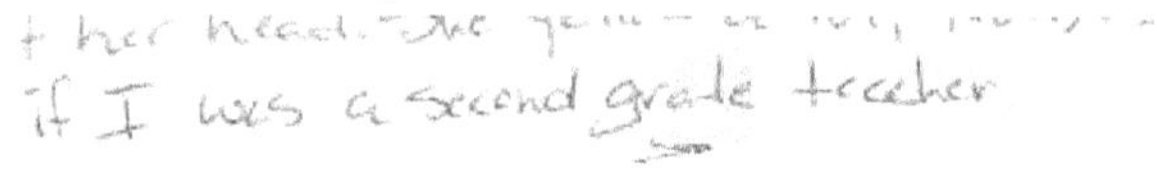

10. Drop in baseline

11. Covering strokes

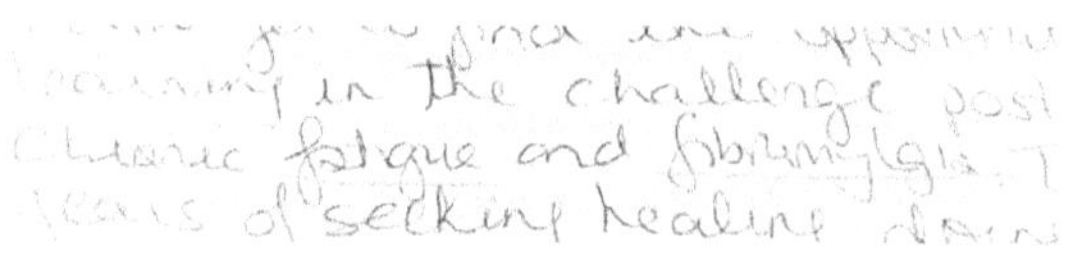

12. Misplaced capital letters

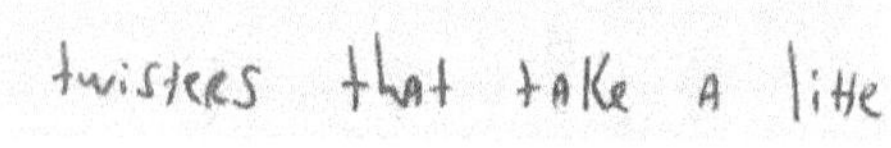

13. Exaggerated spacing between words

14. A jump up in the baseline

15. Slow, precise writing

Once you begin looking for insight into people through handwriting it is your responsibility to do so from a place of compassion and understanding. There is always a multi-dimensional human being, with a full range of feelings, emotions, and motivations behind it. The smaller the sample you have, the less certain you can be of any conclusions and your curiosity will be the key to unlocking the whole story. You are filling in the blanks with what you observe in the writing, but just as if you briefly saw someone holding a cane, you don't, and can't possibly, know the whole story—was that person recently injured, or is it a long-term condition that causes the need for the cane? All you can know, is what you observed. Then, you must ask questions.

BIBLIOGRAPHY

Angela & Quinsey, Vernon & Langford, Dale. (2007). *Psychopathy and the Perception of Affect and Vulnerability. Criminal Justice and Behavior.* 34. 10.1177/0093854806293554

Hayes, R. (1993). *Between the Lines: Understanding yourself and others through handwriting analysis* (1993rd ed.). Destiny Books.

Iannetta, K., Craine, J. F., & Hayes, R. C. (2008). *Danger Between the Lines* (Revised). Kimon Iannetta Trust.

BIOGRAPHICAL NOTES

Teresa Abram is a member and Communications Chair of the American Handwriting Analysis Foundation. She was first introduced to graphology as a teenager through her grandmother, and began analyzing handwriting professionally in 2019. She is the creator and host of *A Most Unusual T Party* podcast which focuses on graphology. She finds fulfillment in raising awareness about the value of handwriting analysis and promoting cursive writing.

handwritingpi@gmail.com

Michael Ondaatje: an analysis of his handwriting

Sheila Lowe, MS, CG, CFDE

I was asked by Professor Robert Lecker to analyze the handwriting of Canadian novelist Michael Ondaatje for an academic book he was writing on the life of this man. In the end, my essay was not made part of the book and I offer it here.

Despite his fame, I have never read any of Mr. Ondaatje's work nor, as far as I am aware, seen films he has written, including his best known work, *The English Patient.* Thus, the following comments are based solely upon my examination of his handwriting using the gestalt method of analysis. This method views the handwriting as a whole picture, which, considering the particular writing style Mr. Ondaatje uses, is important. As you will see, his handwriting defies picking out and interpreting individual elements such as the way he crosses his t's or dots his i's, or the way the writing slants.

The method used for analysis

Gestalt handwriting analysis is based on the principles of gestalt psychology and concerns the configuration of the handwriting on the page. Configuration is defined as *an organized whole that is perceived as different from the sum of its parts.*

Applied to handwriting, the whole is comprised of the spatial layout on the paper, the form (letter designs), and the writing movement, which includes speed, pressure, and rhythm. These three 'big pictures' of handwriting (space/form/movement) are comprised of numerous components, but to simplify for the purposes of this essay, we can accept some basic generalities.

1. Spatial arrangement–the layout of the handwriting on the page—examines the amount of space between letters and words, the space between lines, and margins that frame the text. Space is the most unconscious part of writing and reflects the sense of order the writer keeps in his life and environment. It also casts light on his social and intellectual behavior.

2. Form refers to the writing style, be it the copybook style he learned in school, or a simplification of those letter forms, a stripping away of nonessential strokes and loops that are not needed for legibility. Or, one might making the writing more elaborate, dressing it up with wide loops and swirls–features that draw attention to themselves. Others use printed styles, manuscript (upper /lower case) or all-capital block printing. Writing form is the most conscious aspect of handwriting and reveals the writer's level of ego functioning.

3. Writing movement is seen in the velocity, or speed of execution; in the depth component of pressure on the page, and the overall rhythm (contraction /release) of the handwriting. Movement is another unconscious aspect of writing and demonstrates the writer's libido or intrinsic energy.

Unlike the empirical, or trait-stroke method, which is the other main school of handwriting analysis, in the gestalt method there is no "this means that" interpretation of personality traits. As mentioned above, gestalt is the whole picture and is not easily broken into pieces. If you see someone standing against a wall you see, not a collection of body parts—arm, legs, torso, eyes, nose, mouth, etc., but the whole person. That is the gestalt.

Trait stroke

The trait-stroke method assigns a personality trait name to individual types of handwriting stroke. For example, "resentment strokes," (straight strokes on the beginning of a word, "yieldingness strokes" (rounded strokes). For thinking style the analyst may check off a list of traits such as "comprehensive thinking" or "cumulative thinking," or "analytical thinking, (interpreted in the way the letters 'm' and 'n' are formed). Or Loyalty (how the i is dotted), or Dignity (the height of the d and t stems).

This empirical method may be preferred by left-brain thinkers who see handwriting as discrete pieces that can be constructed into a picture, it fails to obtain the same depth of understanding as the holistic gestalt method.

For example, to simply state that if a writer crosses his t's high he has high goals is insufficient without interpreting what that means within the context of a specific handwriting. And when the style of writing is entirely lacking the standard form and is more on the order of hieroglyphics, as in the case of Michael Ondaatje, the trait-stroke method falls short.

We can say with certainty that Mr. Ondaatje did not learn to write the way he does from a school copybook. This can be viewed in a positive light. Although his handwriting cannot easily be read, the gestalt reveals tremendous originality and creativity–his unwillingness to 'color inside the lines.'

However, because the gestalt method approaches handwriting as a whole, it is difficult to explain exactly what led to my conclusions. With that caveat, I will do my best to describe some of the more general aspects of Mr. Ondaajte's handwriting and my interpretation of them. This sample was darkened.

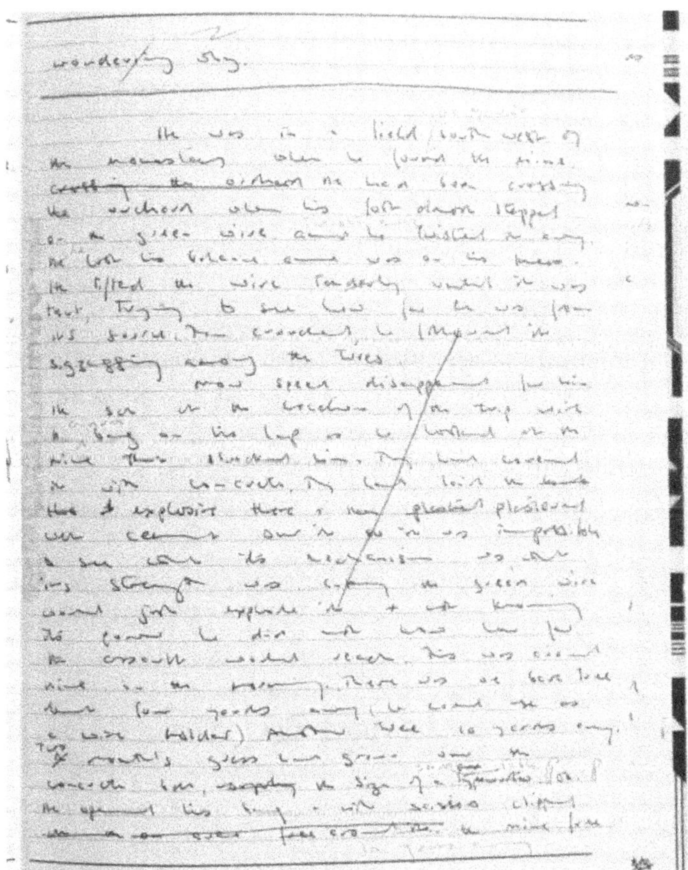

The handwriting sample used for this analysis was apparently taken from a notebook Ondaatje kept for notes on *The English Patient.* Other samples that I found through Google Images were consistent with this one. I did not see the original, but the scan or photograph was of sufficient quality and quantity to make an examination and reach some conclusions. That the handwriting was done on lined paper can have some affect on the final product.

This part of the page is enlarged to better see the writing.

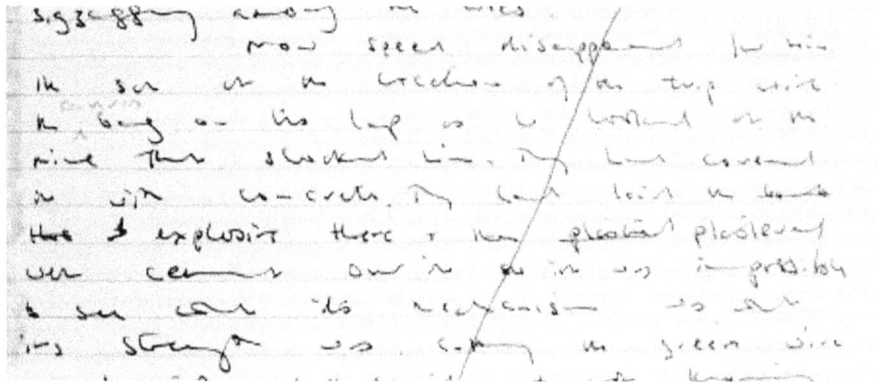

We start with the spatial arrangement, which shows a fair sense of organization. The left margin hugs the left edge of the page. This might be construed as being due to the smaller-than-standard writing space of a notebook or diary. I reject this interpretation because plenty of space remains on the right margin. The line ends, but it would be possible to extend the writing into the area between the end of the line and the right edge of the paper. Thus, the left margin, which represents the writer's past, is important. Because the writing avoids the right edge, the tendency is to hold back, and stick to the familiar–who and what he knows.

In handwriting analysis, the standard for average word space is the width of a letter 'm' in the writing under consideration. In this handwriting, the word spaces are far wider. The extreme spaces erect a wall between the "I" of him and the "you" of others. Already, we see a strong need—a *demand*—for personal space or elbow room. This man does not suffer fools gladly. He would not tolerate anyone breathing down his neck or attempting to micro-manage him. Additionally, the left-tending letter slant suggests, not that he fears social contact, but he feels little need for it. For this reason, there are times when he likely comes across as chilly and even defensive.

Just as his handwriting is stripped to its essentials, there is tremendous efficiency in the writer's ability to strip everything down to its barest essentials. This insistence on immediately getting to the bottom line is reminiscent of Detective Joe Friday in the 1950's TV show, *Dragnet.* Friday was well known for his line, "Just the facts, ma'am." In the same way, Michael Ondaatje rejects listening to superfluous meanderings. Laying out every little detail feels repetitious for him and he simply doesn't want to waste his time that way. He picks up most of what he needs to know through his strong intuition. Whether it's about an event, a conversation, or an idea, you had better do your homework before approaching to him, and leave out anything irrelevant to the discussion.

To describe this writing style as 'form' is stretching it. The fact is, his handwriting reveals a *breakdown* of form. Only the basic elements of letters are dashed onto the page and represent his own personal brand of shorthand. Whether or not anyone else can untangle what it's supposed to say doesn't matter to him.

He is capable of handling several matters at once, multitasking with style. Often, though, he works beyond his optimum capacity, skimming the surface and selecting only the most useful facts. He discards whatever doesn't apply to the task at hand. The downside of this habit is, he is likely to overlook some of the important facts and possibly reach an inaccurate conclusion. An assistant or two is needed to collect and sort through piles of research and other materials. Of course, that person would need to learn to read his hieroglyphics, as the boss would not want to take time to explain himself.

The writing form

This flattened manner of indefinite, *formless* writing suggests intellectual responses that are just as amorphous, diffuse, and contradictory. A tendency to say 'yes' and 'no' in the same breath leaves him a way out of every situation. Perhaps it is a multitude of wide-ranging interests that makes it difficult for him to commit to hard-and-fast choices.

There is a measure of revolt, perhaps even anarchy, in this breaking down of established letter forms. Rendered vague and undefined as they are, the letters remain subjectively ambiguous rather than objectively precise. They are experimental and creative, the freewheeling artifacts of a nonconformist.

Yet another aspect of this handwriting form is its need to protect the ego. The avoidance of creating legible letters in the middle zone–an area of handwriting that reveals the ego–demonstrates a need to defend, rather than to assert, the self. Behind this defense is generalized anxiety or a fear of disappearing into nothingness. And yet, the way it is expressed in behavior is the implementation of immediate purpose: "Let's get down to it!" In this way, rather than passively defying authority, it becomes the actively expressed voice of authority itself.

The writing movement is lively and exhibits energy expended more in mental activities than physical ones. The writing glides along the printed baseline, rising only just enough to offer a small clue as to the idea it wishes to express. It's as if the writer felt overburdened and unable to add anything to what he was already dealing with at the time of writing. As this remains true of his handwriting over a long period of time, we might conclude that he sometimes finds the outer world too much to handle. He is more comfortable in his rich internal wanderings than dealing with the more corporeal, pragmatic world around him.

Originality

The originality—indeed, the uniqueness—of Mr. Ondaatje's writing forms exposes a disregard for established norms and conventions. His refusal to adopt a more definite, or at least a more-or-less fixed point of view allows for mobility of thought and action.

He is quick to adapt to changing circumstances, switching direction when obstacles get in the way of his goals. Skilled at doing whatever it takes, going over, under, or around those obstacles, he gets where he needs to go.

Always on the alert, he is open to effectively understanding others. The high degree of smooth disconnections between the letters displays a fluid, cohesive thinking style. Ideas and thoughts flow logically, allowing him to solve problems through associative thinking.

Like the wide word spacing, the separation of the letters is symbolic of Ondaatje's preference for solitude. This might be seen as a "oneness" with self and the world, if not the individuals in that world.

One aspect of the particular type of disconnected letters he uses is mental genius. Because his major orientation is toward the mental sphere more than the social one, he may be viewed as a "brooding" type. Assuming all the handwriting samples I saw are representative of Mr. Ondaatje over time, we can infer that his rich inner life is more meaningful to him than what he might find in the outer world. Yet, living very much in his mind, he can become exhausted through extended cerebration.

As an observer more than a participant, he may feel that he doesn't have the inner strength to spend a lot of time interacting. Again, his handwriting suggests that he is energized more by thoughts and ideas than social discourse or emotions. This is not to say he is an unemotional person. In fact, his handwriting depicts a profoundly sensitive human. When there is good reason to do so, he has the ability to connect with others with great charm.

As if he tunes an internal antenna to his environment, his finely-tuned intuition picks up the thoughts and feelings of those around him in a way that could be thought of as psychic. Ironically, though, while he may have an *intellectual* understanding of emotion, allowing himself to actually experience a full range of emotion can be challenging.

One who comes across as a bit shy and is non-intrusive himself, Michael Ondaatje expects others to respect the clear boundaries he sets. Since his mental activities are given greater priority than personal relationships, he is highly selective in creating a small, carefully chosen group of intimates, building trust in them over a long period of time.

He doesn't mind when others see him as somewhat eccentric. He thinks and does as he pleases and is not in the least bit interested in compromising on something that is important to him. As an independent thinker he feels no need to alter the way he looks at things in order to accommodate others. Further, he is unlikely to ask for help when needed.

An attitude of apparent indifference, or even intellectual arrogance, is a defense he has developed against being bombarded by everything going on around him. Living with this level of sensitivity can make one overwhelmed by the various demands of life. A minimalist lifestyle can be a defense against such demands. Consequently, he creates distance that even those close to him find hard to breach.

Strokes that rise up like little pyramids from the baseline signal curiosity and the need to explore the unknown. Ondaatje is the philosophical equivalent of

Sir Edmund Hillary, climbing the Everest of ideas that are too difficult for others, who give up before they reach the summit.

Early life?

What created this fascinating and complex personality? It seems reasonable to conjecture that, for whatever reason, the writer did not develop a secure connection to his mother very early in life. In such instances, the mother (or other caregiver) might have been absent from the baby, or at work, or maybe had health problems, or was busy with other children. Or something else. Whatever the reason, little Michael probably spent a lot of time quietly playing on his own, reading and developing his imagination or engaging in other solitary pursuits.

With a propensity to woolgather and get lost in his head, it would be no surprise to learn that he was teased by other children as being 'not normal.' The thing is, he knows exactly who he is and does not feel the need to twist himself into a pretzel to please others. Any effort to "normalize" him would have been met with intense resistance. He finds it far more appealing to spend time in the interesting space above his shoulders than conform to expectations.

A deeply complicated and intriguing individual who resists being known and categorized, he would likely be mortified to read this analysis. But I hope he would also relate to it and resonate with the person I have described (even if he didn't want to discuss it...). The world may have a hard time understanding what his handwriting says, but Michael Ondaatje views the world with great clarity. He expects little from others and simply wants to be left to himself without demands and expectations placed on him.

BIOGRAPHICAL NOTES

Sheila Lowe is a certified forensic handwriting examiner who holds a Master of Science in psychology. An award-winning author, she writes nonfiction about handwriting psychology and two fiction series. She served as president of AHAF for ten years and is a member of the board of directors of the Scientific Association of Forensic Examiners. She teaches and lectures around the world and is often featured in the media when handwriting is in the the news.

sheila@sheilalowe.com

Conscious, Preconscious & Unconscious Determinants in Handwriting

Marc J. Seifer, Ph.D.

Werner Wolff wrote in his classic treatise *Diagrams of the Unconscious*:

> *We cannot bring to consciousness why we incline a certain letter, why we put the dot over the i in a certain place, why we emphasize a curve.... While the direction of the total movement is conscious and single steps are preconscious, its form and quality are unconscious.*

Where the child uses mostly his conscious for the creation of letter forms, the adult has learned to write preconsciously, that is, habitually. A well-developed adult script will display numerous preconscious forms known as automatisms. These habitual psychomotor patterns often contain symbolic imagery, as they are a meeting ground for conscious and unconscious determinants.

The last area, the unconscious, can be understood from a number of perspectives: neurophysiological, such as left-brain/right-brain; Werner Wolff's "principle of configuration," which includes Dan Anthony's research on touch points; and Klages' *"formniwo"* (form level).

Conscious, preconscious, and unconscious criteria form a complex matrix that reflects neurological organization and corresponding psychological states of consciousness. This idea, from Pulver's point of view, neatly connects Freud's superego, ego and id with the upper, middle and lower zones of the writing trail: the middle zone corresponding to conscious activity, the lower zone to unconscious activity, and the preconscious, since it houses the superego, would appear in the upper zone.

Where the low form level writer appears to be at the mercy of a chaotic unconscious, the high form level writer is connected more fully to the subterranean center of being. Other unconscious elements that influence form level would include temperament and IQ. Environmental factors and educational training would, of course also play a role.

Conscious, Preconscious & Unconscious

Freud assumed that humans were basically unconscious beings. Therefore, the conscious, for Freud, was a tool for the unconscious. When this mechanism becomes automatic, then whatever was conscious becomes preconscious. This procedure is set up in a hierarchical way so that the conscious is again freed up when the preconscious kicks into gear.

Take, for instance, playing a guitar and singing. The act of playing the musical instrument must first become a preconscious activity before the musician can sing. This is achieved through practice. Handwriting operates the same way. What is often not realized is that the very process of language is also a preconscious activity. One does not spend time searching for words when one talks. They appear automatically, that is, preconsciously. What one wants to say reflects conscious and intentional aspects. What one actually says, including Freudian slips, may reveal unconscious activity as well. Freud's model is set up as follows:

Conscious: an apparatus for achieving:
1. Awareness of environment and also interior states of consciousness.
2. Access to motility, e.g., voluntary movement (and thus the ego).

Preconscious which houses:
1. All memories that can be remembered.
2. The automatisms, or habitual psychomotor patterns.
3. The censor, and thus the defense mechanisms (and superego).

Unconscious which houses:

1. All memories that have been forgotten or repressed (linked to the id).
2. The true psychic reality, one's deepest desires, creative ability, and the soul.

Figure 1. Superb clarity in the middle zone is expressed in the handwriting of Bernard Baruch. The conscious is emphasized in the handwriting of this great financier.

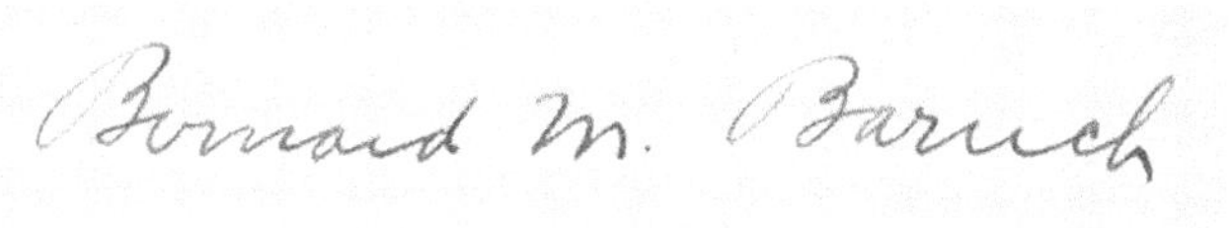

Paradoxically, one can utilize the conscious apparatus but not be "conscious" or aware. Sleepwalking would be an example, as would be driving past one's exit on a highway. In the first instance, the person is walking unconsciously; in the second instance, the person is driving preconsciously. Handwriting, for the most part, like typing, is a preconscious procedure. The hierarchical arrangement of the psyche becomes evident because while the fingers move preconsciously, the conscious is considering the concepts and words that are being written down the page.

The more spontaneous the writer, the more automatic the handwriting and the more the creative unconscious will be reflected. Conversely, the less spontaneous the writing (e.g., the more slowly it is written, or the more stylized), the less automatic the writing and the less the creative unconscious will be expressed.

In slower and/or more stylized handwritings, conscious premeditation is evident. There is a fear of accessing the unconscious, and thus, the defense structure is more pronounced. That is to say, a different part of the preconscious is being expressed, the censor/defense structure. The person is more repressed.

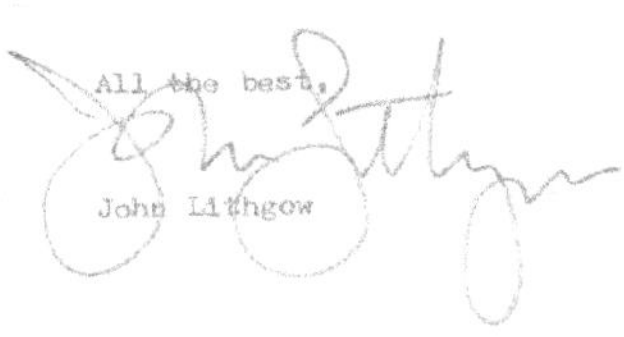

Figure 2. Interesting trizonal dynamics are expressed in the handwriting of the versatile actor, John Lithgow able to play both the hero and also the evil antagonist. The conscious sphere of the middle zone is abstract. Note the high level of simplification and the primary thread in the writing. The preconscious

superego is emphasized in the upper zone as is a rather dynamic and insatiable id emphasized in the unconscious/lower zone

Figure 3. J. Edgar Hoover.

The middle zone of conscious reality is legible, but this is predominantly a lower zone/unconscious handwriting with no emphasis whatever on the upper zone suggesting an inferiority complex. Note the grasping heart-shaped capital J in the signature of "the man who kept the files."

The problem for Freud, and with his typology, is that the Will is ignored. The conscious should also reflect intentional aspects, but for Freud, these were always unconscious procedures. The conscious was simply a way for the unconscious to express itself. Freud did leave a little room in his schema because the conscious was also the mechanism for accessing motility (movement), which included voluntary movements.

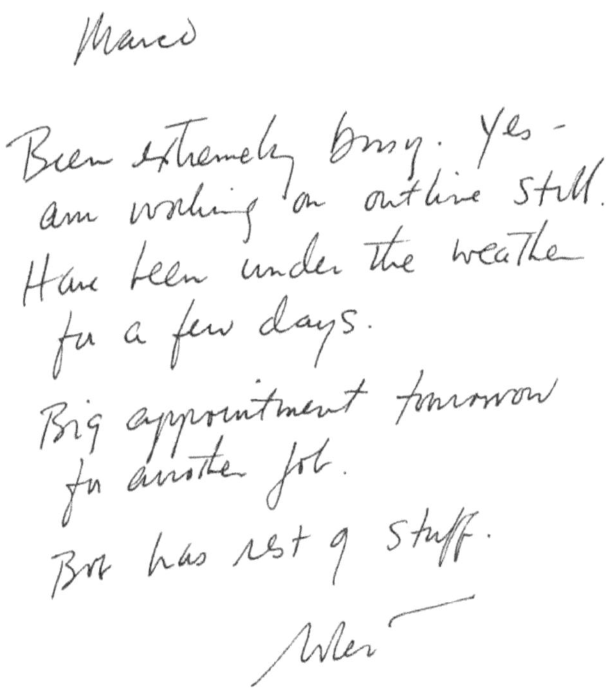

Marco

Been extremely busy. Yes - am working on outline still. Have been under the weather for a few days.

Big appointment tomorrow for another job.

Bob has rest of stuff.

The preconscious, the access route between the conscious apparatus and repressed desires held in the unconscious, is also a battleground. The battle takes place in something called the censor. If repressed desires are thwarted, they will seek other avenues of escape, either through a weakened censor at night through dreams, or by converting the energy through the body into psychosomatic, nervous, or stress-induced illnesses, or by skirting around the censor. This last procedure which houses the defense mechanisms is known as pre-logical or symbolic activity. It shows up in the handwriting as peculiar repetitive symbols.

This spontaneous writer has easy access to the unconscious. The signature, which is a combination of conscious and preconscious activity spells out the name Robert with easy use of primary thread. This signature reflects the sheer brilliance of the artist.

Neurophysiology

The left hemisphere thinks sequentially and programs language. This is the more conscious hemisphere. The right hemisphere thinks intuitively and programs music and pictures. This is the more unconscious hemisphere. It is the author's contention that aspects of the preconscious are linked to the corpus callosum, the connecting fibers between the two hemispheres. It takes eight years for the corpus callosum to develop. A more repressed person would have less access to the unconscious and thus a differently structured corpus callosum than a person who easily accessed the unconscious. **Figure 5.** Preconscious defense mechanisms are evident in the handwriting of this inhibited writer. This person fears the unconscious.

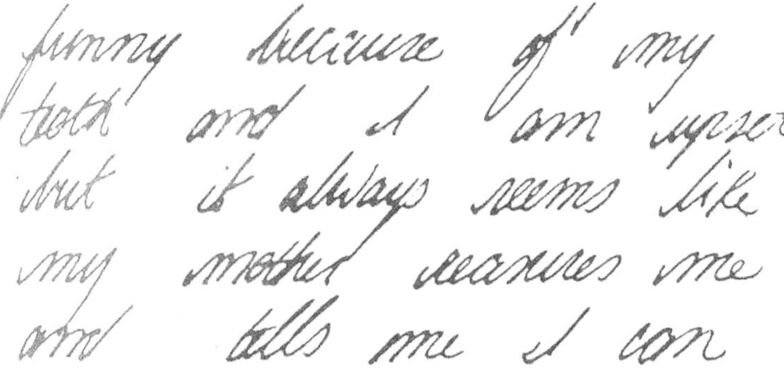

Figure 6. A highly developed linear writer is the author of Sherlock Holmes, Sir Arthur Conan Doyle. Superb utilization of space reveals the excellent balance between left and right brains and conscious and

unconscious processes. Holmes may have been the quintessential empirical left-brained scientist, but Doyle had another side to him. Drawn to psychic phenomena, Doyle heartily believed in ESP, a right brained activity. Although his writing is highly linear, the overall gestalt pattern, along with the pastosity of the writing stroke would counterbalance and reflect right brain activity.

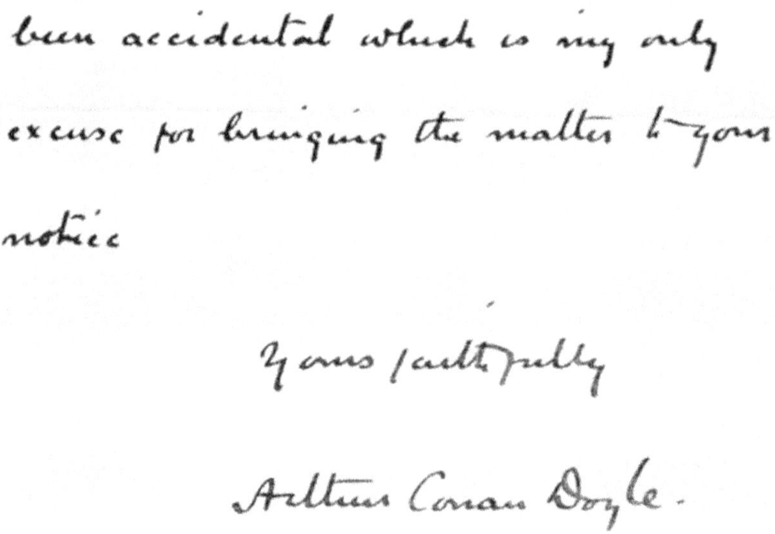

been accidental which is my only
excuse for bringing the matter to your
notice

Yours faithfully

Arthur Conan Doyle.

A more spontaneous and/or released handwriting suggests right brain dominance. A slower and/or more contracted handwriting suggests left brain dominance. Sequential thought would tend to be left brain types.

A purely right brained handwriting would be that of Walt Disney.

Figure 7. Walt Disney certainly was right-brained type thinker. The abstract unconscious is revealed in the top more spontaneous signature suggestive of Disney's various cartoon characters. His CONSCIOUS grasp of reality and ability to express his ideas lucidly to the public correspond more with the bottom signature.

Walt Disney

Walt Disney

Form Level

Klages writes that, "The life of a handwriting lies in the strength of its form." The best way to analyze a coordinated integration of conscious, preconscious, and unconscious forces would therefore involve the study of form level.

Klages generalized by classifying handwritings into either positive or negative categories. A form level score was arrived at by looking at the gestalt first and then considering these aspects of handwriting:

Rhythm, arrangement of space, originality

Klages linked a person's form level in handwriting to other natural processes such as the "perfect expression" of form as seen in the "purely natural form of an organism." Six divisions were created ranging from very high, to average to very low (Karohs, 1964). There is a relationship, Klages maintains, between the shapes of plants and animals and the shapes created by humans through the movements and forms of handwriting. The key difference is that man is influenced by an extra component, the mind, which is non-physical, as opposed to the physical forces which create the physical forms of life.

Manifesting from the writing's gestalt, the concept of originality, or lack thereof, is a key factor. The opposite of originality, which Klages lists as "negations of forms," includes "banality of form, stereotypical forms and school-type forms." How much of originality is conscious and how much is unconscious? This is not an easy question to answer. The concepts of naturalness and spontaneity certainly come into play here, but conscious intent is probably always a factor in complex original creations.

Excessive features reduce form level, whereas harmonious features enhance it. All trait and trait clusters are modified by the form level and every trait has within it ambivalent or antithetical components. Thus, even positive traits may have negative aspects. For instance, if a so-called democrat is liberal, he may also be lax; if a leader is strong, he may also be stubborn. The same trait could thus demonstrate different response patterns in different situations.

Although form level can often be ascertained at a glance, the components that make up form level are rather complex. Sonnemann notes that form level is the "overriding factor" which modified each trait in a handwriting. For instance, the same graphic could have an entirely different meaning in a low form level handwriting as compared to when it is found harmoniously interwoven into a higher level writing (Sonnemann, 1950). The same could be said for flourishes, wavy baselines, use of printscript and use of thread. Form level, according to Mendel is the "yardstick" which allows for differentiation of the same characteristic in two writers. The question then arises as to whether or not it really is the same characteristic.

The overall arrangement, according to Mendel, can be analyzed in terms of the handwriting's general layout on the page. Does it appear orderly or disorderly? Crowded or dispersed? Is it legible or illegible.

Time is a key factor. How much time does the writer allow himself in the act of writing? Graphologically, this is linked not only to speed, but also to simplifications and rhythm. A disturbed rhythm may in part be due to the person's general inability or unwillingness to spend the time necessary to execute the letters in a completely clear and well-paced fashion. Compare the rapid neglected writing of JFK to that of his brother Robert Kennedy .

Figure 8. At right is John F. Kennedy's signature and to the left, is the very small signature of Robert F. Kennedy (enlarged). Both signatures are from the early 1960's. A key typical neglected aspect to signature of John F. Kennedy is the removal of the upper loop of the "d." Apparently, he was idealistic in most matters except for the bedroom. The J resembles an anchor perhaps as a preconscious symbol of his link to the sea. The last name is illegible suggesting ambivalent feelings towards the father. The neglect in the handwriting is probably also associated with his rush to get it out so that he would have time to do something else.

Robert Kennedy's squinched handwriting reflects his feelings of having to grow up in the shadow of two dynamic older brothers. Through this smallness, attention is also drawn to him. The angles in the simplified K reflect his aggressive streak.

Figure 9. Bill Clinton is conscious to a great extent in his signature as compared to being unconscious of his tight retraced capital I. He is a man

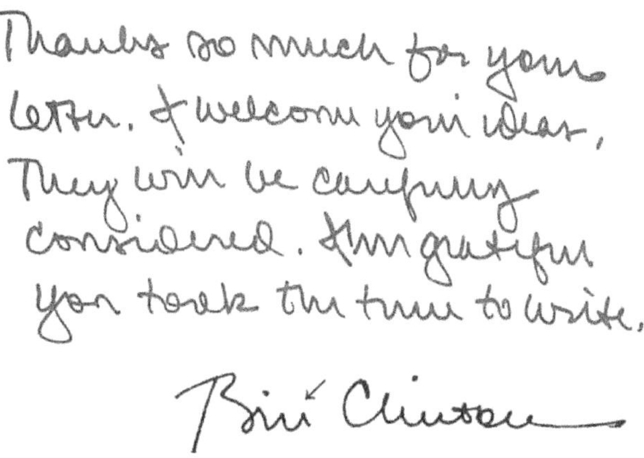
Thanks so much for your letter. I welcome your ideas. They will be carefully considered. I'm grateful you took the time to write.

Bill Clinton

of opposites. High intelligence and even genius is revealed in the simplified double l's which is a form of primary thread, made even more amazing by the fact that it is written by a left-handed writer. He is generous and future oriented, yet this same trait may result in rash decisions.

Preconscious symbols also frequently arise in handwriting, and oftentimes these symbols relate to a person's hobbies or profession.

Figure 10. The signature on the left is that of a lady who plays the violin. The signature on the right is that of Karl Menninger, the famous physician.

Figure 11. In looking at conscious, preconscious, and unconscious aspects

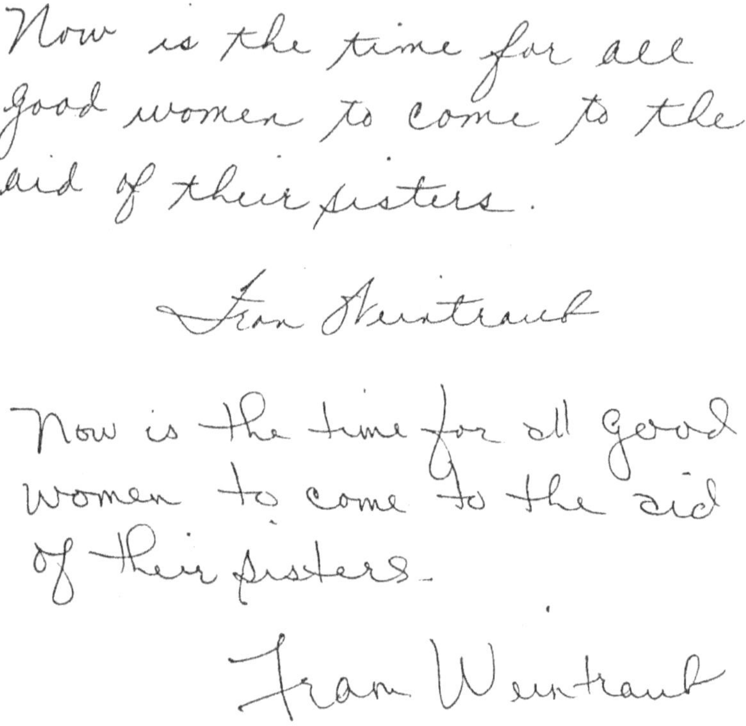

to the writing trail, take the example of Fran, top writing. Surprised at its commonplace style, when I asked if she had any other styles, she rattled off the bottom sample as quickly as could be.

Note how she changed the word "man" to "woman" and how the highly creative letter "a" emerges. The slant also changed from a conforming rightward slant to one that was upright, more in accord with standing on one's own feet. Here we see a dramatic example of how social forces can impinge on both conscious and unconscious factors involved in one's handwriting.

Roman writes that Klages breaks down Rhythm into three divisions:

Rhythm of Movement, which takes into account the periodicity or repeating element in the writing: the extensions into the vertical and horizontal dimensions, the smooth or jerky nature of the stroke and the quality of the speed.

Rhythm of Form, which involves the interrelationship of the parts: simplification or elaboration, originality or letters, types of connections, naturalness, linear or pictorial style.

Rhythm of Arrangement, which involves the spatial distribution of the graphic pattern as a whole: the margins, figure/background relationship, spacing and trizonal components.

Figure 12. Three instances of the Greek E. The most aesthetically successful use of the Greek E can be seen in the top handwriting. This writer

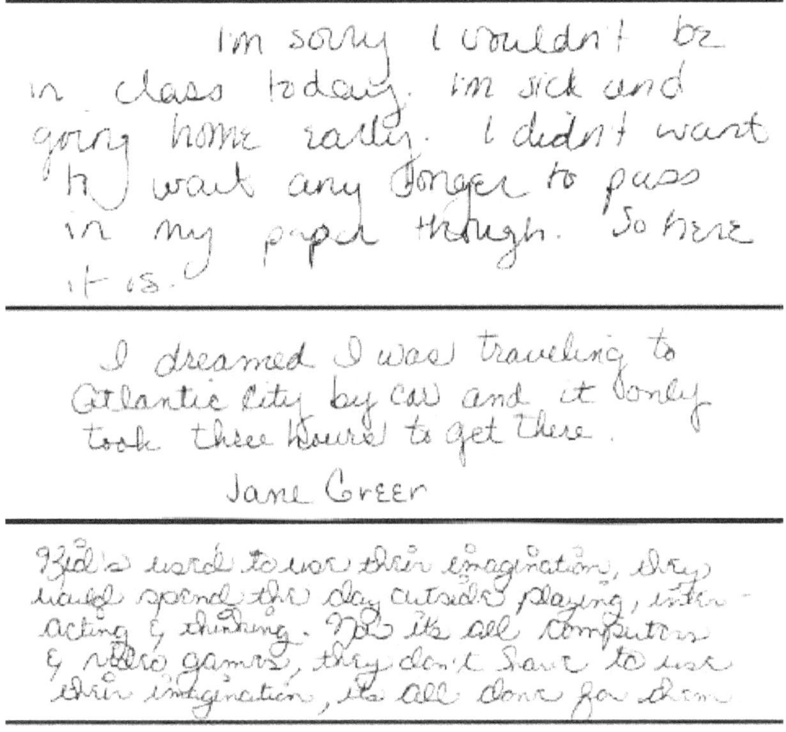

has preconsciously adapted this letter into the overall writing pattern. All three individuals chose the Greek E consciously in order to be noticed and/or in attempts to express themselves in a more original way. The bottom writer, doing her best to control and redirect chaotic and powerful id forces makes an awkward, possibly compulsive use of this letter as it leans back against the rest of the writing. Note also that it rises above the rest of the lowercase letters and has been added along with the circle i-dot. These graphics have a powerful symbolic meaning for this troubled individual. Interestingly enough, unlike in the case of the other two writers, the letter "E" or "e" does not appear in her signature.

Practice is also a factor. Mendel notes that "only a person who does a great deal of writing, who is daily confronted with the need to create more easily executed characters" will develop (or tend to develop) his handwriting. Simplification will tend to arise and new forms will be created. This can occur either spontaneously or consciously. The use of the Greek E, the circle i-dot, the "th" combination where the t-bar becomes the beginning of the "h" and the connection of the i-dot to the next letter are four instances where conscious, preconscious, and unconscious are factors. The Greek E and circle i-dot always (or almost always) begins as a conscious procedure. The "th" combination, on the other hand, often occurs spontaneously without conscious thought, although it might also be consciously adopted into the writing style because of the elegance of the procedure. The last instance, where the i-dot becomes connected to the next letter, probably arises unconsciously. However, over time, and ironically, the person may consciously notice this stylization and therefore move to emphasize it.

Concerning the rhythm of spatial arrangement, Professor Jean-Charles Gille-Maisani writes that, "What a man does not say is as important as what he does say." Harmony can be perceived in the "distribution of the masses."

A person who makes use of a significant amount of blank spaces portrays a need for mental clarity. These kinds of writers which Gille-Maisani calls "aerated writers" tend to be "reflective in thought and judgment." They are also objective as they can "stand back" and perceive. Conscious intent is evident. They may be "steady and critical, capable of restraint," yet at the same time suffer from feelings of "isolation and distancing," which would be the unconscious element.

Figure 13. An example of aerated writing.

In the opposite situation, a person who "entangles lines" may be one who "compensates by a debased extraversion," and thus might be "exces-

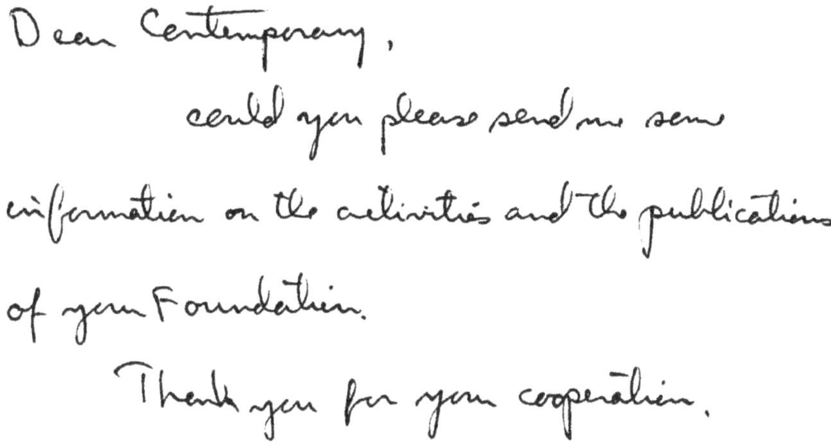

Dear Contemporary,

could you please send me some information on the activities and the publications of your Foundation.

Thank you for your cooperation.

sively open to change" (Gille-Maisani, 1992). However, even though entanglement occurs unconsciously, the person clearly makes no conscious effort to alleviate the situation. Illegible writings fall into a similar category. The person must consciously know that the writing cannot be read but makes no conscious effort to change.

The psychophysiology of handwriting, its relationship to conscious, preconscious, & unconscious processes

The higher the Form Level the greater the use of advanced centers of the brain. Dan Anthony links Form Level score to the following graphic characteristics (Anthony, 1983).

Organization	Alignment control	Rhythm	Spontaneity
Simplification	Lower zone	Pressure	Speed

Graphologically, high Form Level scores translate into dynamic handwritings that display excellent rhythm, good use of trizonal dynamics harmonic use of pressure, sound organization and rightward trend (see Robert, Figure 4). Handwriting analysis, therefore, has a dual nature, analysis by looking at the whole and then breaking down the process into its constituent parts.

Both Sonnemann and Mendel discuss the concepts of vertical and horizontal axes. Up and down movements, the vertical dimension, relates to a person's "self-orientation and available values." The downstroke called the "stable axis" and portrays, according to Mendel, the "backbone of the writer." This backbone reflects conscious procedures. The horizontal or mobile axis expresses one's "attitude towards the future and our fellow man" and also the exteriorization of libidinal drives, what Sonnemann calls "orientation to reality" and the process of objectification of choice, e.g., making conscious what is unconscious.

These two processes, the up and down movement and the one from left to right, occur in time, and relate to what Klages called the rhythm of movement. A periodicity or a repeating element should appear in a natural way, displaying the rhythm of space, or the principle of configuration as Wolff describes it.

Rightward trend involves the process of externalization, whereas leftward trend involves contact avoidance. The first is future-oriented and conscious, the second is past-oriented and unconscious.

During the act of writing, complex letter-forms are created. At the same time, thoughts, words, sentences, and paragraphs are being formed in the mind of the writer. If handwriting were not a predominantly preconscious automatic process, then thinking and writing simultaneously would not be possible. Handwriting is thus mainly a preconscious activity (Seifer, 1989). Concepts, choices of words, capital letters and the beginnings of words and sentences are most conscious, whereas the gestalt and/or rhythm of spatial arrangement, connecting strokes, diacritics, ending strokes and other incidental aspects are more unconscious.

The left-handed writer adds a whole other level of complexity as a releasing movement for a righty away from the body is a contracting movement for the lefty, which would be towards the body. Similarly, a left slant for a lefty from a physiological point of view is easier and more relaxing, and the reverse is also true, namely that a right slant is more of a release for a righty and more difficult to achieve for a lefty. When thinking about the factors of contraction/release, keep in mind handedness.

Contraction involves movement towards the body, and thus ego emphasis, volitional processes, control over emotions and cognitive functions. Release involves spontaneity, object emphasis, impulsivity, and fantasy life. The body of the letter, the person's backbone, the expression of volitional control are linked to the downstroke. The upstroke is mainly just a way to get to the next downstroke. Thus, downstrokes are more linked to conscious procedures and upstrokes are more linked to unconscious procedures. Sonnemann clearly points out that if all the upstrokes of a handwriting are eliminated much of the writing is still legible, whereas if all the downstrokes are eliminated, then the writing becomes illegible.

It is at this point that brain organization comes into consideration. Language is centered in the left hemisphere and pictures are more centered in the right. Where consonants are more left brain centered, "vwls r mr rght bn cntrd." It is fair to say that downstrokes are more linked to left brained thinking and upstrokes more linked to right brained thinking. This conclusion is supported by Jeanette Farmer who suggests that more contracted writers are more left-brain dominant. and more released writers are more right-brained (Farmer, 1994).

Since rhythm is the balance between contraction and release, it is also the balance between up and down, self and not-self, conscious and unconscious and left and right hemispheres of the brain. The process of writing, therefore, involves a constant interaction between left hemisphere and right. As the hand goes up and down, contracts and releases, there is a corresponding alternating and interlinking pattern between the two hemispheres of the brain.

All the lobes of the cerebral cortex are involved as well. The front of the brain, or frontal lobes, programs the highest intellectual functions and also goal direction. The back of the brain, or occipital lobe, processes vision; the temporal lobe, above the ears, houses language; the motor cortex at the top of the brain controls motor movements; and the parietal lobe, at the rear, essentially in-between the occipital, temporal and motor cortex coordinates the entire process, e.g., eye-hand coordination.

High form level handwritings such as that of Arthur Conan Doyle show superb organization, highly advanced automatisms, and an excellent integration of all five lobes of the cerebral cortex, with integration between the two hemispheres (Seifer, 1988).

The other type of upstroke which displays pressure is the beginning stroke on such letters as the "a" and "w." This stroke also involves actualizing unconscious processes. However, since the stroke is unnecessary and is usually eliminated in mature handwritings, it reveals more a left-brained pedantic tendency to impose outmoded traditions. The writer is held back by the past, by the unconscious. Some writers (Korda and Bettelheim) generate and convert this energy in a more productive way.

Figure 14. Beginning Strokes. Michael Korda, author, (at top) and Bruno Bettelheim, psychoanalyst. Strong ego emphasis is expressed in these bold upstrokes. Since most upstrokes lack pressure, in these instances there is a tendency for the writer to express or make conscious that which is normally unconscious. Aging and probably in ill health, Bettelheim committed suicide approximately 15 years after this signature, at the age of 86. Note the pessimistic tumbling at the end.

Michael Korda

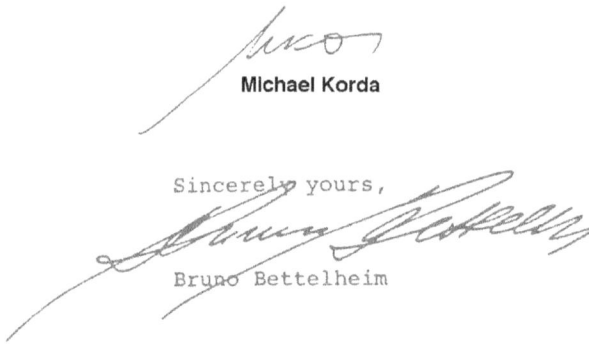

Sincerely yours,

Bruno Bettelheim

Figure 15. This is the highly creative signature of the rather abstract rock and roll artist Frank Zappa. The A's have had to have utilized conscious design, and yet to come up with such an incredibly unique way to create the letter A, access to the unconscious must also have been used. This signature is the mark of true genius.

Jacoby associates connectedness with the writer's adaptability to the inner or outer world (Jacoby, 1939). Connecting strokes are associated with connection to the future.

Disconnection involves the elimination of the upstrokes, isolation and a corresponding break from the future. "These individual upstrokes," Jacoby writes, "are the very lines of connection or bridges between the ego (or self) and the world." Thus, the degree of connection measures the degree of social adaption, self-coordination, and spiritual connection. A natural degree of connection suggests a flexible preconscious and the ability of the psyche to express unconscious processes in a productive way. Too much connection, when it is a negative, can be associated with too much loquaciousness and "one-track mindedness" (Sonnemann, 1950).

Connectedness, which is usually positive, is linked to conscious and unconscious processes and to left and right hemispheres of the brain. In general, the arcade connection implies more repression of the unconscious and the garland connection suggests a more expressive or receptive unconscious. Frank Zappa's extraordinary arcade connection in the center of his signature would certainly be an exception to that rule!

Figure 16. Beginning Strokes. Note the childlike beginning strokes on the a's. This writer is a 35-year-old female social worker who was particularly interested in cases of incest. She was very dominant in class, so the primitive

II Murray was a
Harvard and he didn't have any
until he was working toward his
in England. He read Jung's
and was transformed. He

nature of her script came as a shock. Here beginning upstrokes portray a pedantic attachment to her past. A good possibility exists that she may have been molested as a child.

Diagrams of the unconscious

Practice is also a factor. Mendel notes that "only a person who does a great deal of writing, who is daily confronted with the need to create more easily executed characters" will develop (or tend to develop) his handwriting. Simplification will tend to arise and new forms will be created. This can occur either spontaneously or consciously. Arthur Conan Doyle's right-flying t-bars, Bill Clinton's double "l's" in his signature and Fran's creative "a's" are cases in point. Although all three graphics are preconscious automatisms, the first two most likely arose spontaneously, whereas the last one may have had more conscious input in its initial creation.

Arrhythmic disconnections are associated with a schism within the nature. People who have been adopted, people who have never connected emotionally with the mother, schizophrenic individuals, and epileptic split-brain writers all display this graphic variable (Seifer, 1974). Lack of rhythmic connections shows a lack of a natural ability to access the creative/spiritual side of the unconscious, and/or corresponding parts of the right hemisphere of the brain. Obviously, Form Level will be affected in a negative way if there are arrhythmic disconnections. These people are more at the mercy of the chaotic side of the unconscious. The conscious is totally undeveloped.

Figure 17. The handwriting of the brilliant German graphologist Werner Wolff. English was Wolff's second language. Note the two different f's in the

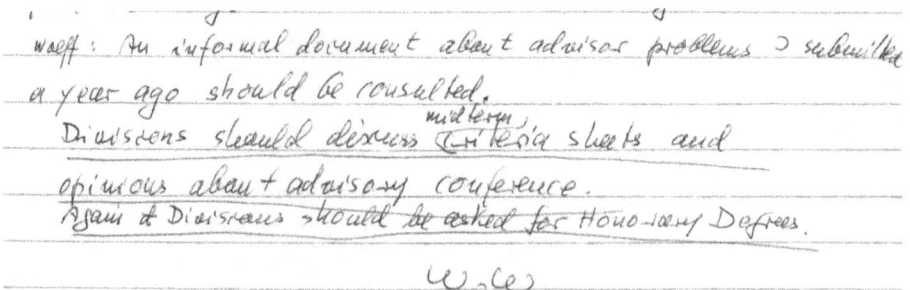

Wolff: An informal document about advisor problems I submitted a year ago should be consulted.
Divisions should discuss midterm criteria sheets and opinions about advisory conference.
Again & Divisions should be asked for Honorary Degrees.
W.W.

word Wolff, top left. Staying on this first line, note how the ending t's rise above the rest of the writing. It is doubtful that Wolff is aware of this idiosyncrasy. There is no way to know what it really means, but to me, it seems these rising t's are linked to Wolff's observant behavior. Note also the abundant garlands in the m's and n's. Werner Wolff was, of course, finely tuned to being open to the forces from the unconscious. Note also the rhythmic W.W. signature. (Thanks to Kate Wolff, Werner's wife, for this sample.)

An integrated handwriting with connections either on paper or through air strokes would display high Form Level scores, naturalness, organization, and rhythm of spatial arrangement. These writers can consciously access their unconscious. They are aware of their dreams, for instance, and they utilize and trust the unconscious.

Dear Marc,

Thanx for remembering me. I'm now down in Washington, working for the Environmental Protection Agency, and really enjoying it here. I'll take a subscription — I'll try anything once!

Keep in touch,

Mitch

63 N.E.
Washington, D.C. 20002

Figure 18. The conscious shows up in the intent of the overall design, the large middle zone and the use of circle dots for periods and i-dot on his signature (see arrows).

The versatile connecting strokes display mental dexterity. High Form Level is revealed in the rhythm of the spatial arrangement. Note how the "balancing, organizing and designing proclivities" are revealed when touch points are located: i-dots line up three at a time in several different ways. Although the baseline changes from one line to another, the gestalt is still rhythmically connected. This man graduated number 1 in his high school class and got 800's (perfect scores) on his SAT's (scholastic aptitude tests). By playing with a ruler in attempts to tap into the unconscious of the writer, a different view of the handwriting emerges.

The conscious in the handwriting shows up in the intentional aspects. Preconscious procedures are the most automatic. The unconscious shows up in the Form Level, diacritics, incidental details, and rhythm of spatial arrangement. In turn, each of these processes also have neurological correlates. Due to the complex nature of personality, the complex process of handwriting, and due to the multi-leveled nature of these three concepts, one can see that this paper is only a starting point.

BIBLIOGRAPHY

Anthony, Daniel. *The Graphological Psychogram.* Newark, NJ, 1969.

Anthony, Daniel. *Is Graphology Valid?Readings in Psychology Today,* 343-348. Del Mar, California: CRM Books, 1969.

Farmer, Jeanette. "Measuring Handwriting to Identify Thinking & Behavioral Styles Four Quadrants of the Brain." *JASPG*, IV, 1995/96, 69-97.

Freud, Sigmund. *Wit & the Unconscious.* New York: Basic Books, 1938.

Gille-Maisani J-G. *The Psychology of Handwriting.* London: Scriptor, 1991.

Hartmann, Heinz. *Ego Psychology & the Problems of Adaption.* New York: University Press, 1952.

Jacoby, H.J. *Analysis of Handwriting.* London: George Allen & Unwin, 1939.

Karohs, Erika. *Ludwig Klages: From His Works.* Pebble Beach, California, 1964.

Klages, Ludwig. *Handschrift and Charakter.* Leipzig: Verlig von Johann Publ., 1929.

Klein, Felix. "Ludwig Klages Translations." *NSG Newsletter*, 11, issues 3-6, 1983.

Klein, Felix. "The Guiding Image." In *Oxford 1987: First British Symposium of Graphological Research*, edited by Nigel Bradley, 51-61. Derbyshire, Great Britain, 1986.

Luria, Alexander. *The Working Brain.* New York: Basic Books., 1973.

Luria, Alexander. *Higher Cortical Functions in Man.* New York: Springer, 1970.

Rapaport, David. "Activity & Passivity of the Ego With Regards to Reality." In *Collected Works*, New York: Basic Books, 1956/1967.

Roman, Klara. *Handwriting: A Key to Personality.* New York: Noonday Press, 1970.

Seifer, Marc. "Form Level." *Journal of the American Society of Professional Graphologists*, VI, 185-200, 2004.

Seifer,Marc."Formiveau Theoretische Betrachtungen." In*Graphologie Und Personlichkeits-Diagnostik*, 29-47, 2005. Munich: Angewandte

Seifer, Marc. "The Telltale Hand: How Writing Reveals the Damaged Brain." *Cerebrum: Dana Forum for Brain Science*, 4, #4, (2002), 27-42.

Seifer, Marc. "Conscious, Preconscious & Unconscious Determinants in Handwriting." *British Institute of Graphologists Tenth Anniversary Symposium Proceedings,* edited by Cathy Bryant, 23-51. Cambridge, England: BIG Press, 1993.

Seifer, Marc. "The Preconscious in Handwriting." *JASPG*, I, (Fall, 1989), pp. 63-80.

Seifer, Marc (1988) "Handwriting & Brain Functioning." In *Experiencing Graphology,* edited by A. Carmi & S. Schneider, 95-123. London: Freund Publishing House.

Seifer, Marc."Handwriting and the Psychosexual Stages of Development." In*Oxford, 1987: The First British Symposium on Graphological Research. Derbyshire,* edited by N. Bradley, 128-145. Great Britain: British Institute of Graphology, 1987.

Seifer, Marc. *The Preconscious in Handwriting.* International Graphology Institute, Haifa, Israel (translated into Hebrew.) 1985.

Seifer, Marc. "The Preconscious in Handwriting." In *NSG Newsletter,* (April, 1975), 1-3.

Seifer, Marc and David Goode."Handwriting: A Measure of Muscle Tension in Schizophrenics and Normals." *National Society for Graphology Newsletter*, pp. 1-3, 1974.

Seifer, Marc. *The Definitive Book of Handwriting Analysis.* Franklin Lakes, New Jersey: Career Press, 2009.

Seifer, Thelma, & Seifer, Marc. "A Right Brain Approach to Handwriting Analysis." *JASPG*, II, (1991 Fall): 108-130

Sonnemann, Ulrich. *Handwriting Analysis as a Diagnostic Tool.* New York: Grune & Stratton, 1950.

Tenhouten, Warren, Marc Seifer, and Patricia Siegel. "Alexithymia & the Split Brain." *Psychiatric Clinics of North America*, (September, 1988): 331 338.

Wolff, Werner. *Diagrams of the Unconscious.* New York: Grune & Stratton, 1948/1965.

This article was adapted from Conscious, Preconscious & Unconscious Determinants in Handwriting, by Marc J. Seifer in *British Institute of Graphologists Tenth Anniversary Symposium Proceedings.* Cathy Bryant, (Ed.) Cambridge, England: BIG Press, 1993, pp. 23-51.

BIOGRAPHICAL NOTES

Past editor of the *Journal of the American Society of Professional Graphologists,* Marc J. Seifer, Ph.D. has lectured on graphology at Oxford and Cambridge Universities in England, in Jerusalem, Federal Reserve Bank Boston, URI Crime Laboratory and University of British Columbia. A forensic documents examiner, and founding member of the American College of Forensic Examiners, he has worked for the Public Defenders, Rhode Island Attorney General's Office and numerous attorneys. Author of *The Definitive Book of Handwriting Analysis,* with articles in *Lawyer's Weekly, Cerebrum and Psychiatric Clinics of North America*, Dr. Seifer has testified in civil, criminal, and federal court.

mseifer@verizon.net

For information about our organization or courses in handwriting analysis, you are invited to visit www.ahafhandwriting.org
or email ahaf@ahafhandwriting.org

A

B

C

D

E

F

G

H

R

S

T

U

W

www.ingramcontent.com/pod-product-compliance
Lightning Source LLC
Chambersburg PA
CBHW020150090426
42734CB00008B/769

* 9 7 8 1 9 7 0 1 8 1 3 6 4 *